SAPPHO AND THE
GREEK LYRIC POETS

SAPPHO AND THE GREEK LYRIC POETS

Translated and Annotated by
WILLIS BARNSTONE

Introduction by William E. McCulloh

Drawings by Tzalopoulou Barnstone

(Expanded edition of GREEK LYRIC POETRY)

SCHOCKEN BOOKS • NEW YORK

Sappho and the Greek lyric poets / translated by Willis Barnstone.
p.   cm.
Bibliography: p.
Includes index.
1. Greek poetry—Translations into English. 2. Sappho—Translations, English. 3. English poetry—Translations from Greek.
I. Barnstone, Willis, 1927–
PA3622.B3S27 1988
884'.01' 08 —dc19

Manufactured in the United States of America

ISBN 0-8052-0831-3

ACKNOWLEDGMENTS

Certain of these poems first appeared in the *Antioch Review, Arizona Quarterly, Chelsea Review, Chicago Review, Evergreen Review, Wesleyan Cardinal* and *The World's Love Poetry*.

Contents

Preface to the New Edition   ix

Introduction, by William E. McCulloh   1

A Note on Selection, Texts and Translation,
  by Willis Barnstone   15

THE GREEK PERIOD

THE HELLENISTIC PERIOD

Contents

THE ROMAN PERIOD

THE BYZANTINE PERIOD

AUTHORS AND ANONYMOUS WORKS OF INDEFINITE PERIOD

SAPPHO

Preface to the New Edition

Sappho and the Greek Lyric Poets combines two earlier volumes — *Sappho* (1965) and *Greek Lyric Poetry* (1962) — in one revised and expanded version. Like two Spanish *picaros*, whom Cervantes or Quevedo might have invented, each volume has gone separately from master to master, acquiring new guises, tricks, and innovations. After the original masters at Doubleday Anchor and Bantam Classics, their new houses were New York University Press, Indiana University Press, Schocken Books, and now, fittingly, since publishers also combine, Schocken/Pantheon, where at last the distinctive lives of these books have come together. En route, at each new house, they acquired different jackets as well as condordances, illustrations, and special essays — a garb admittedly a bit too respectable for young itinerants. Somehow the books have survived twenty-five years, episodically, on their wits.

To marry — and these *picaros* have taken vows — implies reform, the loss of some old ways, and the acquisition of pretended virtues. It has not been easy to give up some of the luxuries of a single life. So Sappho has lost her Greek voice. (The original *Sappho* volume contained facing Greek texts.) Moreover, there were witnesses to her earlier life, the ample *Testimonia*, which contained all the extant ancient biographical accounts of her life. These too had to go. Yet, in defense of her monolingual and unwitnessed state, her earlier scholarly presence does exist in the first edition of *Sappho*, at least in libraries, for those who would examine her more carefully. But, in addition to the companion lyrics of other Greek poets, Sappho now sings with more fragments of her own. I have deciphered eleven fragmentary poems from the almost indecipherable, moving them from incoherence to a minimalist modernity. On the basis of text and ancient context, I have tried to make sense out of pieces of lines that are beautiful and suggestive even in their senselessness, without resorting to the daring earlier rewritings of J. M. Edmonds or the deft restorations of Mary Barnard. In the light of recent Sappho scholarship and personal taste, I have carefully gone over all the texts, making many small, and sometimes substantive, revisions. The other Greek voices occasionally sing in altered form, but on the whole they retain their original sound.

Two books, then, have come together, with the entire corpus of their poetry intact. The Sappho canon is expanded; and *Sappho and the Greek Lyric Poets* contains the largest collection of Greek lyric poetry in English.

Willis Barnstone
Indiana University
Bloomington, 1988

SAPPHO AND THE
GREEK LYRIC POETS

Introduction

Suppose, in our time, the War actually comes. With no current refinements wasted, the elephantine blasts, fire storms, and fallout finish their appointed tasks. Several decades later the literary archaeologists from Tierra del Fuego and the Samoyedes rake loose from London's heaps part of a volume of literary criticism in which stand, entire, Yeats' lines "My fiftieth year had come and gone"—and the "Second Coming," with a few single lines quoted amid the unknown critic's comments. Then a gutted Pittsburgh mansion yields two charred anonymous sheets of a poem whose style—what can be seen of it—resembles Yeats. A fragmentary dictionary cites, as a rare alternate pronunciation of fanatic: "Fá-na-tic. Thus in W. B. Yeats' 'Remorse for Intemperate Speech.'" There are similar further recoveries, equally scanty. So much for the poet whom T. S. Eliot has called the greatest of the twentieth century.

But this has happened already, in time's glacial cataclysm, to the greatest lyric poet (so men say) of the West before the thirteenth century—to Sappho. And to Archilochos, whom some ancients paired with Homer. And to many others, the Herricks, Donnes, and Herberts of Greece's first lyric flowering. For however much one may take it as unmerited grace that one has at least Homer, at least the iceberg tip of the fifth century and its epigones, one must still question the providence which allowed from the vastly different age between—the Lyric Age of the seventh and sixth centuries[1]—only Pindar and the scraps for one other small book. That uniquely organic outgrowth of successive literary styles and forms in Greece—forms which are the ineluctable basis for most Western litera-

---

[1] Thus the title given it by A. R. Burn in *The Lyric Age of Greece* (London, 1960).

[1]

ture[2]—is thus desperately mutilated for us in what seems to have been its most explosively diverse and luxuriant phase.

Homer is the culmination of a long and now invisible tradition of heroic poetry which was the literary voice of a monarchical society. His heroes are the archetypal ancestors of the royalty in whose courts the epic lays flourished and whose values the bard celebrated. But, like Bach, he seems to have written in times which had already moved past his own poetic world. The city-state was beginning to displace the tribal monarchy. The conflict between monarchy and aristocracy had begun, and perhaps also that conflict between aristocracy and commons which led to the great tyrannies (somewhat like the dictatorships of our century) and—at least in some cities—to democracy. But most important for poetry, the poet had begun to emerge as an individual speaking for himself, not an impersonal celebrant of ancestral glory and doom.

While the elder Bach composed his *Art of Fugue "ad maiorem Dei gloriam,"* his sons were breaking the homophonic trail toward the secular divinity of the Beethoven symphony. And within the lifetime of "Homer" (though dates are of course uncertain), Archilochos, the first Western man whom we know as a personality, and the first European lyric poet of whom fragments remain, was fusing and transforming popular and anonymous song and dance into the personal poem. So it is with Archilochos that we must begin, the first historical Western personality, and for us, the impoverished heirs, the inceptor of European lyric.

The Forms of Greek Lyric

But here an academic detour is required. What we shall call Greek "lyric" poetry is in fact a cluster of several quite distinct types, each with its own tradition and development. "Lyric" means literally "accompanied by the lyre," and implies poetry that is sung, not spoken. Now it is

[2] See for example Gilbert Highet, *The Classical Tradition* (New York, 1957).

[2]

likely that all forms of Greek poetry originated in ritual performances which blended word, music, and dance. But in historical times only one branch of that poetry retained all three elements: the choral ode. *Choros*, for the Greeks, meant a performing group which both danced and sang. (Compare "choreography.") *Ôide* meant song. Chorodic poetry, then, remained closer to its ritual origins than did any of the other forms. It was associated with a variety of public ceremonies. Already in Homer one finds most of these mentioned or described.[3] There is the *Thrênos*, or dirge for the dead (the lament for Hektor, *Iliad* XXIV, 746ff.), which survives today as the requiem mass. There is the *Paian*, or hymn to Apollo (*Iliad* I, 472-4), of which some hymns of Hölderlin and Shelley are modern mutations. Of the *Hymenaios* or wedding song (*Iliad* XVIII, 493), Spenser's "Epithalamion," "O Promise Me," and the charivari are schizoid remnants. And compare the *Hyporchêma* or mimetic-narrative dance (*Odyssey* VIII, 261ff.) with *The Seven Deadly Sins* of Weil-Brecht-Balanchine. The *Prosôdion*, or processional song (still surviving in some religious services), is not found in Homer. Nor is the dithyramb, originally an intoxicated improvisation in honor of the god of ecstasy, Dionysos. According to Aristotle, though his claim is much disputed,[4] it was the dithyramb which took on dramatic form and became tragedy. If so, this is the most portentous of all chorodic forms: the bulk of European drama is its grandchild.

In the sixth-century choral odes came to be written in celebration of human, rather than divine, excellence. The *Enkômion* praised great men. Victors in the great athletic contests of Greece were honored in the *Epinîkion*. For those to whom the decathlon is not a revelation of one of the cardinal excellences of man, it seems curious that such should have been the occasion for the poetry of Pindar, who has been called "one of the four spiritual reasons for

---

[3] The classification given here is taken from C. M. Bowra's full discussion in the introduction to his *Greek Lyric Poetry* (Oxford, 1936. 2d ed., 1962).

[4] As, for example, in A. W. Pickard-Cambridge's *Dithyramb, Tragedy, and Comedy* (Oxford, 1927).

[3]

setting ourselves to the toil of mastering the Greek language."[5]

Throughout this apparent wilderness of chorodic types there are three nearly universal common features. First, the language is usually ornate and complex, with some features of the Doric dialect. Second, the typical choral ode (apart from drama) is composed of a series of paired and metrically identical stanzas, with each pair separated from the next by a stanza of similar but not identical metrical character. The pair consists of a strophe and antistrophe, or "turn" and "counter-turn." (These terms are thought to refer to the fact that the dance movements in the second stanza of each pair were exactly reversed from those of the first.) The third, dividing stanza is the epode. The metrical patterns in chorodic poetry are more complex than those of any other Greek poetry—in fact, more complex than any other European poetry except free verse. And the patterns of no two odes are identical. Diversity and regularity, freedom and balance, have never been more perfectly fused.

The third feature common to nearly all choral odes is the material of which the odes consist.[6] There are moral maxims. (In Pindar these can become abrupt revelations.) Individuals involved in the festival or celebration are mentioned. And—most important for literature—a myth is retold, often, as in Pindar, from a striking viewpoint, with daring ellipses and compressions in the narrative—the antipode to Homer's way. Alkman's *Partheneion*, the earliest choral ode to survive *in extenso*, exhibits all three of these elements.

There have been modern attempts at close imitation of the Greek choral ode. Among these are the choruses of Swinburne's *Erectheus* and Arnold's *Merope*, Gray's Pindaric odes, and some of the choruses in the Helena section of Goethe's *Faust II*.

With the elimination of the dancing chorus one reaches the second of the two forms of poetry which are, in the Greek sense, genuinely lyric: the solo song, or monody.

[5] Lewis Richard Farnell, *The Works of Pindar* (London, 1930), I, vii.
[6] Bowra, *Greek Lyric Poetry*, Introduction.

Monody is much closer to the usual modern lyric in its relative simplicity and its preoccupation with the poet's personal concerns. But ancient monody ranged more widely—into politics and satire, for example—than one would expect of "lyric" poetry. And unlike much modern lyric, the poem is never an utterly private communing of the poet with himself; it is always conceived of as addressed to an audience. The audience here, however, is usually not that of an official public occasion, but a private gathering—of disciples (Sappho), or of companions at a drinking party or *symposion* (Alkaios, Anakreon).

Monodies were composed of a single line or short stanza-pattern repeated throughout the poem. Unlike the choral lyric, the same stanza-pattern could be re-used in many poems, and the types of stanzas were limited. Two of the finest types are the Sapphic (employed by its eponym, for example, in the poems translated by Willis Barnstone under the titles "Prayer to Aphrodite" and "Seizure") and the Alcaic (in which Alkaios's "Winter Evening" and "A Nation at Sea" were written[7]). Some idea of their character may perhaps be grasped in Tennyson's imitations:

Sapphic: Faded every violet, all the roses;
          Gone the promise glorious, and the victim,
          Broken in this anger of Aphrodite,
              Yields to the victor.

Alcaeic: O mighty-mouthed inventor of harmonies,
          O skill'd to sing of Time and Eternity,
              God-gifted organ voice of England,
                  Milton, a name to resound for ages.

Among modern imitations, one of Ezra Pound's earlier poems, "Apparuit," is in Sapphics, and a number of Swinburne's imitate monodic meters. But the one modern who consistently transcended imitation in his use of Greek monodic forms, who has earned a place with Horace for having snatched the lyric club from the Greek Hercules, is Hölderlin.

[7] All titles used in this introduction are those given by the translator. The originals are usually untitled.

[5]

In addition to poetry accompanied by music there are two further kinds of Greek verse which one today might roughly class as lyric. Both may originally have been sung, but early lost their music. Iambic poetry, allegedly the invention of Archilochos, was composed of lines predominantly in iambic or trochaic (the reverse of iambic) rhythms. It was at first chiefly employed, as one can see in Archilochos, Semonides of Amorgos, and Hipponax, for personal abuse, satire, and polemic. But even in Archilochos its range was wider (see for example the fragment "Moderation"). Solon used iambics to defend his political and economic policies at Athens.

The greatest offspring in Greek of iambic poetry was the dialog in Athenian drama. The drama is thus a hybrid of the chorodic and iambic traditions. But it has been further maintained that even Shakespeare's blank verse originally came, by way of Italian Renaissance imitations, from ancient drama and thus originally from the iambic poets.[8]

Finally, there is the elegiac poetry. Coleridge's adaptation of Schiller gives some idea of its basic unit, the elegiac couplet:

> In the hexameter rises the fountain's silvery column;
>   In the pentameter aye falling in melody back.

The first line, the hexameter, has six feet of dactyls, often replaced in various feet by spondees (two long syllables). The second line, misnamed the "pentameter," is simply a hexameter with the second half of the third and sixth feet silent.

Of all forms of "lyric" verse, the elegiac has had the most nearly continuous existence, from the late eighth century or earlier into modern times. From the beginning it was used for highly diverse purposes.[9] 1) Like monody, it served to embellish the symposium. There it could speak of love and current political and military affairs, as it does in Kallinos, Mimnermos, and the collection attributed to

---

[8] Highet, *Classical Tradition*, p. 131.
[9] The categories here are approximately those of Bowra in his article "Elegiac Poetry, Greek," *Oxford Classical Dictionary* (Oxford, 1949).

Theognis. 2) It was used for long military and political harangues, such as those of Tyrtaios and Solon, and for historical narrative. 3) It was used in dedications inscribed on statues and other gifts to the gods. 4) It appeared on epitaphs, the short inscriptions on grave-markers. Simonides's epitaph for the Spartan dead at Thermopylae is the most famous (it was quoted in the 1960 Presidential campaign) of a noble company. 5) The form of the lament, especially in its later hybrid, the pastoral elegy, is the one best known in modern times. (Milton's "Lycidas" and "*Epitaphium Damonis,*" Gray's "Elegy," Shelley's "Adonais," Arnold's "Thyrsis.")

The elegiac form was transplanted into Latin and grew nobly in the Augustan period under the care of such men as Propertius and Ovid. It struggled bravely through the Middle Ages until the Renaissance gave it new life, and it survived into the nineteenth century for its finest harvest (apart from its mutation into the English heroic couplet) since the Augustans, in Goethe's *Roman Elegies,* and those of Hölderlin. Since then the couplet form itself has languished. But the spirit passed from Hölderlin into those poems supreme among all which bear the name elegy, the *Duino Elegies* of Rilke.

Development of Greek Lyric

So much for the forms of Greek lyric and their afterlife. It is time now to return to Archilochos and treat of the temporal phases of lyric. The subject is by nature erratic and fragmentary, and the following brash survey of the principal remains will suffer even more heavily from these defects. For full and proper treatment, the reader should consult the bibliography.

We have seen that the social changes in the late eighth century contributed to the development of the poem as individual expression. But much is owing to the innovating personality of Archilochos himself. Born a bastard, of a Greek father and a Thracian mother, he was an outsider from the start. His life as a free-lance soldier, moreover, intensified his alienation from group traditions. Thus thrown upon himself, he rejected the values of the aristocracy, particularly that supreme aristocratic value, Honor (which at the time was roughly chivalric in character). Honor, to the conventional aristocrat of his age, was something worth dying for, since death was in any case inevitable, and an "honorable" death gave one at least the secular immortality of renown. Says Sarpedon to Glaukos in the *Iliad* (XII, 322ff.), "Man, could we survive this war and live forever, deathless and strong, I would not be fighting out in front, nor would I urge you to this fray which gives us glory. But death in myriad forms is closing in—no mortal can slip past it. Come with me; no matter if another will boast over us, or we over him."

Archilochos, as his fragment "On His Shield" makes clear, chose another way. To throw away one's shield in a hasty retreat was not worse than death. It was simple common sense. What counted was not the deathless fame, but the tangible delights of the present, precious moment. Together with future glory Archilochos discarded the equally impalpable worth of present reputation; it was better to make enemies than to appease. Some would hold that the short fragment here titled "Proverb for a Great Scoundrel" refers in fact to the poet himself. If so, the image of the self-reliant, self-enclosed hedgehog is an apt one for this first on Europe's honorable roll of prickly, renegade poets.

Archilochos' revolution did not of course transform the whole of subsequent poetry. It seems to have been the regions of the Eastern Greeks, the Aiolians and Ionians of Asia Minor and the islands, which proved most receptive to the new spirit. Meanwhile at Sparta, the heart of the younger Western, or Dorian branch of Greek culture, Tyrtaios was composing martial elegies in which an older communal ethos still lived. The Spartans were the nearest approximation among the Greeks to the collectivist mentality. It is therefore fitting that their gift to the Lyric Age should have been the most collective of forms, the choral ode.

To be sure, as earlier mentioned, the choral ode had existed, in a sense, from the beginning of cult, and thus perhaps ever since the tribal organization of man. But the wealthy patronage of the Spartan state during its years of peaceful abundance, in the later seventh century, attracted talented poets and gave them the means to produce their choruses for the public festivals. Significantly, most of the earlier of these commissioned poets were from the East, the older and subtler culture. The Eastern influence and the years of peace are perhaps the explanation for the un-Spartan playfulness and charm of the first surviving choral poet, Alkman.

Even in the choral form—a clear mark of the Lyric Age —one hears the voice of Alkman the individual. One of the most impressive aspects of that voice is its vivid perception of nature. Alkman was apparently the first to distinguish four seasons (rather than three). And, as in the poem "Rest," he shows a sense for the life of the inanimate world. "Rest" has suggested to some a parallel with Goethe's "Über allen Gipfeln." But it has further links with Rilke and Jeffers.

Until Simonides, choral poetry after Alkman is attested only in a bitterly small collection of scraps. Stesichoros, a native Dorian (this time from the far West, from Sicily), is credited with the introduction of greatly extended mythical narratives into the choral ode. The loss of his *Oresteia* or *Helen* was perhaps as irreparable as we should judge the perishing of Keats's "Eve of St. Agnes." Ibykos (he too from the far West) has at least left us with enough to establish that we have certainly lost much fine poetry.

With Ibykos we must touch on a matter which needs less belaboring today than it might have in the past. Much of Greek love poetry is about homosexual love. Greek society in general, and particularly in Dorian lands, was so arranged that women could not readily become full emotional companions of men. Marriage was often a purely practical affair entered upon by a man in his middle thirties for the purpose of raising a family. The wife was essentially a housekeeper. Consequently the deepest erotic experiences were frequently—and for the poetry of the Lyric Age, predominantly—homosexual, between older and younger men, and between older and younger women. Often, of course, the affairs were mere adventures in the flesh. At other times they were as luminous and mature as any of the heterosexual passions of later ages. In our century Kavafis and George have shown in their poetry, as nearly as is possible in a different society, what pederasty could mean to the Greeks.

Ibykos brings choral poetry down to somewhere in the middle of the sixth century B.C. We must return to the end of the seventh for the commencement and, at the same time, the climax of monody.

Here Eastern Greece (Asia Minor and the islands)—the Aiolic island of Lesbos in particular—is the focus of creation. Alkaios and Sappho, both aristocrats of Lesbos, were contemporaries, and both in their own way reveal at its most intense the subjective individualism of Archilochos, now winged with lyric meters and those melodies which for us must be unheard.

The times were bad for aristocrats—both Alkaios and Sappho were exiled by a middle-class tyranny—and much of Alkaios' poetry is that of a militant reactionary. Other poems, archetypes of their kind, are devoted to the delights of the drinking party, whether as refuge from the outer political darkness or as a brief forgetting of the darkness of death.

In the poems of Sappho hardly a whiff of politics appears. Her persistent subjects are family, private friends and foes, and love. One view holds that she was head of a cult which was at the same time a finishing school for girls of the aristocracy—a cult devoted to poetry and Aphrodite—no mere symbol of beauty and love, but the genuine goddess. From within the group of her pupils she may have found her favorites. With these perhaps she shared that epiphany of her goddess of which she sings in her only wholly surviving poem, "Prayer to Aphrodite."

Simplicity and directness are the manner of all monody, in contrast to choral poetry. In Sappho these qualities are at their highest. For many, therefore, Sappho in her precious rags will stand above Pindar in his full effulgent robes at the thin-aired pinnacle of ancient lyric.

More than a full generation after Sappho comes the next and last personality in ancient monody. Anakreon, again from the East, but this time Ionia, became in popular legend a sort of poetic Silenus: a lovable, drunken, old infatuate. But, somewhat incongruously, this Silenus displays a deft, ironic wit which later imitators (the many anonymous authors of the *Anakreonteia*), playful and delightful as they often are, could not fully reproduce. It is, from our retrospective vantage, hard to believe that readers for centuries could have accepted the *Anakreonteia* as Anakreon's own.

The monodic strand in the Lyric Age comes to an end in a series of anonymous *Skolia* or drinking songs. These *Skolia* are the only native Athenian contribution, apart from Solon, to the poetry of the Lyric Age. Some of them are quite strong and vivid, but one could not guess from them that the fifth century in literature was to belong to Athens.

Three figures close the great period of Greek lyric. All three were choral poets chiefly, and were closely associated through family ties or rivalry. Simonides was uncle of Bakchylides. Pindar strove, sometimes bitterly, with both.

Simonides, eldest of the three, seems in many ways more modern, more a man of the fifth century, than the other two. Such things as his poem in criticism of Kleoboulos and his lecture-poem to Skopas on the limits of mortal virtue reflect a critical, intellectualist strain in Simonides, a readiness to modify received standards not, as with Archilochos, by mere subjective vehemence, but by rational judgment. His short fragment on "Arete" (virtue or excellence) is one of several poems which show a tendency toward dealing with abstract entities rather than traditional mythological divinities.

Like Pindar and Bakchylides, Simonides frequented the mansions of the great where his skills were welcomed and rewarded. But he seems to have given his ultimate sympathies to Athenian democracy, the fifth century's wave of the future. In his style he was celebrated for the controlled, vivid sobriety which can be seen in the long fragment on Danaë and Perseus.

Bakchylides survived in an even more fragmentary state than his uncle until 1896, when Egyptian sands surrendered a papyrus containing a tolerable proportion of his works. The odes of Bakchylides, as we can now see, are fluent, attractive, and often of great power.

Pindar, who deserves—even in translation—a volume of his own (and has received it in Richmond Lattimore's fine versions), must here be dealt with even more inadequately than all who have gone before. Unlike Simonides, he was not at home in the new currents of the fifth century. Like Homer and Bach, he is the culmination of a tradition—the chorodic—which the times were leaving behind. He was most in his element not at democratic Athens, but in Aigina and Thebes (the chief city of his native Boiotia)— the cultural dinosaurs of the age. Proud, aloof, assured of his genius, and wonderstruck by the brief, god-sent radiance of mortal excellence, he is deservedly the "Theban eagle." For some of those who cleave the knotted oak and swirling ocean of his Greek, there is no greater lyric in the world.

After Pindar there is much that is brilliant, touching, and entertaining in the lyric forms, but the highest energies in Greek literature are now found in drama, history, oratory, and philosophy. There were of course still practitioners of chorody and monody; even Aristotle tried his hand at the former and wrought yeomanly. But a new musical style increasingly subdued the text to mere libretto. The predominant form for pure poetry was henceforth the elegiac epigram.

Elegiac poetry and iambic poetry after Archilochos have been left to one side in our review thus far. Most of the significant poets in both *genres* have been mentioned above in the initial discussion of the forms of Greek lyric. It should be noted that a fraction of the poetry of Archilochos and Anakreon is in elegiacs, and that a few iambic lines of Anakreon survive. The elegiac epigrams of Simonides are, next to the work of Theognis, the largest body of elegiac poetry by one man to survive before the third century. Judging from the remains, the epigram, apart from anonymous inscriptions, did not greatly flourish in the latter part of the fifth and in the fourth centuries. The epigrams some think to be Plato's, if in fact they do belong to this period, are the one bright patch in these years.

But in the third century, at the hands of Asklepiades, Kallimachos, and their successors, epigram acquired new range and freshness. The short, pointed poem, usually in elegiacs—whether erotic, epitaph (real or simulated), satirical, or gnomic—became a popular lyric form.

And so it remained for all the succeeding centuries of Greek as an ancient language. Scholars and litterateurs, while Rome was refocusing the world, continued to refine a form which had lost touch with any vital, transforming, outside forces. But frozen as it was, the epigram could still gleam, most brightly in such men as Meleagros, Philodemos, Marcus Argentarius, grim Palladas—and even in the sixth-century A.D. Byzantine, Paulus Silentiarius. Gathered four times or more in successive collections, the harvest of epigram which is the *Greek Anthology* was stored in roughly its present form by Constantine Cephalas in the tenth century.

The death which came thus slowly to the Greek lyric can come to no other poetry with such apt grace. For in no other poetry does the conviction of the bitter, lesser glory of mortal works dwell so near the center. (The Roman poet mars his work by hollow boasts of immortality; the later West has Christianity flowing ambiguously in its heart.)

Greek lyric lives, of course, in another way—as part of the enriching stream from which each new age of poetry draws. "Death by Water" in *The Waste Land* is a form taken from the *Anthology*. Pound writes poems after Ibykos and Sappho. Salvatore Quasimodo translates the Greek lyricists. And those researchers of atomic rubble, with whom we began, could find a fit Hellenic epitaph for all our troublesome days in Yeats' lines for his own tomb:

> Cast a cold eye
> On life, on death.
> Horseman, pass by!

William E. McCulloh

A Note on Selections, Texts and Translation

Fire, religion and time have treated the lyric poetry of ancient Greece very poorly. Texts have disappeared by intention and through neglect. Today there is little hope of finding original papyrus manuscripts in Greece, for papyrus cannot easily survive in even the relatively dry climate of Greece.[1] Only in waterless parts of Egypt, in the rubbish heaps of antiquity, may ancient documents still be preserved, buried in tombs or with ancient cities under the sand. Indeed, there is always hope that the sands of some provincial city of Egypt will yield a new poem or fragment, such as the odes and dithyrambs of Bakchylides or Alkman's choral ode found in 1896 at Oxyrhynchos.

In what has survived—a small percent of the important lyric poetry—we still have enough to comprise one of our great achievements in the arts. For we have poems by Sappho, Pindar, Bakchylides, Meleagros, Archilochos, Simonides, Alkaios, Anakreon and many others. The largest single collections are the victory odes of Pindar and the more than four thousand poems in the *Greek* or *Palatine Anthology*. A very large proportion of Greek lyric poetry survives as exempla quoted in studies of Greek and Latin scholars.

A single line in Greek by Sappho or an elegiac couplet ascribed to Plato may be precious to us in its own right:

WORLD

I could not hope
to touch the sky
with my two arms.   (Sappho)

[1] In 1961, for the first time, original papyrus was found in continental Greece, at Dervani (Lagada). See Herbert Hunger, "Papyrusfund in Griechenland," *Chronique d'Egypte* 37, no. 74 (July 1962).

[15]

or

> I am a sailor's tomb. Beside me lies a farmer.
> Hell is the same, under the land and sea.   (Plato)

But lines from Greek lyric poetry may also be precious when they are all we have left from which to form an image of an ancient poet. Because, therefore, the number of poems from shorter lyric poetry is so limited, I have translated virtually all the true lyric poems and intelligible fragments—monodic and choral—from the poets of the sixth and seventh centuries B.C, with the exception of Pindar and Bakchylides, who are represented only in part. By considering fragments and epigrams one may perhaps read enough lines from poets like Archilochos, Anakreon, Alkaios, Ibykos, Alkman, to see them in at least clear profile. Of the later poets, found in the *Greek* or *Palatine Anthology,* I have tried to make a generous selection of the better poems.

But the very fact that ancient papyri and later copies of Greek lyrics have been so maltreated makes one all the more mindful of omissions, and these too should be stated. From Pindar I have translated only a selection of the odes and fragments. Pindar's victory odes, a book in themselves, may be read in the luminous translations in Richmond Lattimore's *The Odes of Pindar.* There is also the serious omission of some longer elegiac and iambic poems. Thus while Tyrtaios, Semonides, Solon and Xenophanes are well represented, they have been denied inclusion of one or more of their significant extant compositions.[2] It is a tangible omission, however, which a later edition may hopefully correct. Another edition might also include a larger selection of sepulchral inscriptions.

[2] In this anthology the *lyric* poem is emphasized. For this reason excerpts are not given from epic poetry or from the plays. In using the word *lyric* no rigid definition is intended, e.g., the early Greek concept of lyric poems for the lyre as opposed to elegiac poems for the flute. Rather, lyric here simply means a short poem that sings. In this sense, and this alone, I have given preference to the more purely lyrical pieces from the Greek poets. The longer poems in elegiac couplets tend at times, like heroic couplets in English, to become essays in verse. This is true of longer poems of Tyrtaios, Semonides, Solon and Xenophanes.

More painful is the omission of many longer poems by Bakchylides. While he is represented here, the entire opus —thirteen epinikia, six dithyrambs and various short pieces—appears in lively translation in Robert Fagles' recent book, *Bacchylides: Complete Poems*, which both fills the gap and conveys the narrative eloquence and pristine imagery of this neglected poet. Bakchylides, like Thomas Traherne, is a relatively recent discovery; though there is as yet no piggyback tradition of praise—indeed, he has not been considered on his own but has been consistently and foolishly downgraded as a secondary Pindar—he is assured of his ancient place in the canon of the nine lyric poets.

The most formidable problem in translating from Greek has been to find a just approximation of Greek stanza forms and meter. It is at least consoling that there can never be a single solution for the transfer of prosodic techniques from one language to another. Poems in ancient Greek were composed primarily to be sung, chanted or recited, to be heard not read. In the original papyrus scripts the words were all run together as in Sans rit. There were no indentations of shorter lines as in later manuscripts, for the poetic lines were also run together. Only capital letters were used. Thus even the question of whether English lines should begin with upper- or lower-case letters has no real precedence in the original scripts, and the most faithful translations would use upper-case letters exclusively. So, the first stanza of Sappho's poem to Anaktoria might read,

SOMESAYCAVALRYANDOTHERSCLAIM
INFANTRYORAFLEETOFLONGOARSIS
THESUPREMESIGHTONTHEBLACKEAR
TH.ISAYITIS

Even the stanzaic appearance of a Sapphic hymn or a Simonidean epigram as printed traditionally in Greek texts was determined by later scholars on the basis of metrical pauses.

I have tried to give order to these translations in several ways. To approximate the easy conversational flow of many of the Greek poems, I have more often given a syllabic rather than an accentual regularity to the lines. An exception is the longer elegiac poem where the forceful dactyls seemed to call for a regular (though free-falling) beat in alternating lines of equal feet. In the matter of diction, it is important to remember that the Greeks, as most poets in the past—a Spenser or Kavafis excepted—wrote in a language which seemed natural and contemporary to their readers.[3] My intention has been to use a contemporary idiom, generally chaste, but colloquial as the occasion suggests.

Until very recently, it has been a uniform practice to impose rhyme on poems translated from ancient Greek. But the Greeks did not use end rhyme as a common poetic device. Rhyme was used only in rare instances, usually for humor or satire (see Palladas, 561), and so rhyme is not used in these translations. In most of the poems I have tried to retain the stanzaic patterns suggested by the metrical stops in the Greek texts. In others I have been more original, or perhaps perverse, in seeking an equivalent of the Greek. I am especially guilty of license where I seek to convey the humor of *Greek Anthology* epigrams.

In most cases the Greek rather than Latinized spelling has been followed, thus Alkaios and Theokritos, not Alcaeus and Theocritus. In recent years the English transliteration of Greek words has become common and it is, I believe, essentially more pleasant and satisfying to read. It is a new practice, however, with rules unfixed, used differently by different hands; I am aware of instances where I have not been entirely consistent where the sin of inconsistency is in the end less gauche than the virtue of absolute order. So, while making the reader aware that Pindar and Plato are really Pindaros and Platon, I have persisted in referring to them as Plato and Pindar. Perhaps in a few years when original places and texts are more familiar to us than English maps and translations, we shall speak of Livorno, not Leghorn, Thessaloniki not Salonika, and even Pindaros not Pindar.

[3] Many writers did use archaic Homeric words and phrases, but this too was at least natural in common poetic usage.

I have used standard recent texts: Lobel and Page, Diehl, Bowra (Pindar), Gow (Theokritos) and Loeb Library editions. I have also gone to Italian, French and modern Greek editions where they have been helpful. For some of the earlier poets, especially Sappho, I have in some cases followed the conjectural reconstructions of Treu (*Sappho Lieder*), Edmonds (Loeb Library) and Page (*Sappho and Alcaeus*)—when the only alternative to the reconstructed text is no poem at all. But I have misgivings about this. However, where a mutilated text can be used, it often offers, quite accidentally, very striking effects; in such poems as Sappho's "Age and Light," "Dream" and "The Laurel Tree," the very poverty of the lacuna-ridden text contributes a poignancy and quality of modernity which the reconstructed text lacks.

In innumerable cases there are variant readings in the Greek texts. I have usually followed the more recent editions.

A word about titles. All the poems included here have titles, yet few of these are traditional in the Greek. Why use titles then in English translations? Most of the poems and fragments are quotations found in other ancient writings. Though sometimes merely grammatical in nature, the context in which the poem appears usually gives additional information about the complete poem. The titles here are primarily informational, based on contextual information or on common ancient allusions with which a modern reader may be unfamiliar. Hopefully, titles will serve to replace lengthy footnotes and make the poems more complete.

Ideally, poetry in translation should one day lead a reader to a reading of the poem in the original tongue. The poem in its native phonemes, we often forget, was primarily a poem, and a good one, presumably, if chosen for translation. A poem in translation should be faithful, if to anything, to this primary quality of the original— that of its being an effective poem.

With this in mind we may say something about the general possibilities of poetry in translation. Many banal ideas are commonly held about the disadvantages of poetry in translation—this despite the modern additions to our language of verse translations by Lattimore, Fitts, Fitzgerald, Wilbur, Lowell or Auden. Poems may be poorly translated, as they may have been poorly written originally, but they are not necessarily poorer or better than the original—though the translator must secretly and vainly aim for the latter. The quality of the poem in translation will depend on the translator's skill in writing poetry in his own language in the act of translating. If he is T. S. Eliot translating Saint-Jean Perse or Mallarmé translating Poe or the scholars of the King James Version translating the psalms, the result may indeed be superior —or at the very least equal. Only one thing is certain: the poem in translation will be different. The translator's task, then, is to produce a faithful forgery. The quality and resemblance of the new product to the old lie somewhere between such fidelity and fraud.

But it is said that certain memorable lines or phrases cannot be expressed in any other language. Yet it should also be said that while at times we must lose, at others we gain, and the good translator will take advantage of the text, improving upon the weaker lines of the original, while doing his best with the best. More important, it is forgotten that translation provides an opportunity for languages to interact upon each other, for one tongue to alter and enrich the possibilities of expression in another. In the past some translated works have changed both literary language and tradition: notably the Petrarchan sonnet, Luther's Bible, Judith Gautier's haiku. Milton went as naturally to the King James Version for vocabulary as Shakespeare turned to Holinshed for plots; when Rimbaud's *Illuminations* were translated into English, the tradition of our literature was expanded to the extent that diction and subject never before found in English were presented to us.

In a word, the quality of a work in translation is dependent on the translator's skills. His forgery is not necessarily better or worse than the original or than other works in his own language; it is only necessarily different

—and here the difference, if new and striking, may extend the verbal and thematic borders of his own literature. And as a corollary to his work the new poem may also be seen as an essay into literary criticism, a reading, a creative *explication de texte*.

Discussion of translations of poetry usually confuses *kind* with *value*. One type of translation is thought to be intrinsically superior to others, be it free translation, close translation, poetry *after*, imitation, metaphrase, paraphrase, etc. In the critic's mind the quality of a translation often depends on how closely it conforms to his own preferred method. This error of descriptive rather than evaluative criticism—where kind determines value—probably occurs more often in regard to poetry translation than in any other form of literary criticism. But in the end, method is secondary, and determines neither the virtues nor sins of a poem. The translator need only clearly and honestly indicate his method—whatever it is—and then be judged, not on this choice, but on the quality of the new poem. If the new poem is good, the translator as artist will be performing his ancient function of retelling in his own form, a given content he has overheard from the immediate or the distant past.

Willis Barnstone
Indiana University

The
Greek Period

Archilochos

According to the most probable view, Archilochos lived during the latter half of the eighth century B.C. (The event referred to in "An Eclipse of the Sun" may have occurred either in 711 B.C. or 647 B.C.) He was the son of Telesikles, a nobleman of the island of Paros, and a slave-woman: hence, a bastard. He took part in the Parian colonization of the island of Thasos and seems to have spent most of his life as a soldier in the pay of his country. The only striking event in his life which has been preserved in the tradition is the "Lykambes affair." Lykambes, a nobleman, promised his daughter Neoboule to Archilochos and then went back on the promise. Archilochos took revenge in the poetic invective which has ever since been regarded (too narrowly) as his special gift. The legend that the potency of his satire produced the suicide of Neoboule, or Lykambes, or the whole family, is probably only legend. In later years, according to some interpreters of the fragments, Neoboule became a prostitute and even made advances to Archilochos, who rejected her with bitter comments on his former love. Archilochos died in battle. A cult in his honor was later established on Paros, and, by the third century B.C., his shrine had become a center for scholars.

Chief works: 1) elegies dealing with warfare, consolation ("On Friends Lost at Sea"), personal expression, conviviality; 2) epodes (stanzas composed of several distinct meters) of personal or satirical content, often employing illustrative narratives— especially fable ("An Animal Appeals to Zeus"); 3) poems in iambic or trochaic meters, of satirical, personal, hortatory or narrative content. (The trochaic tetrameter was the popular equivalent of the more aristocratic narrative meter, the dactylic hexameter.)

Archilochos' language is chiefly the Ionic of his day, but in the elegies it is strongly influenced by Homeric diction.

As suggested in the Introduction, the ambiguous

[25]

social position of Archilochos probably helped to
make him the spokesman par excellence of the new
spirit of the Lyric Age. This spirit included a
preoccupation with the "now," "here," and "I" (as
Adrados has said*), rather than with an archetypical
past. It further manifested a greatly increased sense
for man's helpless subjection to circumstance
("Providence," "Moderation").

Archilochos exercised considerable influence in
various ways over Kallimachos (iambics), Catullus
(satire), and Horace (epode).

The iambus was invented by
Archilochos of Paros.
CLEMENT OF ALEXANDRIA, Miscellanies†

Of the three iambic writers in Aristarchos' canon,
the one who achieves the greatest mastery is
Archilochos. We find in him the most developed
sense of expression, with terse and vigorous
phrasing, and abundance of blood and muscle.
QUINTILIAN, Guide to Oratory

I would shun the poisonous tooth of slander.
Though removed in time, I have seen the
cantankerous Archilochos in poverty because he
fattened on the abuse of enemies.
PINDAR, Pythian Odes, 2

In this grave lies Archilochos whom the Muses
guided to the writing of furious iambics to preserve
the supremacy of Homer's dactyls.
ADRIANOS, Palatine Anthology

◆◇◆◇◆◇◆◇◆◇◆◇◆◇◆◇◆◇◆◇◆◇◆◇◆◇◆

* Francisco R. Adrados, *Líricos griegos: elegiacos y yam-
bógraphos arcaicos* (Barcelona, 1956), I, 15.
† Clement is in error here.

1 THASOS AND SICILY
                              This wheatless island
stands like a donkey's back. It bristles
with a tangle of wild woodland.
                              Oh,
there is no country so beautiful,
no sensual earth that keys my passion
as these plains around the river Siris.*

2 AN ISLAND IN THE NORTH AIGAIAN
All, O all the calamities of all the Hellenes
are set loose on this battleground in Thasos.

3 THE DOUBLECROSS†
Let brawling waves beat his ship
against the shore, and have the mop-haired
    Thracians
take him naked at Salmydessos,
and he will suffer a thousand calamities
as he chews the bread of slaves.
His body will stiffen in freezing surf
as he wrestles with slimy seaweed,
and his teeth will rattle like a helpless dog,
flopped on his belly in the surge,
puking out the brine. Let me watch him grovel
in mud—for the wrong he did me:
as a traitor he trampled on our good faith,
he who was once my comrade.

4 PAROS FIGS
Say goodbye to the island Paros,
farewell to its figs and the seafaring life.

---

* These two separate fragments are found together.
† This poem is also ascribed to Hipponax.

5   THREAT

                    Let the stone of Tantalos
no longer overhang this island.

6   WAR

Look, Glaukos, how heavy seawaves leap skyward!
Over the Gyrai rocks
hangs a black cloud, a signal of winter storm.
                    From the unforeseen comes fear.

7   A VESSEL OF WINE

Go take your cup and walk along the timber deck
of our roaming ship; drain the hollow casks
of all their red wine. How can we stay sober
on the watch when all the rest are drunk?

8   A DROWNING

They laid down their lives
in the arms of waves.

9   SHIPWRECK

The vessel wavered on the cutting edge
        between the stormwinds and the waves.

10   PRAYER AT SEA

Often, when their vessel was threatened by the
        gray salty sea,
they prayed to Athene of the lovely braids for
        sweet return.

11   ON FRIENDS LOST AT SEA

If you irritate the wound, Perikles, no man
in our city will enjoy the festivities.
These men were washed under by the thudding
        seawaves,

and the hearts in our chest are swollen with pain.
Yet against this incurable misery, the gods
give us the harsh medicine of endurance.
Sorrows come and go, friend, and now they strike
   us
and we look with horror on the bleeding sores,
yet tomorrow others will mourn the dead. I tell you,
hold back your feminine tears and endure.

12   ON THE LACK OF PROPER BURNING
      AND BURIAL FOR HIS BROTHER-IN-LAW
      WHO WAS SHIPWRECKED
      If only his head and handsome limbs
      had been wrapped in white burial cloth
      and touched by Hephaistos' hand of fire.

13   AN ECLIPSE OF THE SUN
      Nothing in the world can surprise me now. Nothing
      is impossible or too wonderful, for Zeus, father
      of the Olympians, has turned midday into black
         night
      by shielding light from the blossoming sun,
      and now dark terror hangs over mankind.
         Anything
      may happen, so do not be amazed if beasts
      on dry land seek pasture with dolphins in
      the ocean, and those beasts who loved sunny hills
      love crashing seawaves more than the warm
         mainland.

14   DAWN
      Dawn was rising full white.

15   GIRL
      A spray of myrtle and beauty of a rose
      were happiness in her hands, and her hair
      fell as darkness on her back and shoulders.

16   ON PASIPHILE, A FRIEND OF ALL
      As the figtree on its rock feeds many crows,
          so this simple girl sleeps with strangers.

17   SUDDEN LOVE
      And to fall upon her heaving belly,
      and thrust your groin into her groin,
      your thighs between her thighs.

18   ON THE MALE ORGAN
      Feeble now are the muscles in my mushroom.

19   LIKE A DONKEY
      His penis is swollen
      like a donkey from Priene
      taking his fill of barley.

20   QUALITIES OF A GIRLFRIEND
      She is a common woman for rent,
      but what sensuality and fat ankles.
      O fat whore for hire!

21   RICHES
      Enormous was the gold he amassed
      from many years of work,
      but all
      fell into the luscious arms
      of a common whore.

22   PROVIDENCE
      Let the gods take care of everything. Many times
      they resurrect a man whom disaster left lying
      face down on the black earth. Many times they
          topple

a man and pin him, back to the soil, though he
was solid on his feet. A multitude of evils
batters him as he wanders hungry and mad.

23   ON DEAD ANIMALS
Many of them, I hope, will be dried up
by the sharp rays of the sun in its zenith,
by the sun in the time of the Dog Star.

24   PROVERB FOR A GREAT SCOUNDREL
The fox knows many tricks,
the hedgehog only one. A good one.

25   HIS TWO VIRTUES
I am a servant of the kingly wargod Enyalios
and am also skilled in the lovely arts.

26   WINE OF NAXOS IS LIKE NECTAR
BUT HIS JAVELIN IS MUCH MORE
My javelin is good white bread and Ismarian wine.
When I find rest on my javelin I drink wine.

27   ON THE SHORT-HAIRED WARRIORS IN THE
LELANTINE WAR BETWEEN CHALKIS AND
ERETRIA WHO AGREED NOT TO USE MISSILE
WEAPONS
Perhaps fewer bows will be stretched and slings
        hurled
when Ares begins battle on the noisy plain,
but then the mournful labor of the sword is worse.

This is warfare in which the spear-famed islanders
from Euboia are godlike and easily masterful.

28   APHRODITE IS CENSURED
Passionate love relentlessly twists a cord
under my heart and spreads deep mist on my eyes,
stealing the unguarded brains from my head.

29   ON HIS SHIELD
Well, what if some barbaric Thracian glories
in the perfect shield I left under a bush?
I was sorry to leave it—but I saved my skin.
Does it matter? O hell, I'll buy a better one.

30   MY KIND OF GENERAL
I don't like a general
who towers over the troops,
lordly with elegant locks
and trim mustachios.
Give me a stumpy soldier
glaringly bowlegged,
yet rockfirm on his feet,
and in his heart a giant.

31   CHARON THE CARPENTER
The gold booty of Gyges means nothing to me.
I don't envy that Lydian king, nor am I jealous
of what gods can do, nor of the tyrants' great
powers. All these are realms beyond my vision.

32   MERCENARY FRIENDSHIP
Glaukos, soldier of fortune, will be your friend
until he begins to fight.

33   WEDDING DEDICATION
When Alkibia became a married woman, she gave
    the holy veil of her hair to Queen Hera.

34   ON THE DAUGHTER OF LYKAMBES
I pray for one gift: that I might merely touch
Neoboule's hand.

35   LOVE
I live here miserable and broken with desire,
pierced through to the bones by the bitterness
of this god-given painful love.

O comrade, this passion makes my limbs limp
and tramples over me.

36   THIRST
I want to fight you
just as when I am thirsty I want to drink.

37   ON A HANGING
They hung their heads to one side, choking,
and disgorged their remaining arrogance.

38   QUALITY IN LOVE
How can I like the way she makes love?
Give me sweet figs before sour wild pears.

39   OLD AGE
A life of doing nothing is good for old men,
especially if they are simple in their ways,
or stupid, or inane in their endless blabber
as old men tend to be.

40   PERIKLES THE GUEST
                    Like the Mykonians, Perikles,
                        you drink our unmixed wine
            and pay for nothing.

[33]

You broke into this party, uninvited, and act as if
    among old friends.
Your stomach has tricked the brains in your skull
    and now you are shameless.

41   ON THE PEOPLE'S CENSURE

No man, Aisimides, who bows to the mud-slinging
    mob has ever been capable of profound
    pleasures.

42   ON WRONGDOERS

              One big thing I understand:
I know how to spit back with black venom
against the man who wrongs me.

43   THE ROBE

Your telltale robe is bulging, you poor tramp,
and the men you love sit beside you.
The ditchdigger is in on your fancy story
and so is your husband Ariphantos.
Lucky Ariphantos didn't catch the fumes
of that stinking billygoat thief,
for while he was staving off the potter
    Aischylides,
the digger dug out your cherry,
and now your swollen belly tells the tale.

44   AFTER THE DROWNING
    OF HIS SISTER'S HUSBAND

Now, I have no desire for poetry or joy,
yet I will make nothing better by crying,
nor worse by seeking good foods and pleasure.

[34]

45   MODERATION

O my soul, my soul—you are mutilated helplessly
by this blade of sorrow. Yet rise and bare your
    chest,
face those who would attack you, be strong, give no
    ground.
And if you defeat them, do not brag like a loud-
    mouth,
nor, if they beat you, run home and lie down to cry.
Keep some measure in your joy—or in your
    sadness during
crisis—that you may understand man's up-and-
    down life.

46   ON THE DEATH OF TWO FRIENDS*

Broad earth, now you entomb Megatimos and
    Aristophon
    who were the two tall columns of this island
    Naxos.

47   ON A LEWD SERVANT

And wandering about the household
was that hateful chattering eunuch.

48   PERIKLES TO ELPINIKE

Lady, you are much too old
to rub yourself with perfume.

49   AN ANIMAL APPEALS TO ZEUS†

O father Zeus, you who control the cosmos, and
    oversee the actions of man,
his criminal and lawful acts, you also judge the
    arrogance and trial of wild beasts.

* Ascription to Archilochos is uncertain.
† Probably a fox.

50   JUSTICE

My lord Apollo, single out the guilty ones,
and in your customary way, destroy them all.

51   PERFUME

               Her breasts and her dark hair
were perfume, and even an old man would love her.

52   TO A GIRLFRIEND'S FATHER

Father Lykambes, what is this new silliness?
            Are your natural brains
gone wholly bad? The neighbors laugh openly
        at your absurd life,
and you persist in chattering like a cricket.

53   ON DROWNED BODIES

Let us hide the dreadful
gifts of lord Poseidon.

54   DEATH

When dead no man finds respect or glory from men
of his town. Rather, we hope while alive for some
favor from the living. The dead are always scorned.

Kallinos

The content of the fragments indicates that Kallinos was active roughly in the middle of the seventh century B.C. *The Cimmerians were barbarians from the Crimea and Southern Russia who for a time threatened to overwhelm parts of Asia Minor, including the Greek cities of the coast. Kallinos lived in Ephesos, one of these cities. The surviving fragments—like those of Tyrtaios—show essentially an adaptation of Homeric style and language to the demands of the present (as if one were to create war propaganda from the King James Version of the Old Testament prophets). The only major change from Homer is the exclusive focus on courage as sacrificial patriotism rather than a means chiefly for the acquisition of individual glory. All the fragments are elegiac.*

(On Elegy)   Among the best writers in this meter Proklos includes Kallinos of Ephesos, Mimnermos of Kolophon, and also Philetas the son of Telephos, from Kos, and Kallimachos the son of Battos.

PHOTIOS, Library

❖❖❖❖❖❖❖❖❖❖❖❖❖❖❖❖❖❖❖❖❖❖❖❖❖❖

55   A CALL TO ARMS AGAINST THE
CIMMERIAN INVADERS

When will you show some courage, young
   comrades?
How long will you lie back and do nothing?
Lazing in shabby peace on our land bled by war,
have you no shame before the neighboring
   townsmen?

Let each man hurl his spear once more before he
   dies,
for glory dazzles on our helmets when we battle

the enemy for farmland and children and true wife.
Death will come only when the web of destiny
is spun.
    So move out, charge into the barbarous ranks
with spear held high and shield gripping a brave
    heart.
From death there is no escape; all men face the
    dark,
even those with blood of gods in their veins.

Often a man flees from the clash and thud of
    spears
and comes home to fall into sudden doom,
but he is neither loved nor missed by his
    townsmen.

Yet when a hero dies the great and small shed
    tears;
by a whole people a brave warrior is mourned.
In life he seems a demigod before the crowd;
as a marble pillar they look upon his strength,
for all alone he does the great deeds of an army.

56   TO ZEUS
Pity the people of Smyrna,
and now recall
if they ever burned for you
the choice thighs of oxen.

Tyrtaios

Tyrtaios was active at Sparta during the Second Messenian War, that is, some time in the seventh century B.C. *The legend that he came originally from Athens seems to be false. His works included marching songs (now lost) and elegies. In the remains of the latter, martial exhortations predominate, as with Kallinos. And like Kallinos, Tyrtaios modifies the Homeric tradition in the direction of a more corporate and collective ethos. He came at the time of Sparta's transition from an ordinary Greek city to a severely disciplined military commune.*

The Spartans swore that they would take Messene or die themselves. When the oracle told them to take an Athenian general, they chose Tyrtaios, the lame poet, who rekindled their courage, and he took Messene in the twentieth year of the war.

Suda Lexicon

And Philochoros says that when the Spartans overpowered the Messenians through the generalship of Tyrtaios, they made it a custom of their military expeditions that after the evening meal when the paean had been sung each man would sing a poem by Tyrtaios, and the leader would judge the singing and give the winner a prize of meat.

ATHENAIOS, Scholars at Dinner

❖❖❖❖❖❖❖❖❖❖❖❖❖❖❖❖❖❖❖❖❖❖❖❖❖❖❖❖❖

57   SPARTAN SOLDIER

It is beautiful when a brave man of the front ranks
    falls and dies, battling for his homeland,
and ghastly when a man flees planted fields and
    city
    and wanders begging with his dear mother,
aging father, little children and true wife.

[39]

He will be scorned in every new village,
reduced to want and loathsome poverty; and shame
    will brand his family line, his noble
figure. Derision and disaster will hound him.
    A turncoat gets no respect or pity;
so let us battle for our country and freely give
    our lives to save our darling children.
Young men, fight shield to shield and never
      succumb
    to panic or miserable flight,
but steel the heart in your chests with
      magnificence
    and courage. Forget your own life
when you grapple with the enemy. Never run
    and let an old soldier collapse
whose legs have lost their power. It is shocking
      when
    an old man lies on the front line
before a youth: an old warrior whose head is white
    and beard gray, exhaling his strong soul
into the dust, clutching his bloody genitals
    in his hands: an abominable vision,
foul to see: his flesh naked. But in a young man
    all is beautiful when he still
possesses the shining flower of lovely youth.
    Alive he is adored by men,
desired by women, and finest to look upon
    when he falls dead in the forward clash.
Let each man spread his legs, rooting them in the
      ground,
    bite his teeth into his lips, and hold.

58   FRONTIERS

You should reach the limits of virtue
before you cross the border of death.

Semonides

Born on Samos, Semonides may have become associated with the island of Amorgos as leader of a colony there. He probably was active in the second half of the seventh century B.C. *His works included iambic poems (a rather long satire on women is extant) and two books of elegies. In the iambics his language is Ionic.*

In his response to the experience of human subjection to the gods (a topic particularly characteristic of the Lyric Age) Semonides differs from Archilochos. The earlier poet had concluded upon a fusion of activism and resignation. But Semonides deduced instead a code of passivity and hedonism.

Amorgos is one of the Sporades islands and was the home of the iambic poet Semonides.

STRABON, *Geography*

Semonides, son of Krines, from Amorgos, writer of iambic verse. Originally he was from Samos but during the colonization of Amorgos he was sent by the Samians as a leader. He built three cities in Amorgos: Minoa, Aigialos and Arkesime. He lived 390 years after the Trojan War. According to some, he was the first to write iambic verse, and he wrote the *History of the Samians* in two books of elegiac verse, and other diverse poetry.

Suda Lexicon

I know that you have lived a thousand things worthy of iambic satire, and so bad that even Archilochos himself could not stand to write about even one of your outrageous acts, even if he called in as collaborators Hipponax and Semonides.

LOUKIANOS, *The Liar*

❖❖❖❖❖❖❖❖❖❖❖❖❖❖❖❖❖❖❖❖❖❖❖❖❖❖❖❖

59   THE DARKNESS OF HUMAN LIFE

My child, deep-thundering Zeus controls the end
of all that is, disposing as he wills.
We who are mortals have no mind; we live like
        cattle,
day to day, knowing nothing of god's plans
to end each one of us. Yet we are fed
by hope and faith to dream impossible plans.
Some wait for a day to come, others watch
the turning of years. No one among the mortals
feels so broken as not to hope in coming time
to fly home rich to splendid goods and lands.
Yet before he makes his goal, odious old age
lays hold of him first. Appalling disease
consumes another. Some are killed in war
where death carries them under the dark earth.
Some drown and die under the myriad waves
when a hurricane slams across the blue salt water
cracking their cargo ship. Others rope a noose
around their wretched necks and choose to die,
abandoning the sun of day. A thousand black
        spirits
waylay man with unending grief and suffering.
If you listen to my counsel, you won't want
the good things of life; nor batter your heart
by torturing your skull with cold remorse.

60   LIFE AND DEATH

Later we will have a long time to lie dead
yet the few years we have now we live badly.

61   REMEMBRANCE OF THE DEAD

If we were sensible we would not spend
more than a day of sorrow for the dead.

62   ON MATRIMONY

Man gets nothing brighter than a kind wife
and nothing more chilling than a bad hag.

63   BREVITY OF LIFE*

One verse by the blind poet of Chios is indelible:
"The life of man is like a summer's leaf."
Yet few who hear these words take them into their
    heart,
for hope is rooted in every youthful soul,
the lovely flower of youth grows tall with color,
life will have no end,
or there is no place for growing old, for death;
and while in health, no fear of foul disease.
Poor fools! in islands of illusion,
for men have but a day of youth and life.
You few who understand, know when death is near
the food you give your soul must be supreme.

* Ascribed by Edmonds to Semonides. The "blind poet" is Homer.

Terpandros

Traditionally regarded as the first to make the choral lyric a developed art form, Terpandros was a fellow countryman of Alkaios and Sappho. But he was earlier by about a generation (his period of activity was the middle of the seventh century B.C.) and seems to have worked chiefly at Sparta, where he only briefly preceded Alkman. He is credited with increasing the strings of the lyre from four to seven. No fragments survive whose authenticity is uncontested.

Furthermore, Pindar claims that Terpandros was the inventor of *skolia* (drinking) songs.

Music was first established in Sparta by Terpandros.
PLUTARCH, *On Music*

The Spartans were fighting among themselves and sent to Lesbos for the musician Terpandros; he came and made their minds tranquil and stopped the quarrel. After that whenever the Spartans listened to a musician, they would say, "He is not the equal of the poet of Lesbos."
Suda Lexicon

✧✧✧✧✧✧✧✧✧✧✧✧✧✧✧✧✧✧✧✧✧✧✧✧✧✧✧

64   HYMN TO ZEUS
Zeus, inceptor of all,
of all things the commander,
Zeus, I bring you this gift:
the beginning of song.

65   TO APOLLO AND THE MUSES

Let us pour a libation
to the Muses, daughters
of Memory, and to Leto's
son, their lord Apollo.

66   SPARTA

The Muse sings brilliantly and
spears of young men flower.
Justice, defender of brave works,
goes down the street of light.

Alkman

*The first fully visible representative of the choral
ode lived at Sparta, and was active probably during
the middle of the seventh century* B.C. *It is possible
that he was (like several other poets of his time)
brought in from the East—in Alkman's case, from
Sardis in Lydia (Asia Minor).*

*His works were arranged in six books. They
included* partheneia, *hymns and* prooimia *(hexameter
preludes to recitations of epic poetry). His language
is strongly Doric, with Aiolic and Homeric influences.*

*Alkman in his fragments seems a poet of wayward
and playful sensitivity. The long and difficult
fragment of a* partheneion *("Song for a Choir of
Virgins") illustrates this sensitivity in the vivid,
glancing personal references, while "Rest" and
"Lakonian Wine" may serve to show its range in
nature and conviviality.*

Do not judge the man by the gravestone. The tomb
you see is small but it holds the bones of a great
man. For know that this is Alkman, supreme artist
of the Lakonian lyre, who commanded the nine
Muses. And twin continents dispute whether he is of
Lydia or Lakonia, for the mothers of a singer are
many.

ANTIPATROS OF THESSALONIKE

❖❖❖❖❖❖❖❖❖❖❖❖❖❖❖❖❖❖❖❖❖❖❖❖❖❖❖❖

67   ARS POETICA
I know the tunes
of every bird,

but I, Alkman, found my words and song
in the tongue
of the strident partridge.

[46]

68   REST
Now chasms and mountain summits are asleep,
and sierra slopes and ravines;
creeping things nourished by the dark earth,
hillside beasts and generations of bees,
monsters in the depths of the purple brine,
all lie asleep,
and also tribes of flying birds.

69   ON THE FEATS OF A YOUNG GIRL
Often at night along the mountain tops,
when gods are reveling by torch light,
you came carrying a great jar
(like one shepherds use) but of heavy gold.
You filled the jar with milk
drawn from a lioness, and made a great cheese
unbroken and gleaming white.

70   ON THE WORM
The dappled worm is the murderer
within the eye of blooming vines.

71   IN MYTHOLOGY
Dew, a child of moon and air,
causes the deergrass to grow.

72   SONG FOR A CHOIR OF VIRGINS*

THE WHOLE CHOIR

There is a vengeance from the gods,
but happy is the man who weaves
the fabric of his days with peace,
and without tears.

* The choir consists of ten virgins. The half-choirs speak in the first
person singular, in friendly rivalry, each praising its own half-choir
leaders.

AGIDO'S HALF-CHOIR

But I sing
of Agido's light. I see her
like the sun who shines on us
by order of Agido.

HAGESICHORA'S HALF-CHOIR

Our splendid
leader will not have us praise
or abuse her, for her brilliance
is as if among a herd of cattle
one had set a champion racehorse,
sinewy, strong, with thunder-ringing hooves,
a creature from a dream with wings.
Do you see? The horse is Venetian,
and the mane of our cousin
Hagesichora is a blossom
of the purest gold,
and below is her silver face.
Can I tell you this more clearly?
There you have Hagesichora.
In beauty she may be second to Agido
but she will run like a
Skythian horse against a Lydian racer.
For as we carry Orthria's plow
so the Pleiades of dawn will rise
and strive against us
like the burning star of Sirios
through the ambrosial night.

AGIDO'S HALF-CHOIR

All our wealth of purple dye
or the dappled snake of full gold
about our wrist or our Lydian
wimple that is the sweet glory
of all these tender-eyed girls,
no, nothing will keep them off.
Not Nanno's soft braids,
nor Areta's godlike beauty,
neither Thylakis nor Kleësisera.

HAGESICHORA'S HALF-CHOIR

You need not go to Ainesimbrota
and say: let Astaphis be mine,
have Philylla look my way,
and Damareta and darling Ianthemis.
For Hagesichora is our saviour.
Is Hagesichora of the lovely
ankles not right here with us?

AGIDO'S HALF-CHOIR

Yes, she waits by our Agido,
and commends our ceremonies.
O gods, receive our prayers,
for you determine everything
accomplished. My choir leader,
I tell you I a girl shrieked
in vain like an owl
from the roof tops.

HAGESICHORA'S HALF-CHOIR

But my great wish
is to please the Lady of the Dawn
who has healed our sore wounds.
Only Hagesichora could give
her girls the peace they desired.

THE WHOLE CHOIR

A great chariot simply follows
the course of its trace-horse;
in a vessel all must swiftly
heed the shouting of the helmsman,
so our combined choir may not
sing more sweetly than the Sirens—
for they are gods—but how we sang,
we ten girls with even one away!
And her song is like a swan
by the Xanthos river, and she
with the splendor of her blond hair.

73 SUPPLICATION
The girls fell to their knees, helpless—
like small birds under a hovering hawk.

74 HOME OF THE NORTH WIND
The Rhipé mountain flowering with forests
is the breast of black-flowing night.

75 TO THE DIOSKOUROI
Kastor and noble Polydeukes, you trainers
of swift stallions, are extraordinary horsemen.

76 TO HERA
I pray to you, Hera,
and bring you as my offering
a delicate garland of marigold
and galingale.

77 ON THE POET ALKMAN
He is no boorish farmer or
a clumsy pigkeeper or even
a sheep-chaser. He was not born
in Thessaly or Erysiche
but in Sardis on the high hills.

78 ON A POETESS
Aphrodite commands and love rains
upon my body and melts my heart

for Megalostrata to whom the sweet
Muse gave the gift of poetry. O
happy girl of the goldenrod hair!

79   ALKMAN'S SUPPER

Get him that enormous caldron on the tripod
so he can bloat his stomach with every food.
It is cool but soon will boil with good soup
which gobbler Alkman likes sparkling hot,
especially in the cold season of the solstice.
The glutton Alkman abstains from fancy dishes
but like the demos eats a plain massive meal.

80   WEDDING FEAST

Seven couches and as many tables
spread with poppy cakes and linseed and
sesame, and among the wooden flagons
were honey cakes for the young.

81   THE FOUR SEASONS

Three seasons were created: summer
and winter and a third in autumn,
and even a fourth—the spring—
when the fields are heavy with crops
and a glutton still goes hungry.

82   LAKONIAN WINE

I know the wine from the Five Hills,
wine from Oinos or Denthiades
or Karystos or wine of Onogla
or Stathmi—unboiled, unfired wines
of fine aroma.

83   ON THE KALCHA FLOWER

She wears a gold chain
made from slender petals
of purple kalcha flowers.

84 THE JOURNEY
Narrow is our way of life
and necessity is pitiless.

85 ON TANTALOS
The guilty man sat
among pleasant things under a hanging rock,
and from his chair he looked
and then the vision faded.

86 APHRODITE
You are from the beautiful island Kypros
and from the sea-surrounded city Paphos.

87 WANDERING LOVE
It is not Aphrodite but riotous Eros who is
playing like a child,
scuttling down across the tips of meadow ferns.
Please, do not crush them.

88 TO THE MOON GODDESS
I am your servant, Artemis.

You draw your long bow at night,
clothed in the skins of wild beasts.

Now hear our beautiful singing.

89 I AM OLD
O girls of honey-sweet voices, my limbs are weak.
They will not bear me. I wish, ah, I wish I were
a carefree kingfisher flying over flowering foam
with the halcyons—sea-blue holy birds of spring.

90 MAN'S LESSONS
Experience and suffering
are the mother of wisdom.

91 ON HIS POETRY
Muse of the round sky, daughter of Zeus,
I sing my poems loud and clear to you.

92 WINDFLOWER
Bright-shining.

93 CALM SEA
The calm sea falls dumbly
on the shore
among a tangle of seaweed.

Alkaios

Alkaios' poetry is deeply involved in his political vicissitudes. The greater part of his life was spent in fighting reform movements which shook the established aristocracy of his native island Lesbos. He was born around 630 B.C. Some twenty years later the reigning tyrant, Melanchros, was overthrown by Pittakos and the brothers of Alkaios. Alkaios was for a time involved in the alliance with Pittakos, and even fought with him against the Athenians at Sigeion (near Troy). But a break came, and Pittakos allied himself with Myrsilos to govern Mytilene while Alkaios went into exile at Pyrrha (another town on Lesbos). At the death of Myrsilos, Alkaios returned home but was soon in exile again, this time apparently traveling widely, as far as Egypt. (His brother served in the army of Babylon under Nebuchadnezzar, in campaigns which led to the capture of Jerusalem, 597 B.C.) Some time after 590 B.C. Pittakos forgave Alkaios, and the latter probably returned home.

Alkaios' works consisted of at least ten books, chiefly monodic. Hymns, political, erotic and sympotic poems predominate. He wrote in the Aiolic dialect, in a direct and emphatic style.

In his political poems Alkaios shows considerable similarity to Theognis. Both were hard-core aristocrats, convinced of the superiority of their class and cause, identifying private values with public right. (Alkaios seems to have gone so far as to support revolution against the established government.)

The influence of Alkaios is probably most seen in three places: the appropriations of Alkaios' forms and subjects by Horace; the recurrent metaphor (in poetry and elsewhere) of the "ship of state"; and the convivial poem (compare "Winter Evening" with Horace, Odes 1.9, and Milton, Sonnet XX).

Alkaios is rightly awarded the golden quill in that part of his work where he assails tyrants; his ethical

value is also great; his style is concise, magnificent,
exact, very much like Homer's; but he stoops to
humor and love when better suited for higher themes.

QUINTILIAN

❖❖❖❖❖❖❖❖❖❖❖❖❖❖❖❖❖❖❖❖❖❖❖❖❖❖❖❖❖❖

94   INSTANT
      I already hear the flowering spring.

95   PRAYER TO THE CONSTELLATION
      DIOSKOUROI, PATRON DEITIES OF
      MARINERS
      Come with me now and leave the land of
      Pelops, mighty sons of Zeus and Leda,
      and in kindness spread your light on us,
                  Kastor and Polydeukes.

      You who wander above the long earth
      and over all the seas on swift horses,
      easily delivering mariners
                  from pitiful death,

      fly to the masthead of our swift ship,
      and gazing over foremast and forestays,
      light a clear path through the midnight gloom
                  for our black vessel.

96   WINTER EVENING
      Zeus rumbles and a mammoth winter of snow
      pours from the sky; agile rivers are ice.

      Damn the winter cold! Pile up the burning logs
      and water the great flagons of red wine;
      place feather pillows by your head, and drink.

      Let us not brood about hard times. Bakchos,
      our solace is in *you* and your red wines:
      our medicine of grape. Drink deeply, drink.

97   SUMMER STAR
Wash your gullet with wine for the Dog-Star
        returns
with the heat of summer searing a thirsting earth.
Cicadas cry softly under high leaves, and pour
        down
shrill song incessantly from under their wings.
The artichoke blooms, and women are warm and
        wanton—
but men turn lean and limp for the burning Dog-
                Star parches their brains and knees.

98   WHY WAIT FOR THE LIGHTING
       OF THE LAMPS?
Let us drink. Why wait for the lighting of the
        lamps?
Night is a hair's breadth away. Take down the great
        goblets
from the shelf, dear friend, for the son of Semele
        and Zeus
gave us wine to forget our pains. Mix two parts
        water, one wine,
and let us empty the dripping cups—urgently.

99   DRINK, SONG AND SHIPS
Why water more wine in the great bowl?
Why do you drown your gullet in grape?
I cannot let you spill out your life
on song and drink. Let us go to sea,

and not let the wintry calm of morning
slip by as a drunken sleep. Had we
boarded at dawn, seized rudder and spun
the flapping cross-jack into the wind,

we would be happy now, happy as swimming
in grape. But you draped a lazy arm
on my shoulder, saying: "Sir, a pillow,
your singing does not lead me to ships."

[56]

100 COSTUME

But let them hang braided garlands
of yellow dill around our necks,
and drape strands of redolent myrrh
across our breasts.

101 ON HIS BROTHER'S HOMECOMING

You have come home from the ends of the earth,
Antimenidas, my dear brother; come
with a gold and ivory handle to your sword.
You fought alongside the Babylonians
and your prowess saved them from annihilation
when you battled and cut down a warrior giant
who was almost eight feet tall.

102 THE LYRE

Daughter of the rock and the gray sea,
                    you fill all hearts
with triumph, tortoise shell of the sea.

103 BIRDS

                    What birds are these
wildgeese—flying from precincts where the earth
                    and oceans end—
with their enormous wings and speckled throats?

104 ON MONEY

Aristodemos wasn't lying
when he said one day in Sparta,

"Money is the man; and a poor man
can be neither good nor honorable."

105   TO THE RIVER HEBROS

Hebros, most beautiful river near Ainos,
you carry a shining bath of Thracian foam
out into the purple sea. And many girls
            stand near you,

and with soft hands rub oil on the smooth flesh
of their beautiful thighs. And they pour
your water over themselves like a sooth-
            ing unguent.

106   HELEN AND THETIS

Helen, your sinful deeds brought a bitter end
to Priam and his lovely children. They say
because of you holy Ilium was destroyed
            by climbing fire.

But the son of Aiakos did not find such a wife
when he summoned the blessed gods to his wedding
and took the delicate sea-nymph Thetis from
            the watery palace

of Nereus, bringing her to the mountain cave
of the centaur Cheiron. There, the love of Peleus
for his sea-nymph led him to lie naked with
            the untouched virgin,

and within the year she bore a son, Achilles;
bravest demigod and splendid driver of
tawny stallions. But for Helen, Ilium and
            her people were destroyed.

107   HYMN TO APOLLO*

Our king Apollo, O child of mighty Zeus,
when you were born your father gave you
a gold headband and a lyre of tortoise shell,
and more: a chariot drawn by swans. You were

* Text is derived from a paraphrase of Alkaios' poem.

to go to Delphi and the Kastalian springs
whose waters are the gift of broad Kephissos,
and there deliver justice to the Hellenes
through the oracles. But when you seized the reins,

you made the swans sail north to the distant land
of the Hyperboreans, and though the Delphians
begged you to return—with paeans of flutes
and circles of girls dancing about the tripod—

Apollo, you remained to rule that people
through the long year. Came the season when the
    tripod
rings loud and clear in Delphi, you turned the swans
to Parnassos. It was high noon of summer

when you glided back from the far northlands;
swallows and nightingales were singing; cicadas
also sang about you; silver brooks poured down
from Kastalia, and the great river Kephissos

threw blue-foaming waves into the bright wind:
    yes,
even the waters knew a god was coming home.

108   THE PEOPLE'S SICKNESS

Poverty—our painful and uncontrolled disease—
you maim great peoples with your sister
    Helplessness.

109   A WOMAN*

Bad,
every misery and disaster I've known, a woman

with a home
of shameful death,

---

* Very fragmentary text but not reconstructed.

incurable decrepitude coming on
and madness in the terrorized heart of the stag,

out of his mind
and ruined.

110 THINGS OF WAR
The great house glitters with bronze. War has pat-
terned the roof with shining helmets,
their horsehair plumes waving in wind, headdress
of fighting men. And pegs
are concealed under bright greaves of brass which
block the iron-tipped arrows. Many
fresh-linen corslets are hanging and hollow shields
are heaped about the floor,
and standing in rows are swords of Chalkidian steel,
belt-knives and warriors' kilts.
We cannot forget our arms and armor when soon
our dreadful duties begin.

111 WALLS AND THE CITY
Not homes with beautiful roofs,
nor walls of permanent stone,
nor canals and piers for ships

make the city—but men of strength.

Not stone and timber, nor skill
of carpenter—but men brave
who will handle sword and spear.

With these you have: city and walls.

112 HYPOCRISY
Father Zeus, in our worst moment of hardship,
the Lydians selflessly gave us two thousand
staters, and gave us hope that we might re-enter
our sacred city

of Mytilene. There we were only strangers,
but in our own homeland the cunning fox
made honeyed speeches for the blackmail gold,
                and then betrayed us.

113   ON PREMATURE POLITICAL ACTIVITY

It is late; for the harvest is in.
Before, we hoped that the full vines
would bring a plenitude of fine grapes,
but the clusters are slow
to ripen and the landlords
picked unripe bunches from the branch.
We have many grapes now—green and sour.

114   ON THE TYRANT PITTAKOS

                One and all,
you have proclaimed Pittakos, the lowborn,
to be tyrant of your lifeless and doomed
land. Moreover, you deafen him with praise.

115   A NATION AT SEA

I can't tell you which way the gale has turned
for waves crash in from west and east, and we
are tossed and driven between, our black ship
        laboring under the giant storm.

The sea washes across the decks and maststep
and dark daylight already shows through long rents
in the sails. Even the halyards slacken as
        windward waves coil above the hull.

What sore labor to bale the water we've shipped!
Let us raise bulwarks and ride out the storm,
heeding my words: "Let each man now be famous."
        Yet base cowards betray the state.

116   TO THE MYTILENIANS
                    The local tyrant
rants and blusters and you are silenced
like a school of frightened neophytes
confronting the dead in holy rituals.

But I tell you, O citizens of Lesbos,
rise up and quench the smoldering logs
before their flames climb and consume you all
in total fire!

117   EARTHQUAKE
The tyrant's craze for absolute power will soon
demolish his country; already the earth trembles.

118   TO THE BASEBORN TYRANT
I say this to him too: he is a strident
lute who would like to be heard at a party
of the well-born people of Lesbos. Better
had he chosen to drink with the filthy herd.
He married a daughter from the ancient
race of Atreus; now let him offend our people
as he did the former tyrant Myrsilos,
until the Wargod makes us revolt. We must
forget our anger and cease these pitiful
clashes between brothers. Only a god
could have maddened our people into war
and so give Pittakos his bit of glory.

119   TO HIS FRIEND MELANIPPOS
Drink and be drunk with me, Melanippos. Do you
think when you have crossed the great fuming
    river,
you will ever return from Hell to see the clean
bright light of the sun? Do not strive for wild
    hopes.

Even the son of Aiolos, King Sisyphos, wisest of
    men,
thought he had eluded death. But for all his brains

Fate made him recross Acheron, and the son of
    Kronos
assigned him a terrible trial below the dark earth.

Come, I beg you not to brood about these hopeless
matters while we are young. We will suffer what
    must

be suffered. When the wind is waiting in the north,
a good captain will not swing into the open sea.

Sappho

*Sappho was the compatriot and approximate
contemporary of Alkaios. Her home on Lesbos was
at Mytilene. She came of a noble family. The names
of some of her family have been preserved:
Skamandronymos was her father, Kleïs her mother.
Her husband was Kerkylas of Andros, and she
named her daughter Kleïs for her mother. One of her
brothers was Charaxos. Political changes led to her
exile (with other members of the aristocracy) around
600 B.C. She spent some time in Sicily before she was
allowed to return home.*

*Her chief concerns, apparently, were with
personal relationships, and these above all among a
circle of young women of the upper class. Among
those whom she loved were Atthis and Anaktoria.
We hear also the names of several rivals: Andromeda
and Gorgo. Fittingly, the goddess whom she
affectionately worshiped was Aphrodite. Indeed the
connection between life and religion was so close for
Sappho that she might have repeated the words of
Eranna in Rilke's poem:*

> . . . denn die schöne Göttin in der Mitte
> ihrer Mythen glüht und lebt mein Leben.

> (For the fair goddess amid her myths glows
> and lives my life)

*The story that Sappho loved a certain Phaon and
died by leaping from the Leukadian rock for love of
him resulted probably from a misunderstanding of a
ritual dirge for the vegetation god Phaon.*

*In appearance she is said to have been small and
dark.*

*The works of Sappho were arranged in seven
books, the seventh comprising wedding songs. They
survived into Byzantine times, but were then
probably destroyed by Christian intolerance.*

*There seems to be a slight difference in style
between some works of Sappho which may have been*

*written for a more public audience (e. g., the
"Wedding of Andromache") and the poems which
are more private and personal in character. The
former show an inclination to admit Homeric forms
and prosody; the latter are purely in the Aiolic
dialect. The intense power of her simple and
euphonious style has been remarked upon from the
ancient critics until now.*

*In her outlook Sappho is notable, among other
things, for her interpretation of love: unlike many
of the poets of the Lyric Age, she regarded love not
as a dangerous obsession, but as fulfillment. And
she elevated love into the criterion of value ("To
Anaktoria").*

*Her influence on later literature, whether in style
or subject, has been considerable. One could start
with the following: Catullus Ll, Ovid's* Sappho
Phaoni *in the* Heroides, *plays by Grillparzer and
Durrell, Rilke's Sappho poems in* Neue Gedichte
and the poems of H.D.

Some say nine Muses — but count again.
Behold the tenth: Sappho of Lesbos.

PLATO

A contemporary of Pittakos and Alkaios was Sappho
— a marvel. In all the centuries since history began
we know of no woman who in any true sense can
be said to rival her as a poet.

STRABON, Geography

❖❖❖❖❖❖❖❖❖❖❖❖❖❖❖❖❖❖❖❖❖❖❖❖❖❖❖❖❖❖

120   THE LYRIC POEM

Come, holy tortoise shell,
my lyre, and become a poem.

121   NOW I BEGIN

I begin with words of air
yet they are good to hear.

[65]

122   HEADDRESS

My mother always said
that in her youth she was
exceedingly in fashion

wearing a purple ribbon
looped in her hair. But
the girl whose hair is yellower

than torchlight need wear no
colorful ribbons from Sardis —
but a garland of fresh flowers.

123   HER INNOCENCE

I do not have a rancorous spirit
but the simple heart of a child.

124   TO ANAKTORIA

Some say cavalry and others claim
infantry or a fleet of long oars
is the supreme sight on the black earth.
I say it is

the one you love. And easily proved.
Didn't Helen — who far surpassed all
mortals in beauty — desert the best
of men, her king,

and sail off to Troy and forget
her daughter and dear kinsmen? Merely
the Kyprian's gaze made her bend and led
her from her path;

these things remind me now
of Anaktoria who is far,
and I
for one

would rather see her warm supple step
and the sparkle of her face — than watch all the
dazzling chariots and armored
                    hoplites of Lydia.

125   ALONE*

The moon and Pleiades
are set. Midnight,
and time spins away.
I lie in bed, alone.

126   TO EROS

You burn me.

127   THE BLAST OF LOVE

Like a mountain whirlwind
punishing the oak trees,
love shattered my heart.

128   SEIZURE

To me he seems like a god
as he sits facing you and
hears you near as you speak
softly and laugh

in a sweet echo that jolts
the heart in my ribs. For now
as I look at you my voice
is empty and

can say nothing as my tongue
cracks and slender fire is quick
under my skin. My eyes are dead
to light, my ears

* Authorship uncertain.

[67]

pound, and sweat pours over me.
I convulse, greener than grass,
and feel my mind slip as I
go close to death,

yet, being poor, must suffer
everything.

129   WORLD
       I could not hope
       to touch the sky
       with my two arms.

130   BEACH COLOR
       The furzy flower of the golden broom
       grew along the shore.

131   LET SLEEPING DOGS LIE
       Don't stir up the small
       heaps of beach jetsam.

132   TO HER GIRLFRIENDS
       On this day I will sing beautifully
       and make you happy, dear companions.

133   FULL MOON
       The glow and beauty of the stars
       are nothing near the splendid moon
       when in her roundness she burns silver
       about the world.

134   THEN
       In gold sandals
       dawn like a thief
       fell upon me.

135   THE CRICKET

When sun dazzles the earth
with straight-falling flames,
a cricket rubs its wings
scraping up a shrill song.

136   PIGEONS AT REST

The hearts in the pigeons grew cold
and their wings dropped to their sides.

137   THE HERALD

Nightingale, with your
lovely voice, you are
the herald of spring.

138   EVENING STAR

Of all stars, Hesperos
is the most beautiful.

139   CEREMONY

Now the earth with many flowers
puts on her spring embroidery.

140   DEAR ATTHIS, DID YOU KNOW?

In dream Love came out of heaven
and put on his purple cloak.

141   TO ATTHIS

Though in Sardis now,
she thinks of us constantly

and of the life we shared.
She saw you as a goddess
and above all your dancing gave her deep joy.

Now she shines among Lydian women like
the rose-fingered moon
rising after sundown, erasing all

stars around her, and pouring light equally
across the salt sea
and over densely flowered fields

lucent under dew. Her light spreads
on roses and tender thyme
and the blooming honey-lotus.

Often while she wanders she remem-
bers you, gentle Atthis,
and desire eats away at her heart

for us to come.

142   A LETTER*

"Sappho, if you do not come out,
I swear, I will love you no more.

O rise and free your lovely strength
from the bed and shine upon us.
Lift off your Chian nightgown, and

like a pure lily by a spring,
bathe in the water. Our Kleïs
will bring a saffron blouse and violet

tunic from your chest. We will place
a clean mantle on you, and crown
your hair with flowers. So come, darling,

with your beauty that maddens us,
and you, Praxinoa, roast the nuts
for our breakfast. One of the gods

* The speaker may be Atthis, whose words Sappho is quoting.

is good to us, for on this day
Sappho, most beautiful of women,
will come with us to the white city

of Mytilene, like a mother
among her daughters." Dearest Atthis,
can you now forget all those days?

143   TO HER FRIEND

Honestly I wish I were dead!
Although she too cried bitterly

when she left, and said to me,
"Ah, what a nightmare it is now.
Sappho, I swear I go unwillingly."

And I answered, "Go, and be happy.
But remember me, for surely you
know how we worshiped you. If not,

then I want to remind you of all
the exquisite days
we two shared; how

you took garlands of violets
and roses, and when by my side
you tied them round you in soft bands,

and you took many flowers
and flung them in loops
about your sapling throat,

how the air was rich in a scent
of queenly spices made of myrrh
you rubbed smoothly on your limbs,

and on soft beds, gently, your desire
for delicate young women
was satisfied,

and how there was no dance and no
holy shrine
we two did not share,

no sound,
no
grove."

144 TO ATTHIS

Love—bittersweet, irrepressible—
loosens my limbs and I tremble.

Yet, Atthis, you despise my being.
To chase Andromeda, you leave me.

145 TO ATTHIS

I loved you, Atthis, long ago
when you were like a graceless child.

146 LONG DEPARTURE

How you will remember one day
those things we did in our youth,
many and beautiful.

We in the city feel its sharpness,
boldness of a man, and remember
a fine small voice.

147 TO APHRODITE

On your dappled throne, eternal
Aphrodite, cunning daughter of Zeus,
I beg you, Lady, don't crush me
with love's pain

but come to me now, if ever before
you heard my remote cry, and yielded,
slipping from your father's gold
house, and came,

yoking birds to your chariot.
Beautiful sudden sparrows took you
from heaven through the middle sky,
whipping wings,

down to the dark earth. Blessed,
with a smile on your deathless lips,
you asked what was wrong now,
why did I call you,

what did my mad heart want to
happen. "Sappho, whom shall I get
to love you? Who is turning
against you?

Let her run away, soon she'll be
after you. Scorn your gifts, soon she'll
bribe you. Not love, she'll love you,
even unwillingly."

So come to me once again and free me
from blunt agony. Labor
and fill my heart with its fire,
and be my ally.

148   TO APHRODITE OF THE FLOWERS,
AT KNOSSOS

Leave Krete and come to this holy temple
where the graceful grove of apple trees
circles an altar smoking with frank-
      incense.

Here roses leave shadow on the ground
and cold springs babble through apple branches
where shuddering leaves pour down pro-
      found sleep.

In our meadow where horses graze
and wild flowers of spring blossom,
anise shoots fill the air with a-
      roma.

And here, Queen Aphrodite, pour
heavenly nectar into gold cups
and fill them gracefully with sud-
    den joy.

149   TO LADY HERA

Lady Hera, while I Pray let your
graceful form appear, which came once
to the dazzling kings of the Atreidai
when they prayed.

The Atreidai accomplished many feats,
first at Illium, and then on the sea
on their voyage back, but could not
reach home again

before imploring you, Zeus of the winds
and Thyone's lovely child: Dionysos.
So be kind, as in former days,
and now help *me*.

150   PARALYSIS

Mother darling, I cannot work the loom
for sweet Kypris has almost crushed me,
broken me with love for a slender boy.

151   DESIRE

          For I am
a slave of the Kypros-born,
who lays a net of trickery.

152   FROM APHRODITE

I tell you, Sappho,
love is my servant.

153   TO EROS

From all the offspring
of the earth and heaven
love is the most precious.

154   THE DEATH OF ADONIS

Our tender Adonis is dying, O Kythereia,
What can we do?
Beat on your breasts, my friends, and tear
your dresses.

155   LOVE TOKEN

Your face is shaded, Aphrodite,
with a kerchief of porphyry
color: a precious gift from Mnasis
of far Phokaia.

156   DIALOGUE

Kypros-born, in dream
we two were talking.

157   TO APHRODITE

For you, Aphrodite, I will burn
the savory fat of a white she-goat.
All this I will leave behind for you.

158   TO APHRODITE

Aphrodite with gold flowers in your hair,
I say if only
some other fate were mine!

159   HEKATE

Hekate, shining of gold,
handmaid to Aphrodite.

160   PEITHO (PERSUASION)

You are the daughter of Aphrodite:
[you confuse us
and we mortals love.]

161   TO THE THE GRACES

O daughters of Zeus,
come to me now,
O Graces of the pink arms.

162   TO THE GRACES AND MUSES

Come, come now,
tender Graces,
and Muses of the splendid hair.

163   MAKING OF THE POEM

Come to me now, O Muses.
Leave your gold house.

164   THE MUSES

To me they brought honor, for they
gave me the secret of their craft.

165   SLEEP

May you find sleep on
a soft girlfriend's breast.

166   BECAUSE OF A RIVAL

Sappho, why do you condemn
the many joys of Aphrodite?

167 A RIVAL

By now they've had
their fill of Gorgo.

168 THE VIRGIN

Like a sweet apple reddening on the high
tip of the topmost branch and forgotten
by the pickers — no, beyond their reach.

Like a hyacinth crushed in the mountains
by shepherds; lying trampled on the earth
yet blooming purple.

169 SAPPHO'S EPITHET

The honey-voiced women.

170 LOOPS OF FLOWERS

Women ripe for marriage
were braiding flowers.

171 BRIDEGROOM

What are you, my lovely bridegroom?
You are most like a slender sapling.

172 WEDDING SONG

Groom, we virgins at your door
will pass the night singing of the love
between you and your bride. Her limbs
are like violets.

Wake and call out the young men,
your friends, and you can walk the streets
and we shall sleep less tonight than
the bright nightingale.

173   AFTER THE NIGHT FESTIVAL

Peace is simply havoc
and my heart is worn out.
[The night] sits down,
but come, my friends.
Soon it will be dawn.

174   SONG OF THE WEDDING BED

[Bride, warm with rose-
colored love, brightest
ornament of the Paphian,
come to the bedroom now,
enter the bed and play
tenderly with your man.
May the Evening Star
lead you eagerly
to that instant when you
will gaze in wonder
before the silver throne
of Hera, queen of marriage.]

175   SONG FOR THE BRIDE

No woman who ever was,
O groom, was like her.

176   AFTER THE CEREMONY

Happy groom, the wedding took place
and the woman you prayed for is yours.

Now her charming face is warm with love.

My bride, your body is a joy,
your eyes soft as honey,
and love pours its light
on your perfect features.

Using all her skill Aphrodite
honored you.

177   A LANKY GROOM

Raise the ceiling and sing.
Hymen!
Have carpenters raise the roof.
Hymen!
The groom who will come in
is tall like towering Ares.

178   DRINKS FOR THE GROOM

The wine bowl was full
with perfect ambrosia.
Hermes took up a jug to pour wine for the gods;
then all gripped their goblets,
spilled out libations
and shouted lots of good luck
to the groom.

179   GOODBYE, BE HAPPY

Goodbye, be happy, bride and groom.

Be happy, bride and honored groom.

180   THE GUARD OUTSIDE THE BRIDAL
       CHAMBER

The doorkeeper's feet are fourteen
yards long. Ten shoemakers used up
five oxhides to cobble each sandle.

181   SHALL I?

I do not know what to do:
I say yes — and then no.

182   ONE NIGHT

All the while, believe me, I prayed
our night would last twice as long.

183   DANCERS

While the full moon rose, young women
took their place around the altar.

In old days Kretan women danced
supplely around an altar of love,
crushing the soft flowering grass.

184   BRIDE

[O beautiful, O charming bride,
now you play with gold Aphrodite
and the roseate-ankled Graces.]

185   LOSS

Virginity, virginity, when you leave me,
where do you go?

I am gone and never come back to you.
I never return.

186   REMORSE

Do I still long
for my virginity?

187   WEDDING OF ANDROMACHE

Kypros!
A herald came.
Idaos. Racing powerfully.

Of the rest of Asia. Imperishable glory! (He said:)
"From holy Thebe and the waters of Plakia,
graceful Andromache coming with the navy
over the salt sea. They come with armbands of gold
and purple gowns and odd trinkets of rare design
and countless silver jars and ivory pins."
So he spoke. And Priam sprang to his feet

and the glowing news went from friend to friend
through the wide city. Instantly the sons of Ilios
hitched the mules to their finely wheeled chariots,
and a throng of wives and slender-ankled girls
climbed inside. Priam's daughters rode alone,
while young men led their horses under the cars.
Greatly.
Charioteers.

Like gods.
Holy.

They all set out for Illium
in the confusion of sweet flutes and crashing
    cymbals,
and girls sang a loud heavenly song
whose wonderful echo
touched the sky.
Everywhere in the streets.
Bowls and chalices.

Myrrh and cassia and incense rode on the wind.
Old women sang happily
and all the men sang out with thrilling force,
calling on Paean, great archer, lord of the lyre,
and sang of Hektor and Andromache like gods.

188   TO HERSELF

It's no easy thing to rival a goddess
for the beauty of her figure
or be more than Adonis.

Aphrodite poured nectar with her own hands
from a gold vial. Then Peitho . . .
was at the shrine at Geraistos.

Darling,
I will go to you.

189   HOMECOMING
You came. And you did well to come.
I longed for you and you brought fire
to my heart, which burns high for you.

Welcome, darling, be blessed three times
for all the hours of our separation.

190   HER RIVAL'S PEDIGREE
A very bright good morning,
Andromeda — O daughter
from kings and sons of kings.

191   RIVAL
I have lost, and you, Andromeda,
have made an excellent exchange.

192   ANDROMEDA, WHAT NOW?
                    Can this farm girl
in farm-girl finery burn your heart?
She is even ignorant of the way
to lift her gown over her ankles.

193   A RING
Silly woman. Yes, it is a ring,
but really, don't be so proud.

194   THE GIRL RUNNER
Someone taught Hero from the island
of Gyara
how to run like a star.

195   ARES' STRENGTH
Ares lets everybody
know that he could
drag off Hephaistos
with his bare hands.

196   BEFORE THE MURDER
It seems untrue but
once Leto and Niobe
were devoted friends.

197   TO THE NIGHTINGALE'S SISTER
Irana, why is Pandion's daughter,
the swallow, awakening me?

198   WEALTH AND VIRTUE
Wealth without virtue is a dangerous neighbor
[but joined they form a mountain of joy].

199   TO AN UNEDUCATED WOMAN
When dead you will lie forever forgotten,
for you have no claim to the Pierian roses.
Dim here, you will move more dimly in Hell,
flitting among the undistinguished dead.

200   TO A HANDSOME MAN
If you love me, stand and gaze at me candidly,
let the grace in your eyes pour forth.

201   CONVERSATION WITH ALKAIOS
          Alkaios
Violet-haired, pure, honey-smiling Sappho,
I want to speak to you but shame disarms me.*

          Sappho
If you cared for what is upright and good,
and your tongue were not concocting trouble,
shame would not be hiding in your eyes
and you would speak out your real desires.

202   APPEARANCES
A handsome man now looks handsome.
A good man will soon take on beauty.

203   RETURN
O Gongyla, my darling rose,
put on your milk-white gown. I want
you to come back quickly. For my
desire feeds on

your beauty. Each time I see your gown
I am made weak and happy. I too
blamed the Kyprian. Now I pray
she will not seek

revenge, but may she soon allow
you, Gongyla, to come to me
again: you whom of all women
I most desire.

204   UNGIVEN LOVE
I am dry with longing
and I hunger for her.

---

* Line 1, or lines 1 and 2, are ascribed to Alkaios.

205 IN TIME OF STORM

Brightness. I ask for good fortune
to reach the harbor, the earth
for our black ships.

We are sailors under great gales,
hoping for dry reefs,
to sail in with our cargo.

The sky is flowing.
Awash in the storm we have many
duties. O dry land!

206 ART

No woman I think will ever outshine
your skill — no woman who will ever
look into sunlight.

207 GOLD

[Like the Golden Fleece,
it is indestructible:]
gold is the child of God.

208 ASIAN DYES

Her gay embroidered gown
draped down to her toes:
fine needlework from Lydia.

209 ON AMORGINE FABRICS

She wore around her the soft
fine linen robes of Amorgos.

210 JASON'S CLOTHING

His cloak was of a cloth
handspun from many colors.

211   WHEN YOU COME
       You will lie down and
       I shall lay out soft
       pillows for your body.

212   COMPARISONS
       Softer than fine robes

       More golden than gold.

       Sweeter than the lyre.

       Far whiter than an egg.

213   THE PREEMINENCE OF LESBIAN POETRY
       Towering over all lands
       is the singer of Lesbos.

214   TO DIKA, NOT TO GO BAREHEADED
       Dika, take some shoots of dill, and loop
       them skillfully about your lovely hair.
       The happy Graces love her who wears flowers
       but turn their back on one who goes plain.

215   THE BEAUTY OF HER WOMEN
       Mnasidika has a lovelier body
       than even our soft Gyrinno's.

216   YIELDING
       No more. Do not try
       to bend a hard heart.

217   TRIAL
       When anger floods into my chest,
       I bite my tongue — not to explode.

218   BECAUSE OF THE PUNISHMENT

Tears came to the eyes
of even the holy gods.

219   A VISION OF SMYRNA

Like the hyacinth
there is a light
blinding my eyes.

220   A RETURN

Safe now. I've flown to you
like a child to its mother.

221   OUT OF ALL PEOPLE

Is it possible
that in some other land you love
some other more than you love me?

222   I WOULD FLY TO THE VERY
FOOT OF YOUR MOUNTAINS

[I would go anywhere
to take you in my arms
again,] my darling.

223   TO HER DETRACTOR

As for him who blames me,
let him walk with madness
and stumble through sorrows.

224   A GIRL

One day I watched a tender girl
picking some wild flowers.

225 HOMECOMING

Soft girl from whom I was
altogether cut off,
I have come home again.

226 WEATHERCOCKS

Those whom I treated kindly
especially injure me now.

227 HAVING REFUSED TO ACCEPT
THE BITTER WITH THE SWEET

I will never find again
honey or the honeybees.

228 REST

The night closed their eyes
and then night poured down
black sleep upon their lids.

229 ENCOUNTER

You were once a tender child. Now, come
and sing. Grant me your beauty, talk,
be generous
with your gracefulness.

We were walking to a wedding. You knew
all that. Now I ask: quickly, send your young
women away. Let the gods have
their way. We

mortals have no road
to high Olympos.

230   TO A FRIEND

When I gaze at you, it is not
even Hermione I think of,
but I am overcome as before the beauty
of blond Helen

among mortal women. Be assured
your presence would free me from cares
on dewy banks where all night
we would stay awake.

231   KLEÏS

I have a small daughter who is beautiful
like a gold flower. I would not trade
my darling Kleïs for all Lydia or even
for lovely Lesbos.

232   FROM HER EXILE

I have no embroidered headband
for you, Kleïs, and no idea
where to find one while Myrsilos

rules Mytilene. The bright
ribbon reminds me of those days
when we were not wasting away

and our enemies were in exile.

233   BETRAYAL

You have done wrong, Mika,
and I will not concur:
you have chosen to be friends
with the house of Penthilos.
Yet now we hear a sweet intrusion,
a voice like honey
from the loud-singing nightingale
in the dewy branches.

234   TO APHRODITE AND THE NEREIDS
Kyprian and Nereids, I beg you
to bring my brother home safely,
and let him accomplish whatever
is in his heart.

Let him amend his former errors
and be a joy to his friends but
a terror to enemies — though never
again to us.

Let him do honor to his sister,
and be free of the black torment
which in other days of sorrow
ravaged his soul.

235   AGAINST DORICHA, HER BROTHER'S
MISTRESS
Kyprian, may she find you harsh
and find no occasion to brag: I
Doricha got my love to come back
        a second time.

236   AGE AND LIGHT
Here are fine gifts, children.
O friend, singer on the clear tortoise lyre,

all my flesh is wrinkled with age,
my black hair has faded to white,

my legs can no longer carry me,
once nimble like a fawn's,

but what can I do?
It cannot be undone,

no more than can pink-armed Dawn
not end in darkness on earth,

or keep her love for Tithonos,
who must waste away;

yet I love refinement, and beauty and light
are for me the same as desire for the sun.

237   DREAM
O dream from the blackness,
come when I am sleeping.

Sweet is the god but still I am
in agony and far from my strength,

for I had hopes to share
something of the happy ones,

nor was I so foolish
as to scorn pleasant toys.

Now may I have
all these things.

238   THE LAUREL TREE
You lay in wait
behind a laurel tree,

and everything
was pleasant:

you a woman
wanderer like me.

I barely heard you,
my darling;

you came in your
trim garments,

and suddenly: beauty
of your garments.

239   FOR PELAGON*

Pelagon the fisherman. His father
Meniskos placed here a fishbasket
and oar: relics of a wretched life.

240   EMPTINESS

I have never found you
so repulsive, O peace.**

241   A WOMAN'S PLEA

I pray for long life and health.
My children, I would escape
from wrinkles and cling to youth.

242   SAPPHO SAYS†

Death is our evil. The gods believe this,
or else by now they would be dead.

243   ON TIMAS‡

Here is the dust of Timas who unmarried
was led into Persephone's dark bedroom,
and when she died her girlfriends took sharp
iron knives and cut off their soft hair.

244   ACHILLES

He lies now in the black earth,
and the many sorrows are ended
which he bore for the Atreidai.§

---

* Probably not by Sappho.
** The word "peace" may be the name "Irana."
† Probably not by Sappho.
‡ Probably not by Sappho.
§ Probably Menelaos.

[92]

245   ARTEMIS*

Artemis swore a severe oath to gold-haired
      Phoibos,
whom Koios's daughter bore after she lay with
      Zeus,
famous lord of high clouds. She swore by his
      beard:
"I shall always be a virgin, hunting on the peaks
of solitary mountains. Come, grant me my wish."
She spoke and the father of the blessed gods
consented. Now gods and mortals call her virgin,
deer-slaying hunter. And Eros, loosener of cords
holding in reluctant thighs, never comes near
      her.

246   THE SWAN'S GIFT

It is said that Leda long ago
found a hidden egg the color
of hyacinths.

247   IT IS LATE

Even if you love me, find
a younger woman. I could
never bear to share my bed
with a man younger than I.

248   BITTERSWEET LOVE

[It brings us pain]
and weaves myths.

249   YOU FORGOT

And I am now wholly
gone into oblivion.

---

* Attributed to Alkaios by Lobel and Page, to Sappho by Max Treu.

250   HER FRIENDS

No, my heart can never change
toward you who are so lovely.

251   EVENING STAR

Hesperos, you bring home all the bright dawn
    disperses,
bring home the sheep,
bring home the goat, bring the child home to its
    mother*

252   TO HERMES

Gongyla, is there no sign of you? No epiphany
of your presence? Hermes came
in a dream. O Lord,

I swear by my ally Aphrodite, I have no pleasure
in being on the earth. I care
only to die,

to watch the banks of Acheron plaited
with lotus, the dewy banks
of the river of Hell.

253   OLD AGE

Of course I am downcast and tremble
with pity for my state
when old age and wrinkles cover me,

when Eros flies about
and I pursue the glorious young.
Pick up your lyre

and sing to us of her who wears
violets on her breasts. Sing especially
of her who is wandering.

---

* In Bruno Snell's reading the bright dawn brings *out* the sheep
and goat, and the child away from its mother.

254   TO HER DAUGHTER
WHEN SAPPHO WAS DYING

It would be wrong for us. It is not right
for mourning to enter a home of poetry.

255   HER WEALTH

[The golden Muses gave me
true riches: when dead
I shall not be forgotten.]

256   SOMEONE, I TELL YOU

Someone, I tell you,
will remember us.

[We are oppressed by
fears of oblivion

yet are always saved
by judgment of good men.

Therefore, I tell you,
stand upright for me.]

257   HADES*

In all the dominions of the gods
only Death allows no place for sweet hope.

258   EROS

Now in my
Heart I
see clearly

* This is also attributed to Alkaios.

A beautiful
face
shining,

etched
by love.

259   SAPPHO, I LOVED YOU

Andromeda
forgot,

and I too
blamed you,

yet Sappho
I loved you.

In Kypros I am Queen
and to you a power

as sun of fire
is a glory to all.

Even in Hades
I am with you.

260   DAWN

The queenly dawn.

Solon

A member of the Athenian aristocracy, Solon had
begun his poetic activity earlier than ca. 600 B.C.
For it was at this time that he wrote an elegy to his
fellow citizens urging them to the reconquest of
Salamis. But the most notable part of his life, and
the subject of a good deal of his surviving poetry,
was his involvement in the Athenian Social Question.
In the conflict between the landed grandees and the
dispossessed peasants (many of whom had been
enslaved through debt) Solon took a middle position.
In 594-593 B.C. he was elected as an Archon with
extraordinary powers to carry out social and
constitutional reforms in an effort to avoid civil war
and revolution. Among other things, he abolished
existing debts, established a council of four hundred
as a counterweight to the aristocratic council of the
Areiopagos and gave each class of the citizenry a
certain voice in the political affairs of the country.
After making his laws (and his name of course has
since become a synonym for legislator), he bound
the people to retain them unchanged for ten years,
and went abroad for the duration. As one would
expect, Solon displeased both sides by his
moderation, and in fact the détente he had effected
came to nothing in the end: Athens spent a good
part of the sixth century under a tyranny based on
the support of the commoners. However, even under
the tyranny much of the substance of his reforms
was retained, and the Solonian spirit, with its insight
and discretion, prepared the way for the later
brilliant and precarious forms of Athenian
democracy.

The poetry of Solon, which constitutes the first
Athenian literature, includes elegiac and iambic
verse. The subject matter is political and moral, but
also sometimes convivial and erotic.

It seems that the three most democratic aspects of
Solon's rule were: first and greatest, the prohibition
of loans on the person; second, the right of redress

for those who were wronged; third, the right of
appeal to courts of law, which more than all else
strengthened the people. Once master of the vote,
the people became master of the constitution.
                              ARISTOTLE, *Constitution of Athens*

He died in Kypros at the age of eighty. He left
orders with his family to have his bones taken to
Salamis and there burn them to ashes and scatter
them over the soil.
                              DIOGENES LAERTIOS, *Life of Solon*

And when Kroisos (Croesus) stood on the pyre, in
such an evil moment, it is said that he remembered
how truly inspired was Solon's saying that no mortal
is happy.
                              HERODOTOS, *Histories*

✧✧✧✧✧✧✧✧✧✧✧✧✧✧✧✧✧✧✧✧✧✧✧✧✧✧✧✧✧✧

261   APOLOGIA OF HIS RULE

Where did I fail? When did I give up goals
for which I gathered my torn people together?
When the judgment of time descends on me,
call on my prime witness, Black Earth, supreme
excellent mother of the Olympian gods,
whose expanse was once pocked with mortgage
        stones,
which I dug out to free a soil in bondage.

Into our home, Athens, founded by the gods,
I brought back many sold unlawfully as slaves,
and throngs of debtors harried into exile,
drifting about so long in foreign lands
they could no longer use our Attic tongue;
here at home men who wore the shameful brand
of slavery and suffered the hideous moods
of brutal masters—all these I freed. Fusing
justice and power into an iron weapon,
I forced through every measure I had pledged.
I wrote the laws for good and bad alike,
and gave an upright posture to our courts.

Had someone else controlled the whip of power,
a bungler, a man of greed, he would not
have held the people in. Had I agreed
to do what satisfied opponents, or else
what their enemies planned in turn for them,
our dear city would be widowed of her men.
But I put myself on guard at every side,
spinning like a wolf among a pack of dogs.

262   CIVIL WAR IN ATTICA
I know it, and sorrow lives in my heart
that the oldest land of Ionia is burning.

263   THE SIGNS OF DICTATORSHIP
The power of hail and snow springs from a cloud,
    and thunder from the fire of lightning.
Strong men destroy a city, and a tyrant
    enslaves a people through their ignorance.
A ship once out of port is hard to capture:
    know this now before it is too late.

264   TO PHOKOS
(*On his refusal to assume dictatorial
powers from which there is no retreat.*)
If I have spared my country
by not descending into tyranny and unrelenting
        violence;
if I have not piled odious dung on my good name,
I am unashamed.
No, I contend that my policy
won far greater victories with common man.

265   INDIFFERENCE TO WEALTH
Vast silver, gold, wheatlands, horses, mules
    are only equal to the wealth
of him whose belly, ribs and feet are warm,
    who may be poor but enters love

with men or women when he comes upon
    the proper season in his youth.
This is plenitude for man. No one goes down
    to Hades with fabulous belongings.
Even ransom will not spare him from repugnant
    disease, evil old age and death.

266   VIRTUE AMONG THE POOR
Many malicious men are rich. Many good men
    suffer through poverty. Yet who would trade
virtue for gold? While the name of virtue endures
    money drops from hand to hand, lasting little.

267   SOLON BEFORE THE CROWDS IN ATHENS
I am a herald from lovely Salamis. In place
    of talk I bring a song: an ornament of words.

268   A CITY OF TEN THOUSAND IN TEARS
May I meet death without tears. But let my death
    bring sorrow and mourning to my friends.

269   LESSON IN CITIZENSHIP
You must obey the law of the land,
whether you think it right or wrong.

270   THE EROTIC MAN
In the tender flower of youth he loves a boy,
    desiring his thighs and delicious mouth.

271   THE GODS
The mind of the eternal gods
    can not be seen by man.

272 MORTAL MAN
     No mortal is happy, and all men on earth
        who look upon the sun are wretched.

273 TEN AGES IN THE LIFE OF MAN
     A boy who is still a child grows baby teeth
        and loses them all in seven years.
     When God makes him fourteen, the signs of
        maturity begin to shine on his body.
     In the third seven, limbs growing, chin bearded,
        his skin acquires the color of manhood.
     In the fourth age a man is at a peak in
        strength—a sign in man of excellence.
     The time is ripe in the fifth for a young man
        to think of marriage and of offspring.
     In the sixth the mind of man is trained in all
        things; he doesn't try the impossible.
     In the seventh and eighth, that is, fourteen years,
        he speaks most eloquently in his life.
     He can still do much in the ninth but his speech
        and thought are discernibly less keen;
     and if he makes the full measure of ten sevens,
        when death comes, it will not come too soon.

Mimnermos

Mimnermos was active around 600 B.C. or some ten years later. He was a citizen of either Kolophon or Smyrna. The milieu of his poetry is that of the Anatolian Greek city, fighting against Oriental domination, but already under various sorts of Oriental influence, including that of intermarriage. Mimnermos' name is apparently itself Oriental. He is symptom and spokesman of the decadence of Ionia, enervated by despair and by pleasure.

His works included a Smyrneid (long poem on the history of Smyrna) and a collection of elegies probably addressed to Nanno (a flute-girl who accompanied the performance of his poems) and dealing in part with his love. In his erotic elegies Mimnermos is one of the ancestors of the later love-elegists of Alexandria and Rome.

Mimnermos discovered the sweet sound and soft
breath of iambic pentameter, after much suffering.
He loved Nanno. . . . reveled with Examyes and
irritated the oppressive Hermobios and hostile
Pherekles because he hated their verse.

HERMESIANAX IN PHOTIOS, *Library*

If as Mimnermos says, there is not joy without love
and play, then you should live with love and play.

HORACE, *Epistles*

❖❖❖❖❖❖❖❖❖❖❖❖❖❖❖❖❖❖❖❖❖❖❖❖❖

274   CENSURE OF AGE

What good is life when golden love is gone?
Frankly, I would rather be dead than ignore
a girl's warm surrender, her soft arms in bed
at night: lovely flower of youth that all women
and men desire!
            When old age comes
a man feels feeble and ugly and crawls under
a crushing sorrow.

[102]

                He loses the simple joy
of looking at the sun.
Children despise him.
He is repulsive to young women—in this sad
blind alley which God has made of old age.

275   TIME

When a man's good hour is past
though he once shone among mortals
he is neither honored nor loved.
Not even his own children favor him.

276   NOW

Be young, dear soul. Soon others will be men
    and I being dead will be black earth.

277   A PLEDGE

Between us, dear friend,
let there always be truth,
most just of all things.

278   FOR THE GOLDEN FLEECE

Jason went to the city of King Aietes
where the sun's swift rays are stored
in a gold chamber by the ocean's lips.

279   REFUGE AGAINST TALK

Be happy in your own soul. Among pitiless
    townsmen
    one will always abuse you, another speak praise.

280   A WARRIOR OF THE LYDIAN WARS

No man could match his strength or heroic heart,
    so the elders told me who had seen him

[103]

cutting through the phalanx of massed Lydian
    cavalry,
  swinging his ashwood spear on the plain
of Hermos. Pallas Athene could find no fault
    with the stinging courage in his heart
when he plunged first-line into the bloody clash,
    rushing through the rain of bitter shafts.
No man ever battled more bravely than he
    when he darted forward like a ray of sun.

281   HELIOS AT NIGHT

The sun works every day and there's no rest
    for him or for his horses once
the rose-fingered dawn leaves the ocean waters
    and begins to scale the firmament.
For with night the sun is swept across the waves
    in a hollow cup of gleaming gold,
a wondrous bed with wings, forged by Hephaistos;
    it speeds him sleeping over salt foam
from the Hesperides to the Ethiopian desert.
    There his fleet chariot and horses wait
till Dawn comes, early child of morning.

282   EXPECTATION

Like fragile shoots in the polyflowered spring
    growing quickly in amazing sun,
we love the blossom of youth for a brief season
    knowing from the gods nothing of evil
or good. Yet near us loom black Keres, and
    painful old age, or worse, death.
The fruit-tree of our life ripens swiftly like
    a morning sun. But our brilliance gone,
we are soon better dead than alive. Our heart
    is torn, our home is dark with poverty.
One man longs for a son and goes down childless
    into Hell; another shrivels in murderous
disease. No man on earth eludes the net
    of unending sorrows sent by Zeus.

283   EXPEDITION

We left the craggy city of Neleian Pylos
and came on ship to handsome Asia
and lovely Kolophon our base.
There we brashly mustered our immense army
    in dreadful pride,
and set out along the river flowing inside
    the forest.
Aided by the gods
we captured the Aiolian city of Smyrna.

Phokylides

*Perhaps a contemporary of Solon and Mimnermos
(ca. 600 B.C.), Phokylides was a citizen of Miletos.
He wrote a series of maxims, each with the "seal"
of the author (i.e., each beginning with a formula
which included the author's name). Some have seen
in this pride of authorship a sign of the new
consciousness of the individual. Phokylides wrote in
dactylic hexameters instead of elegiacs. (The verses
known as the* Carmen Phokylideum *are an
interesting 230-line succession of maxims written
by either a Jew or a Christian ca.* A.D. *100.)*

To prove this we might consider the poetry of
Hesiod, Theognis and Phokylides, who are declared
to be the best counselors ever known in matters
of human life.

ISOKRATES, *To Nikokles*

Archilochos may be reproached for his subject
matter, Parmenides for his prosody and Phokylides
for his poverty of expression. . . . Yet each deserves
praise for his special innate ability to stir and lead
his audience.

PLUTARCH, *On Listening*

❖❖❖❖❖❖❖❖❖❖❖❖❖❖❖❖❖❖❖❖❖❖❖❖❖❖

284   APPEARANCE OF WISDOM
Many empty-headed clods pass by like sages
when they walk with chin erect and stern eyes.

285   ON THE PROBLEM OF CHOOSING A WIFE
In the words of Phokylides: the tribes of women
come in four breeds: bee, bitch and grimy sow,
and sinewy mare with draping mane. The mare
is healthy, swift, roundly built and on the loose.

The Greek Period

The monster-looking sow is neither good nor
      rotten,
and the bristling bitch lies snapping at the leash.

Yes, the bee is best: a whizz at cleaning, trim
and good in cooking. My poor friend, I tell you,
for a bright, balmy marriage, pray for a bee.

Asios

Of Samos. Sixth century B.C. *Wrote genealogies, satirical hexameters, elegiacs, etc.*

In the epic poems of Asios, son of Amphiptolemos of Samos, Phoinix had two daughters by Perimede, daughter of Oineos. These were Astypalaia and Europa.

PAUSANIAS, *Description of Greece*

You are blind to history, Sir Potbelly. You are an ass-licker, and to recall the old Samian poet Asios, an ass-kisser.

ATHENAIOS, *Scholars at Dinner*

❖❖❖❖❖❖❖❖❖❖❖❖❖❖❖❖❖❖❖❖❖❖❖❖❖❖❖❖

286   AN OLD PARASITE
Clubfoot, branded like a runaway slave,
the old ass-kisser came like a beggar,
crashing the wedding party of Meles.
He asked for soup and stood among us
like a phantom risen from the mud.

Stesichoros

*A poet who was ranked with Homer by some of
the ancients, Stesichoros was born in Sicily around
630 B.C. and died around 555 B.C. He was active both
at Akragas (where he seems to have come into
conflict with the tyrant Phalaris) and Himera. He
may have made a visit to mainland Greece, and
Sparta in particular.*

*His works were abundant: they were arranged in
twenty-six books by the Alexandrian scholars. They
seem to have involved a confluence of the Doric
choral traditions and the Ionian epic, with an
admixture of local Sicilian legend. Stesichoros
introduced full-fledged narrative into choral poetry,
and told his stories more directly than, e.g., Pindar.
Among the subjects of his narratives were Herakles,
Europa, Helen, the Sack of Troy and the Orestes
legend. Tradition further ascribes to Stesichoros the
innovation of the triadic structure of the choral ode
(strophe, antistrophe and epode). His language was
Doric, with strong Homeric influence.*

*The influence of Stesichoros on the subjects of
sixth-century painting was apparently very great.
Thanks to Stesichoros, Athena was shown fully
armed at birth, Herakles acquired his club, lionskin
and bow, and Geryon his wings. If more of him had
survived, the effect on the literature of modern
Europe would probably have been greater than if
Alkman, Ibykos or even Simonides had been
preserved entire.*

There is a story that while Sokrates was in prison,
awaiting his death, he heard a man sing skillfully a
song by the lyric poet Stesichoros, and begged him
to teach it to him before it was too late, and when
the musician asked why, Sokrates replied, "I want to
die knowing one thing more."

AMMIANUS MARCELLINUS

✦✦✦✦✦✦✦✦✦✦✦✦✦✦✦✦✦✦✦✦✦✦✦✦✦

287   ON THE ILIAD
The white-horsed myth.

288   RECANTATION TO HELEN*
I spoke nonsense and I begin again:

The story is not true.
You never sailed on a benched ship.
You never entered the city of Troy.

289   ON KLYTAIMNESTRA

*Foreseeing the end of
the Aigisthos line.*

She dreamed that a serpent appeared
            with blood-dripping scales,
and from his belly stepped a king
            from the ancient dynasty
of Pleisthenes and Agamemnon.

290   ON THE MARRIAGE
OF HELEN AND MENELAOS
Many quince apples were cast upon the chariot
   of the king,
many leaves of myrtle,
hundreds of roses and thousands of braided violets.

291   ON THE MARRIAGE OF ADMETOS
AND ALKESTIS
            Bring your virgin's dowry
cakes of every kind—sesame, groats, sweet oil—
            and bring yellow honey too.

---

* According to Plato in the *Phaedros,* when Stesichoros was blinded for
having slandered Helen, he, unlike Homer who was blinded for the same
sin, wrote a *Palinode,* a recantation, and immediately recovered his sight.

292   BIRTHPLACE OF EURYTION
Eurytion was born in famous Erytheia
in the hollow of a rock,
near the inexhaustible silver-rooted springs
        of the river in Tartessos.

293   HERAKLES' QUEST OF THE CATTLE OF
GERYON

Then the sungod Helios, child of Hyperion,
soared in his gold-flashing bowl above the ocean
and entered the depths of black holy night,
seeking his mother, young wife and darling
        children.

But crossing the land on foot was Herakles, son of
        Zeus,
on his mission through the shadowy laurel grove.

294   A KING'S PUNISHMENT
On the day of sacrifice,
Tyndareos remembered all the gods but one:
        the gift-giving Kyprian,
and in her rage the queen of love
made his daughters marry two times
and three times,
made them walk out on their husbands.

295   ON SONG AND LAMENT
Apollo loves happy play and cadenced singing
but he leaves groans and mourning to Hades.

Yet how futile even to weep for the dead—
for when dead, a man's glory dies among men.

296   SEASON OF SONG

Forget the wars.
It is time to sing.
Take out the flute from Phrygia
and recall the songs of our blond Graces.

Clamor of babbling swallows:
it is already spring.

Ibykos

Born of a noble family at Rhegium in the toe of Italy in the first half of the sixth century B.C., *Ibykos went to the island of Samos after he had begun his poetic career. It is said that he went to Samos as an alternative to assuming the tyranny which was offered him in his native town. In any case, he went probably at the invitation of the famous Tyrant of Samos, Polykrates, who made his court a center of culture and sophistication— Anakreon was another of Polykrates' guests. Ibykos was said to have been murdered by robbers and avenged by birds who were present at the murder. (See Schiller's ballad "The Cranes of Ibykos.")*

In his work, Ibykos brought about a fusion of the West Greek choral lyric as developed by Stesichoros and the East Greek personalism as seen, e.g., in Alkaios and Sappho. In his early work Ibykos seems clearly to have followed Stesichoros' tradition of lyric narrative ("On Herakles" is probably a fragment from this period). But on moving to Samos, he appropriated erotic themes to the choral form, giving them a more ornate and elaborate expression than they had received at the hands of the monodists. Both subject and style, it may be imagined, suited the tastes of the Polykratean court. His language is the composite language of most choral poetry, with Doric traces.

Caught by robbers in a deserted spot, he was killed exclaiming that the very cranes which flew over at the moment would be his avengers. Some time afterward one of the robbers saw some cranes in the city and cried, "Look! the avengers of Ibykos." Whereupon one of the bystanders enquired into the matter of this speech of his. The crime was admitted, and the robbers brought to justice. Hence the proverb: "The cranes of Ibykos."

Suda Lexicon

As foolish as Ibykos.

PROVERB BY DIOGENES

What extravagant things Alkaios writes on the love
of youths! And as for Anakreon, his poetry is erotic
from beginning to end. Yet to judge from his works
they all were surpassed in this matter by Ibykos of
Rhegium. And the love of all these poets was
sensual love.

CICERO

◇◇◇◇◇◇◇◇◇◇◇◇◇◇◇◇◇◇◇◇◇◇◇◇◇◇◇◇◇◇◇◇

297   LOVE'S SEASON
In spring the quince trees
ripen in the girls' holy orchard
with river waters;
and grapes turn violet
under the shade of luxuriant leafage
and newborn shoots.

But for me, Eros
knows no winter sleep, and as north winds
burn down from Thrace
with searing lightning,
Kypris mutilates my heart with black
and baleful love.

298   MORNING
Dawn that ends our sleep
also wakes
the loud nightingale.

299   LIKE AN OLD CHAMPION
Even now Eros looks at me with tenderness
from under dark eyelids, and casts me spellbound
into Aphrodite's nets where I lie caught
inextricably,

for I swear his mere approach makes me tremble
like an old champion chariot horse, as he
draws a swift cart unwillingly to the race.

[114]

300 RESEMBLING THE BIRDS

In the high branches perch the mottled ducks
and purple cormorants with their sleek throats
and kingfishers of the long wings.

O let my heart always be like the birds
of the purple crest and long wings!

301 ON FLOWERS

Myrtles and violets and yellow cassidonies,
apple flowers and roses and glossy laurel.

302 ON EURYALOS

Euryalos, child of the exquisite Graces
and darling of the lovely-haired Muses,
you were reared by Kypris and soft-eyed Peitho
among the blossoms of the rose.

303 ON FEMININE NATURE
AND PUBLIC DECENCY

Spartan girls
are naked-thighed and man-crazy.

304 CONSTELLATION

Burning across the endless night
like brilliant Dog Stars.

305 ON HERAKLES

I killed the boys on the white horse,
the sons of Molione.

Their bodies were alike; their age
and faces were identical—being
twins and born together
in a silver egg.

306   THE IMPOSSIBLE
When a man is dead one can find
no medicine to bring him life.

307   ON A MAN-MADE PENINSULA
IN SYRACUSE
With mortal hands they joined the island
of Ortygia to the stony mainland,
where once there was a hunting zone
for seasnails and carnivorous fish.

Hipponax

*Hipponax was banished from Ephesos ca. 545 B.C.
He spent much time as a wandering beggar in the
neighboring city of Klazomenai. He seems to have
had quarrels with two sculptors named Boupalos and
Athenis. There are indications of a liaison with the
former's girlfriend Arete.*

*In style and subject matter Hipponax is set off
from the other major poets of the Lyric Age by his
total preoccupation with private topics and his
adoption of the demotic manner. He is for Adrados
an instance of the increasing dissolution of
Hellenism in the Greek cities of Asia Minor.**

*Hipponax wrote choliambs ("lame" iambics, also
known as "scazons," with a dragging final foot in
each line), other iambic and trochaic verse,
hexameters and epodes—not the epodes of a choral
triad, but, as with Archilochos, a quasi-stanzaic form
usually composed of two different kinds of metrical
lines.*

*Hipponax influenced Greek comedy, and was the
fountainhead of several different types of choliambic
poetry: Kallimachos' iambics, Herondas, Kerkidas,
etc.*

O stranger, stay clear of the horrible tomb of
Hipponax, which hurls abuse as thick as hail and
whose very ashes compose iambics in hatred of
Boupalos. You might wake the sleeping wasp
whose bile would not rest even in Hades, but
launches straight shafts of song in lame measure.†
                    PHILIPPOS, *Palatine Anthology*

❖❖❖❖❖❖❖❖❖❖❖❖❖❖❖❖❖❖❖❖❖❖❖❖❖❖❖

* Adrados, *Líricos griegos,* 2: 13.
† Hipponax invented the choliamb, or lame iambic.

308   ON THE SCOUNDREL BOUPALOS
        Hold my coat while I belt Boupalos in the eye.
        I am ambidextrous and never miss a punch.

309   KEEP GOING, MONSTER*
        Keep going, monster, all the long way to Smyrna.
        Pass through Lydia and past the tomb of Attales,
        the grave of King Gyges and the stele of
           Megastrys,
        the funereal monument of Atys, and king of
           Attalyda,
        and turn your belly toward the sinking sun.

310   MIDWIFE
        What navel-snipper wiped you, god-blasted one,
        and washed you as you kicked about the floor?

311   ON A SERPENT PAINTED AT
        THE WRONG END OF A SHIP
        Mimnes, you degenerate artist! Don't paint
        a snake running up the rear end
        of our trireme.†
        Unbearable disgrace and evil luck
        will tag us, slave of slaves. You leave the
           helmsman
        open to being bitten on the shins.

312   PRAYER TO HERMES
        Hermes, dear Hermes, Maia's son from Kyllene,
        I pray to you, for I'm frozen and I shiver.

---

* Attales: brother of Alyattes, King of Persia, whose tomb still exists.
Megastrys: lover of Gyges. Atys: mythical lover of Kybeles. Attalyda:
founder of city of same name. Text is corrupt and with many variations
and interpretations.
    † A galley having three banks of oars.

Give Hipponax a woolen overcoat, a Persian
cape, some sandals and felt slippers,
and sixty gold staters for his inner wall.

Give Hipponax a woolen overcoat. I tell you,
his teeth are rattling in his head!

But from you never even a shabby coat against
    the very cold
or slippers to keep my toes from freezing.

313   WAYS OF PROVIDENCE
Never yet has the blind god, Wealth,
come to my house and said: "Hipponax,
I'm giving you thirty silver minas
and much more." No, he's far too tight.

314   A NEW CHARYBDIS
O Muse, sing to me of that sea-monster,
    Eurymedon's son,*
whose stomach, like a knife, fattens on all it finds.
Tell of his dreadful end, and how by public order
the town will stone him to death beside the sterile
    sea.

315   MEDICATION FOR SADNESS
I will abandon my agonized soul to vice
if instantly you don't send a medimnos
of barley. From the flour I'll make a brew
to drink as medicine against my sorrows.

316   MISERIES
In a Lydian voice she said, "Come quick,
I will plug up your tight asshole."
And she beat my balls with a branch

* Parody of Homer.

as though I were a scapegoat. I tripped,
and stuck on the gallows I suffered
a double torture: a branch lashed
my chest; someone wet me with cowshit
and my ass stank. Beetles came, drawn
by the stinking gook like summer flies.
They fell on me, shoved, filing their teeth
on my bones. The invasion complete,
I ached more than from a Pygelian plague.

317   INJUSTICE
It is outrageous. Now they rail at Kritias,
    the upright islander from Chios,
and condemn him for adultery,
merely because they saw him
wandering in the rooms of a cathouse.

Anakreon

The only great Ionian monodist was born in Teos
in Asia Minor around 572 B.C. Soon after the
capture of Sardis by the Persians in 541 B.C.
Anakreon fled with his fellow townsmen to Abdera
in Thrace, and established a colony there. "On a
Virgin" may date from this period. The Tyrant of
Samos, Polykrates, invited him to come and teach
his son music and poetry. Anakreon and Ibykos thus
both were poetic luminaries of the court of Samos.
Anakreon in particular seems temperamentally
suited to the sophisticated conviviality and
eroticism which was the Polykratean style. In 522 B.C.
Polykrates was killed by Persian treachery, and
Anakreon went to Athens—in a boat, it is said, sent
especially for him by Hipparchos, brother of the
reigning Athenian tyrant Hippias. Hipparchos, who
was a sort of cultural commissar under his brother,
seems to have fostered a style of life much like that
at Samos under Polykrates. Upon the assassination
of Hipparchos in 514 B.C. Anakreon moved to
Thessaly for a time, but was then received back in
Athens (now a democracy) with apparently no hard
feelings over his earlier friendship with the tyrants.
During this period he was a friend of Xanthippos,
the father of Perikles. Anakreon died at the age of
eighty-five, probably soon after 490 B.C. The legend
was that he choked, appropriately, on a grape pip.

The works of Anakreon, in six books, consisted of
lyrics (mainly monodic), iambics and elegiacs. The
bulk of the surviving fragments are lyric. The
language of Anakreon is almost entirely the Ionian
of his day.

The most remarkable feature of the poetry of
Anakreon, the one most commented on, is its
varying tone of playfulness, sophistication,
detachment or irony (as seen, for instance, in "The
Vision of Love," "On an Old Lover" and
"Preparations for Love").

His influence in later poetry has probably been
greater than that of either Alkaios or Sappho. The

numerous two-dimensional projections in the
Anakreonteia *are often delightful, but sweet, not
savory. Horace adapted some themes. But the poetry
of Renaissance France and England is the locus of
the most flourishing Anakreonism. Even though
filtered in large part through the* Anakreonteia, *the
poet's manner is still perceptible in Ronsard, Herrick,
Ben Jonson and others.*

Anakreon's poetic works are entirely erotic.
                                      CICERO, *Tusculan Disputations*

The grammarian Didymos wrote four thousand
books . . . in which he discusses whether Anakreon
was more of a rake than a sot, whether Sappho was
a prostitute, and other questions the answers to
which you should forget if you knew them.
                                      SENECA, *Letters to Lucilius*

Stranger, passing near the tomb of Anakreon,
pour me a libation as you approach,
for in life I was a drunkard.
                                                      ANONYMOUS

✦✧✦✧✦✧✦✧✦✧✦✧✦✧✦✧✦✧✦✧✦✧✦✧✦✧✦

318   ARTEMIS
       On my knees I speak to you,
       Artemis, hunter of deer,
       blond child of Zeus and queen
       of roaming beasts. From pools
       of the river Lethaios you gaze
       across a city of brave men.
       Serenity. You are a shepherd
       of no flock of savage citizens.

319   DICE
       The dice of love are
       shouting and madness.

       [122]

320   THE VISION OF LOVE
On easy wings I glide to Olympos where
I seek my master Eros,
but he no longer lets me run down warm women
as in my doghood days:
he sees my graying beard and passes me by,
while I stand transfixed
in the wind made by his wings of quivering gold.

321   ON AN OLD LOVER
Eros, the blond god of lovers,
strikes me with a purple ball
and asks me to play with a girl
     wearing colorful sandals;

but the girl is from beautiful
Lesbos, and scorns my white hair,
and turning her back runs gaping
     behind another girl.

322   ON A VIRGIN
My Thracian foal, why do you glare with disdain
and then shun me absolutely as if I knew
     nothing of this art?

I tell you I could bridle you with tight straps,
seize the reins and gallop you around the posts
     of the pleasant course.

But you prefer to graze on the calm meadow,
or frisk and gambol gayly—having no manly
     rider to break you in.

323   PREPARATIONS FOR LOVE
Bring out water and wine and an armful
of flowers.
I want the proper setting
when I spar a few rounds with love.

324   KNOCKOUT
        Eros, the blacksmith of love,
        smashed me with a giant hammer
        and doused me in the cold river.

325   THE PLUNGE
        Lord! I clamber up the white cliff
        and dive into the steaming wave,
                    O dead drunk with love.

326   ON A CONSERVATIVE LOVER
        I love and yet do not love.
        I am mad yet not quite mad.

327   DEFINITION OF A WHORE
        Given-to-all and
                        celebrated by the masses,
        a carrier-of-peoples
                        and an apple orchard
        of mad haunches.

328   ON STREETWALKERS
        Although we call these women loose,
        they tighten their thighs around thighs.

329   ON THE FORTUNES OF ARTEMON
        Once he went about in filthy clothes and waspy
            hair,
        with wooden rings on his ears, and wore around
            his ribs
        an unwashed hairy oxhide from an old miserable
            shield.
        Our con-man pimped a living from bakery girls
            and whores,

and got his neck bound to a whipping block where
    the leather
made raw meat of his back—and best, he rode the
    wheel
so that hairs could be torn from his beard and
    scalp.

But now the good Artemon rides like a generous
    lord
in an excellent coach or litter; he wears gold
    earrings
and carries a special ivory parasol like a grand
    lady.

330   CHARIOTEER
O sweet boy like a girl,
I see you though you will not look my way.
You are unaware that you handle the reins
        of my soul.

331   ON DRINKING PARTIES*
I do not like the man who sits by his bowl
                and sobs about the sad wars,
but the rake who loves to rave about fine feats
                in the arts and art of love.

332   A WAY TO THE HEART
                        Come swiftly
and rub aromatic myrrh on her breasts:
the hollow cave around her heart.

333   ON THE ORIGIN OF MULES OR HALF-ASSES
The Mysians were first in perfecting the art
of coupling mare-hopping donkeys with horses.

* Attributed to Semonides by Bergk.

334   OF EFFEMINACY
In the morning they were joined in marriage,
though later in the same chamber
the groom could not join with his wife.

335   DECEMBER
We go through Poseidon's month.
Ponderous clouds sag with water
and furious storms break out
collapsing the rain earthward.

336   ON A HOPLITE
Here, the tomb of Timokritos, a hero in the wars.
It is the coward whom Ares spares—not the brave.

337   ON A GUARDIAN ANGEL
Now I hang in Athene's gleaming temple.
It was I who brought Python safely home
                     from the dreadful wars:
I, his shield.

338   VACILLATION
The bird flashes back and forth
between the black leaves of laurel trees
and the greenness of the olive grove.

339   ON THE SOLDIER AGATHON
All members of this village have come to weep
at your funeral pyre, O courageous Agathon,
who died for Abdera:

for in the chaos of the horrible battlefield,
blood-loving Ares never before slaughtered
a more fearless youth.

[126]

340   ON KLEINORIDES, LOST AT SEA*

You too, Kleinorides, were lost loving your country
as you confronted the wintry blast of the south
    wind.
In the spring season of your life you died unwed;
the seawaves washed away your graceful adoles-
    cence.

341   ENCOUNTER

I looked at her and took off
like a frightened cuckoo bird.

342   CANDOR

                                Personally,
I hate those who are furtive and touchy, morose
in their ways. I have learned that you, Megistes,
are of the innocent; of the childlike ones.

343   ON DEATH

My temples are white, my head largely bald.
Graceful youth has departed from my face,
and my teeth are loose teeth of an old man.
            I have few years left of sweet life.

Therefore I tremble and fear the underworld,
for the lightless chasm of death is dreadful
and the descent appalling: once cast down
            into Hell, there is no return.

344   PREPARATION

Let us hang garlands of celery
                across our foreheads,
and call a festival to Dionysos.

* Also ascribed to Leonidas of Tarentum.

Xenophanes

Born in 565 B.C. in Kolophon (near Ephesos in Asia Minor), Xenophanes fled from the Persian invaders and settled in Elea, in Italy. He died sometime after 473 B.C. He seems to have been partly a philosopher and partly a rhapsode (professional reciter of poems), but the integration of the two roles is not a matter of common agreement. On the philosophical side Xenophanes is remarkable for his vigorous criticism of traditional myth and anthropomorphic religion, and for his espousal of a kind of pantheism. His works included "Silloï" (satiric and parodic hexameters), a poem "On Nature" and elegies. He wrote also two verse histories—of Elea and of Kolophon.

When someone related to Xenophanes that he had seen eels alive in hot water, he said: "Then we can boil them in cold."

PLUTARCH, *Common Notions against the Stoics*

Consider Xenophanes' remark that it is just as impious to say that the gods were born as to say that they died. Both statements imply that at some time they did not exist.

ARISTOTLE, *Rhetoric*

You Xenophaneses, Diagorases, Hippons, Epikouroses, and the rest of that catalogue of odious god-forsaken wretches, go drop dead.

CLAUDIUS AELIANUS

Xenophanes says there are four elements in existing things, and an infinite number of separate worlds. Clouds are made from vapor of the sun carried upward into the air. The essence of god is spherical, in no way resembling man. He is all

eyes and all ears but does not
breathe. He is in his totality mind
and thinking, and is eternal. Xenophanes
was the first to have declared
that all that exists is transitory and
destructible, and that the soul is
breath or spirit.

DIOGENES LAERTIOS, *Lives of the
Philosophers*

❖❖❖❖❖❖❖❖❖❖❖❖❖❖❖❖❖❖❖❖❖❖❖❖❖❖❖❖❖

345   BANQUET DECORUM

Now the floor is scrubbed clean, our hands are
     washed
     and cups are dry. A boy loops garlands
in our hair. Another passes round a phial
     of redolent balsam. The mixing bowl
is bubbling with good cheer, and more fragrant
     wine
     stands potent in the earthen jars.
Incense floats a holy perfume through the room.
     Water is cold, crystal, sweet.
Golden bread is set near on a princely table
     loaded down with cheese and rich honey.
The altar in the center is submerged in flowers
     and the house vibrates with fun and singing.

Gracious men should first sing praises to God
     with proper stories and pure words.
After the libation when we pray for strength
     to act with rectitude (our first concern),
there is no sin in drinking all one can
     and still get home without a servant—
unless too old. We commend the man who shows
     good memory after drink; who seeks virtue
and not to harangue us with the ancient myths
     of noisy wars of Titans, Giants,
Centaurs. These things are worth nothing. The
     good
     lies in our reverence for the gods.

[129]

346 GAY DAYS IN ASIATIC KOLOPHON

They acquired useless luxuries out of Lydia
   while still free from her odious tyranny;
paraded to the market place in seapurple robes,
   often in bright swarms of a thousand.
They were proud and pleased in their elaborate
   hairdo's
   and hid body odor with rare perfumes.

347 THE NATURE OF GOD

There is one God—supreme among gods and
   men—
who is like mortals in neither body nor mind.

348 AGNOSTIC CREDO

The truth is that no man ever was or will be
who understands the gods and all I speak of.
If you stumble on some rocks of the whole truth
you never know it. There is always speculation.

349 PYTHAGORAS AND THE TRANSMIGRATED
SOUL

One day a dog was being thrashed in the street,
and behold, Pythagoras, philosopher of spirits,
   was walking by.
               His heart was in his mouth
for the poor pup.
           "Stop! Stop!" he cried.
"Don't beat him any more.
This is my dear friend's soul.
I recognize the voice when I hear him bark."

350 KNOWLEDGE

The gods did not enrich man
with a knowledge of all things
from the beginning of life.
Yet man seeks, and in time
invents what may be better.

351   THE MAKING OF GODS

1

Man made his gods, and furnished them
with his own body, voice and garments.

2

If a horse or lion or a slow ox
had agile hands for paint and sculpture,
the horse would make his god a horse,
the ox would sculpt an ox.

3

Our gods have flat noses and black skins
say the Ethiopians. The Thracians say
our gods have red hair and hazel eyes.

352   ON WATERS AND WINDS

Sea is a source of water and source of wind.
With no great ocean there would be no wind,
no moving rivers nor rainwater from the sky.
Great ocean is father of clouds, winds, rivers.

353   THE PHYSICAL ORIGIN OF THE RAINBOW

Whom they call Iris—is also a raincloud
which we see as purple, scarlet and green.

354   THE NATURE OF THE UNIVERSE

Everything comes from the earth,
and everything ends in the earth.

355   FIRST PRINCIPLES

All that is born and grows
comes from water and earth.

356   LAMPOON AGAINST HOMER AND HESIOD

Homer and Hesiod emblazoned the gods
with all that is shameful and scandalous
in man:
stealing, adultery and mutual deceit.

357   THE SHAPE OF THE EARTH

At our feet we see this end of the earth
where it rises to meet the firmament.
Below, the world sinks down unendingly.

Simonides

*Pindar's stylistic antipode and sometime rival
was born of good family on the island of Keos
in 556 B.C. Like Anakreon he was one of the poets
invited to Athens by Hipparchos as part of the
program of cultural enrichment inaugurated under
the Peisistratid tyranny. It was probably at Athens
that he wrote the dithyrambs to which only one
brief reference survives. After the fall of the
tyranny—again like Anakreon—he went to
Thessaly under the patronage of several leading
houses. But he was back in Athens by 490, since
he is reported to have defeated the dramatist
Aischylos in a competition to write an epitaph
for those fallen at Marathon. During the period
of the Persian Wars he became as it were the poetic
spokesman for the whole of Greece, as his ode
on the fallen at Thermopylai would suggest. At
Athens he became the friend of Themistokles. In
476 B.C. at the age of eighty he went to Sicily,
where he was welcomed both at Syracuse and
Akragas. (Pindar was in Sicily at this same time.)
Simonides died in Sicily in 468/7 B.C. and was
buried at Akragas. The tradition reports that he
was ugly, and shrewd in money matters.*

*Simonides composed choral poetry in many
genres, especially* threnoi *and* epinikia. *He also
wrote elegies and elegiac epigrams. His dialect was
a mollified Doric in choral lyric, and in elegy—
as usual for this genre—predominantly Homeric.
In contrast to Pindar, his style in choral poetry
was on the whole direct and harmonious. His
epinikia seem, unlike those of Pindar, to have
been sportive and lighthearted. In outlook—
political, ethical, religious—he was more "modern"
and more adaptable by far than Pindar.*

"Still," I said, "I do not find it easy
to disbelieve a wise and inspired
artist like Simonides."

PLATO, *Republic*

[133]

When Simonides was discussing wis-
dom and riches with Hieron's wife,
and she asked him which was better, to
become wise or to become wealthy, he
replied, "To become wealthy. For I
see the wise sitting on the door-
steps of the rich."

ARISTOTLE, Rhetoric

His chief excellence lies in his pathos.
Indeed some consider that in this
quality he surpasses all other
writers in this kind of literature.

QUINTILIAN, Guide to Oratory

✧✧✧✧✧✧✧✧✧✧✧✧✧✧✧✧✧✧✧✧✧✧✧✧✧✧✧✧✧✧

358   MEN OF THE FRONT RANKS

Through their extraordinary courage, the wide
farmlands of Tegea
have not shot fire and smoke into the sky.
For they made their choice
to leave their children in a country green
and sweet with freedom,
and died for this in the wild ranks of battle.

359   ON THE LAKEDAIMONIANS
FALLEN AT PLATAIA

These men left an altar of glory on their land,
shining in all weather,
when they were enveloped by the black mists of
   death.
but although they died
they are not dead, for their courage raises them in
   glory
from the rooms of Hell.

360 ON THE GREEKS FALLEN AT EURYMEDON

With mindless bravura Ares washed his long sleek
arrowheads
in the crimson waters within their chests,
and dust now lies not on the living flesh
of javelineers,
but on the vivid remnants of lifeless bodies.

361 ON THOSE WHO DIED AT THERMOPYLAI

Their tomb is an altar on which stand our bowls
of remembrance
and the wine of our praise.
Neither mold and worms, nor time
which destroys all things, will blacken their deaths.
The shrine of these brave men
has found its guardian
in the glory of Greece. Leonidas, the Spartan king,
lives in the great ornament he left behind
of unending fame and virtue.

362 GRAVE BY THE WATER

We were slaughtered in a Dirphian gully, and our
graves,
near Euripos, were paid for by our nation.
Justice. For in confronting the cruel clouds of war,
we gave away our years of lovely youth.

363 ARETE*

Virtue lives on a high rock
painful to climb and guarded by
a band of pure and evasive nymphs.
No mortal may look upon her
unless sweat pours from his body
and he climbs the summit of manliness.

* Arete: virtue, courage, achievement.

364 INSCRIPTION FOR ATHENIAN HEROES
WHO FOUGHT AT THE ISTHMOS
When her fate rested on the razor's edge,
we gave away our lives to save all Greece.

365 CODE OF HONOR AT THERMOPYLAI
Stranger, go back to Sparta and tell our people
that we who were slain obeyed the code.

366 VICTORY AT MARATHON
At Marathon the Athenians fought for all Greece
and broke the spearhead of Persia's crack troops.

367 ON THOSE WHO DIED WITH LEONIDAS
Leonidas, king of the open fields of Sparta,
those slain with you lie famous in their graves,
for they attacked absorbing the head-on assault
of endless Persian men, arrows and swift horse.

368 AN ORACLE'S DEATH AT THERMOPYLAI
This is the tomb of famous Megistias, slain by
the Persians near the Spercheios River,
a seer who even when aware that death was near
would not desert his Spartan kings.

369 ON MEGAKLES
When I look at the tomb of Megakles
with its dead body,
I pity you, poor Kallia, his father.

370 CROSSING THE GULF OF CORINTH
All these victors from the Tyrrhenian wars
were on their way to Apollo at Delphi
with their first plunder

when they found their grave
on one night, in one ship, in one deep sea.

371   THE ATHENIAN VANGUARD

Athenian sons demolished the Persian army
and saved their country from painful slavery.

372   SOCIAL DICTUM

The city is the teacher of the man.

373   ON IPHIMENES

O Geraneia, tall-air mountain of evil,
I wish you faced the far Danube or Tanais,
river of distant Skythia;
that the Skeironian precipice did not rise
from the sea where Iphimenes sailed around
the broken rock of Molouris.
Now he is a frozen corpse in the gulf,
and this open tomb tells of his bitter voyage.

374   DANAË AND THE INFANT PERSEUS
IMPRISONED IN A CHEST ON THE SEA

A tilting sea and thundering winds
tossed the carved chest and filled Danaë
with terror; she cried
and placed her arm lovingly around
Perseus saying: "My child, I suffer
and yet your heart is calm; you sleep
profoundly in the blue dark of night
and shine in our gloomy bronze-ribbed boat.
Don't think of the heaving saltwave
that seeps in through airholes and drenches
your hair, nor of the clamoring gale;
but lying in our seaviolet blanket
keep your lovely body close to mine.

If you knew the horror of our plight,
your gentle ears would hear my words.
But sleep, my son, and let
the ocean sleep and our great troubles end.
I ask you, father Zeus,
rescue us from our fate; and should
my words seem too severe, I beg you please
remember where we are, and forgive
my prayer."

375   ON LYKAS, A THESSALIAN HOUND
Bitch-hound, hunter, even your dead white bones
terrify the beasts of the field,
for your bravery is common knowledge
from huge Pelion to far Ossa
and on the dizzying sheep-paths of Kithairon.

376   HALCYON DAYS*
During the winter solstice
Zeus orders fourteen days of peaceful weather,
and man has called this windless season holy
for then the mottled halcyon rears its young.

377   ON A STATUE OF PHILON
I am from the island of Corfu.
My name: Philon, son of Glaukos.
And I am here,
because down in Olympia, at the games,
I was champion in boxing two years running.

378   VICTORY SONG FOR THE BOXER
GLAUKOS OF KARYSTOS
Neither the knockout king Polydeukes
nor even Herakles (iron boy of Alkmena)
would put up his guard to the mighty Glaukos.

* "The halcyon nests about the time of the winter solstice, and that is why, when the weather is fine at that time of year, we call the days 'Halcyon days.' " Aristotle, *History of Animals.*

379   A MODEST GRAVE

Sir, you are not looking at the tomb
of some great Lydian king,
for being poor my gravestone is small,
yet still too much for me.

380   ON THE GIRL GORGO

As she lay dying in her dear mother's arms,
Gorgo wept and whispered her last words:

"Stay with my father,
and on a better day bear a second daughter
who will care for you when you are old."

381   ENCIRCLED WOMAN

I am possessed by the fierce noise
all around me
of the purple, tormented sea.

382   HUMAN BANKRUPTCY

I who lie here, Brotachos of Gortyn, was born in
    Krete,
and I did not come here for death but weighty
    business.

383   SACRED HEALTH

Not even lucid wisdom
will give you joy
when sacred health is gone.

384   FLUX

If you are a simple mortal, do not speak
of tomorrow or how long this man may be
among the happy, for change comes suddenly
like the shifting flight of a dragonfly.

385   GREEN
The birds of spring
are the green-necked
singing nightingales.

386   ON DEMIGODS
Born half-divine and sons of mighty gods,
not even these, living in ancient times,
came to old age unscorned and without painful
hardships—nor did they escape from doom.

387   ON AN ATHENIAN DAUGHTER GIVEN
TO A FOREIGN PRINCE IN LAMPSAKOS
This dust lies on Archedike, daughter of Hippias,
despot of Athens and most princely Greek of his
day.
Although a daughter, wife, sister and mother of
tyrants,
she never yielded to snobbery; her heart was
humble.

388   PASSAGE OF TIME
One thousand years, ten thousand years
are but a tiny dot,
the smallest segment of a point,
an invisible hair.

389   ACCOMPLISHMENTS
Without the gods
a man or city can do nothing.
Only God knows everything, and man
suffers for what he does.

There is no evil
man may not expect, and soon
God wipes away the few things
he may have done.

Lasos

Born about 545 B.C. *at Hermione in the Argolid*
of the Peloponnesos, Lasos lived at Athens under
the patronage of Hipparchos, where he introduced
competitions in dithyrambic composition and was
rivaled by Simonides in this genre.

The flute player Skopelinos taught
Pindar the flute, and finding his
pupil of exceptional ability, passed
him on to Lasos of Hermione to
learn the lyre.

THOMAS MAGISTER, *Life of Pindar*

Lasisms: sophistries as the sophistries
or entangled arguments of Lasos.

HESYCHIOS, *Glossary*

❖❖❖❖❖❖❖❖❖❖❖❖❖❖❖❖❖❖❖❖❖❖❖❖❖❖

390 TO THE HERMIONIAN DEMETER
I sing of Demeter and the kore Persephone,
    wife of Klymenos,
and I lead
a choral hymn of honey voices
with all the low notes in the Aiolian harmony.

Theognis

Born in Megara in 544 B.C., Theognis was a
member of the embattled aristocracy. He was in
exile for part of his life, but returned home at some
time. He lived until at least 480 B.C. The subjects
of his poetry seem to have been chiefly two: the
vicissitudes of an aristocrat fallen on evil populist
times and the moral reflections appropriate to such
experience, and the vicissitudes of the poet's
affections—chiefly directed toward one Kyrnos.
However much out-of-balance one may find
Theognis' antediluvian social and moral views, his
vivid expression of keen experience ranks him
among the supreme elegists surviving from the
Lyric Age.

The corpus of poems traditionally assigned to
Theognis (about 1,400 lines) by no means wholly
belongs to him. Much of it consists of imitations and
copies of earlier poets (some of this may be by
Theognis) and of Theognis himself. The collection
may have arisen as a useful handbook of after-
dinner poetry for the man who did not care to produce
his own. The poems addressed to Kyrnos have the
greatest likelihood of Theognidean authorship. The
contents of the collection may be classified as
follows: 1) autobiography; 2) preludes, hymns,
epitaphs, etc.; 3) erotic and convivial verse; 4)
gnomic or "wisdom" poetry: gather-ye-rosebud
sermons, class propaganda, praise of wealth and
dispraise of poverty, expression of aristocratic moral
code—especially the virtues of courage, resignation
and fidelity.

We also have a witness in the poet
Theognis, a citizen of Megara, Sicily,
who said: "In a difficult dispute, a
trustworthy man is equal to gold
and silver."

PLATO, *Laws*

Theognis wrote exhortations; but
scattered among them were dis-
gusting, pederastic love poems and
pieces repugnant to a virtuous life.

The Suda Lexicon

This poet is concerned with no
other matter than the virtues and
vices of man, and his poetry is a
study of man just as a treatise on
horsemanship written by an expert
horseman studies horses.

STOBAIOS, Anthology

The epic verse of Empedokles and
Parmenides, the *Theriaka (Venom-
ous Bites)* and the *Gnomologies* of
Theognis are prose works which
borrow from poetry the use of its
meter and high tone, as if it were
a carriage, to avoid going prosai-
cally on foot.

PLUTARCH, How the Young Should
Listen to Poetry

❖❖❖❖❖❖❖❖❖❖❖❖❖❖❖❖❖❖❖❖❖❖❖❖❖❖

391   SHADOWS

Fools and children you are, mankind! You mourn
  the dead and not the dying flower of youth.

392   EUGENICS

In breeding donkeys, rams or horses, we seek out
  the thoroughbred to get a good strain,
my Kyrnos. Yet now the noblest man will marry
  the lowest daughter of a base family,
if only she brings in money. And a lady
  will share her bed with a foul rich man,
preferring gold to pedigree. Money is all.
  Good breed with bad and race is lost
to riches. Don't wonder our city's blood is polluted
  when noble men will couple with upstarts.

393   LIBERATION

Death, friend Kyrnos, is better to the poor
   than a life cursed with painful poverty.

394   POVERTY

Nothing destroys a good man quicker than
      poverty:
   not malarial fever, Kyrnos, nor old age.
Better to hurl oneself into the abysmal sea
   or over a blunt cliff—than be a victim
of poverty. The poor man can do or say nothing
   worthwhile. Even his mouth is gagged.

395   A LOOSE VESSEL

A ripe young wife and an old husband
make a very sad conjunction.
She is like a ship. Her wild rudder
doesn't respond to him.
Her anchors don't hold.
Often she slips her moorings altogether
to enter at night in another port.

396   TO KYRNOS, A REPROACH

I gave you wings to fly looming high and easy
   over unboarded sea and the entire earth.
At every meal and banquet you will be present
   on the lips of guests. Graceful young men
will sing of you in limpid lovely notes
   to the clean piping of the flutes.
When you go under the dark vaults of earth
   to the mournful chambers of sad Hell,
even when you lie dead you will not lose
   your glory. Your name will be recalled
among men always, Kyrnos. You will wheel high
   over the mainland and Greek islands
and cross the unharvested sea pulsing with fish,
   not by horse but carried to those who love you

in the gifts of Muses capped in violet flowers.
   You will be like a song to the living
as long as there is sun, earth. Yet you ignore me
   and trick me as if I were a child.

397   A SEAMAN'S SORROW
   I heard the sharp cry of the bird, O son of
      Polypas,
   who came to men with the message to plow
in good season; and it wounded my heart black
   that others own my flowering lands,
and not for me are mules dragging the curved
      plow,
   now, in my exile, on the wretched sea.

398   WORDS OF A BEARDED MAN
       RECLINING ON A COUCH
   O beautiful boy, I crave you more than any man.
   Stand where you are and hear my few words.

399   GOOD WILL WASTED
   I knew it before and know it better now:
     don't wait for thanks from the lower classes.

400   HIS FAIRNESS
   I will blame no enemy who is a good man
     nor praise a friend who may be vile.

401   OUR COURSE
   Best of all things—is never to be born,
   never to know the light of sharp sun.
   But being born, then best
   to pass quickly as one can through the gates of
      Hell,
   and there lie under the massive shield of earth.

402 THE WANDERER
   I have spent long days in the land of Sicily, and
      walked
      through the vineyards of the Euboian plain;
   saw the city of Sparta shining by the reedy
      Eurotas.
      Everywhere people took me into their homes
   yet my heart found no pleasure in foreign kindness.
      No place is as precious as one's homeland.

403 THE ATHLETE
   Blessed is the man who knows how to make love
      as one wrestles in a gym,
   and then goes home happy to sleep the day
      with a delicious young boy.

404 GOOD AND EVIL
   Easier to make bad out of good than good out of
      bad.
      Don't try to teach me. I am too old to learn.

405 A CITY IN TRAVAIL
   Kyrnos, the city is pregnant, and I fear it will bear
      a man who will clean up our outrageous pride.
   The people are still well behaved, but the leaders
      plunge along a course of vile corruption.

Apollodoros

Active during the late sixth century B.C.

Under these omens Pindar turned to
the art of poetry, his teacher being
either Lasos, as said before, or the
Athenian Agathokles or Apollodoros.
We are told about Apollodoros that
when he was the leader of the cyclic
chorus, he had to leave the city and
entrusted the training of the chorus
to Pindar, still a boy, who did so well
as to become known throughout
the area.

EUSTATHIOS, *Introduction to Pindar*

❖❖❖❖❖❖❖❖❖❖❖❖❖❖❖❖❖❖❖❖❖❖❖❖❖❖❖❖

406   WHO?
Who can be coming to the edge
of my gates
at this black hour of night?

Hipparchos

Hipparchos was the younger brother of Hippias,
Tyrant of Athens (who succeeded his father
Peisistratos in 527 B.C.). He was as it were the
commissar of culture during his brother's reign,
and was responsible for much of Athens' rapid
advance in the arts. The frivolous decadence of his
private life ended when he was assassinated by
Harmodios and Aristogeiton in 514 B.C.

Because of their esteem and age, Hippias and
Hipparchos, not their half-brothers, held the reins
of power, and since Hippias was the elder and by
nature a clever politician, he was virtual ruler. On
the other hand, Hipparchos was childlike, amorous
and a friend of the arts. It was he who brought
Anakreon, Simonides and other poets to Athens.

ARISTOTLE, *Constitution of Athens*

A great light was born in Athens when Hipparchos
was slaughtered by Aristogeiton and Harmodios.

SIMONIDES, *Inscription for Statues of Tyrannicides*

Hipparchos set up statues of Hermes on the roads
between the city and every community in Attica
. . . so that his citizens would not most admire
the wise sayings inscribed at Delphi, such as "Know
yourself" and "Nothing in excess," but rather be
guided by the wisdom of himself, Hipparchos. Thus
they would read them and partake of his wisdom
while going back and forth to their farms and
homes, and so become enlightened men.

PLATO, *Hipparchos*

❖❖❖❖❖❖❖❖❖❖❖❖❖❖❖❖❖❖❖❖❖❖❖❖❖❖❖❖❖❖

407   INSCRIPTION FROM A STATUE OF HERMES
        This will recall Hipparchos:
        As you walk think of the good.

408   INSCRIPTION FROM A STATUE OF HERMES
        This will recall Hipparchos:
        Never doublecross a friend.

Korinna

This Boiotian poet was probably a contemporary of Pindar, but it is also possible that she lived in the late third century B.C. Until the papyrus finds of this century, she was known only in the scantiest of fragments. Her works included narrative choral lyrics intended for an audience of women, on such subjects as the Seven Against Thebes. Her diction and meter are simple, her dialect chiefly Boiotian.

Daughter of Acheloodoros and Hippokrateia, of Thebes or Tanagra; a pupil of Myrtis and a lyric poet. It is reported that she gained victory five times over Pindar in poetry competitions. She wrote five books as well as Inscriptions and Lyric Nomes.

Suda Lexicon

When Pindar the poet competed at Thebes he ran into ignorant judges, and was defeated five times by Korinna. To show the judges' bad taste, Pindar called Korinna a pig.

CLAUDIUS AELIANUS, *Historical Miscellanies*

When Pindar was still young and proud of his mastery of language, Korinna censured him for his poor taste.

PLUTARCH, *Glory of Athens*

◇◆◇◆◇◆◇◆◇◆◇◆◇◆◇◆◇◆◇◆◇◆◇◆◇◆◇◆◇

409   ON HERSELF

I Korinna am here to sing the courage
of heroes and heroines in old myths.

To daughters of Tanagra in white robes,
I sing. And all the city is delighted
with the clean water of my plaintive voice.

410   THE CONTEST OF HELIKON
        AND KITHAIRON

Kithairon sang of cunning Kronos
and sacred Rheia who stole her son
Zeus, mighty among immortals.

Then the Muses asked the gods to put
their ballot stones in the urn of
gold. All stood up and Kithairon won

the greater part. Hermes shouted loud,
at once proclaiming sweet victory.
The gods adorned his brow with flowers,

and Kithairon rejoiced. But Helikon
was stunned with bitter rage, and tore
a massive boulder from the mountain;

insanely he shouted and lobbed the rock
down on thousands of mortals below.

411   HERMES

When he sailed into the harbor
his ship became a snorting horse.
Hermes ravished the white city
while the wind like a nightingale
sang with his whirling war-axe.

412   ROUT OF THE ERETRIAN FLEET

For you alone, Tanagra,
Hermes came to fight
with his naked fists.

413   ON MYRTIS
       Although I was her pupil,

       Even I reproach Myrtis
       of the crystalline voice.

       She was a mere woman poet,
       yet she challenged Pindar.

414   ON HERSELF
       Will you sleep forever? There was a time,
       Korinna, when you were not a loafer.

Telesilla

Fifth-century B.C. *poet of Argos.*
She wrote hymns to the gods,
mainly for women.

No less renowned than these collective
deeds is the battle in which the
Spartan king Kleomenes was driven
from Argos (with his men) by the
poet Telesilla.

PLUTARCH, *Feminine Virtue*

Above the theater is a temple of
Aphrodite. And in front of the
pedestal of the goddess is a slab
engraved with a figure of Telesilla,
the writer of songs. . . . Telesilla was
famous among women for her poetry
but still more famous for the follow-
ing deed: [her defeat of the Spartans].

PAUSANIAS, *Description of Greece (Argos)*

◇✦✦✦✦✦✦✦✦✦✦✦✦✦✦✦✦✦✦✦✦✦✦✦◇

415   REFUGE FROM RAPE
O Artemis and your virgin girls,
come to us. Run swiftly
to escape the hunter Alpheus.

416   SONG TO APOLLO
O the sun-loving Apollo!

Timokreon

Born on Rhodes, active during first
half of fifth century B.C. *He sided*
with the Persians in the wars and
visited their king. Timokreon, who
crossed poetic swords with Simoni-
des, was reputed to be a glutton.
He composed lyrics and elegies.

When Timokreon became the guest
of the Persian king, he took full ad-
vantage of the food offered him. Once,
when the king asked why he was
stuffing himself, he answered, "So I
can give a great number of Persians
a sound thrashing." The next day he
defeated a large number of them, one
by one, and then stood beating the
air. He explained to his astonished
host that he had all these blows to
spare if any one would come on for
more.

ATHENAIOS, *Scholars at Dinner*

After drinking and eating and slan-
dering to my heart's content, I now
lie here, Timokreon of Rhodes.

SIMONIDES

❖◆◆◆◆◆◆◆◆◆◆◆◆◆◆◆◆◆◆◆◆◆◆◆◆◆◆◆◆◆❖

417 THE SOURCE
Blind money, I wish you were banished
from coastal plains and the sea,
from the deep continent,
and made your home on Acheron's shore
in black Tartaros.
For all the malevolence in man
is caused by you.

Lamprokles

Active at Athens in early fifth century B.C., *he composed dithyrambs and hymns, and was an influential teacher of music.*

Pythokleides was a musician of solemn music, a Pythagorian who taught Agathokles, the teacher of Lamprokles, the teacher of Damon.*

SCHOLIAST, On Plato

In the *History of Harmony*, Aristoxenos claims that the Mixolydian mode was invented by Pythokleides, the flute player. Lysis states that Lamprokles of Athens, understanding that this mode has a disjunction . . . arranged it to proceed from B to B.

PLUTARCH, On Music

◇◇◇◇◇◇◇◇◇◇◇◇◇◇◇◇◇◇◇◇◇◇◇◇◇◇◇◇◇◇

418   ON ATHENA

City-destroying Pallas,
wonderful captain in battle,
constant champion of war,
virgin, child of great Zeus,
you tame unbroken stallions.

---

* The teacher of Perikles and Socrates.

[155]

Pindaros (Pindar)

The prince of choral poets was born in 518 B.C. *at Kynoskephalai in Boiotia, of an aristocratic family. He was educated in his craft chiefly at Athens. In the course of his career he established connections with leading families in many parts of the Greek world. (The relationship between poet and patron during this period, remarks Hermann Fränkel, should be understood within the tradition of the exchange of gifts by guest-friends, rather than treated as a sheerly commercial link.) He went to Sicily in 476* B.C. *and was welcomed both by Hieron of Syracuse and by Theron of Akragas. At least from this time onward Pindar found himself on occasion in competition with Simonides and Bakchylides, and was not always the winner: Bakchylides was commissioned instead of Pindar to write an epinikion for Hieron in 468. Pindar died at eighty in 438* B.C.

The works of Pindar comprised seventeen books, including nearly all choral genres. Only the four books of his epinikian odes have survived in substantial completeness, but the fragments of others fill some eighty pages in Bowra's edition.

The style of Pindar is dense and highly personal, blended from several dialects. His viewpoint is that of an aristocratic conservative, both in religion and politics. The epinikion for Pindar is above all a religious celebration of the glories of god and hero, and (as it were incidentally) their reflection in the achievements of his aristocratic contemporaries.

Pindar has had deeper influence on subsequent literature than any other Greek lyric poet. The modern ode at its greatest is chiefly the descendant of Pindar. But, as Bowra says, "He was capable . . . at times, of a sublimity to which there is no parallel."

A delight to strangers and loved by
friends, Pindar was servant of the
sweet-voiced Muses.

PLATO

[156]

The Greek Period

In lyric poetry would you prefer to be Bakchylides
rather than Pindar? And in tragedy Ion of Chios
rather than—Sophokles? It is true that Bakchylides
and Ion are faultless and entirely elegant writers
of the polished school, while Pindar and Sophokles,
although at time they burn everything before them
as it were in their swift career, are often extinguished
unaccountably and fail most lamentably. But would
anyone in his sense regard all the compositions of
Ion put together as an equivalent for the single play
of the *Oidipous* [or all the works of Bakchylides
as equal to a single ode of Pindar's?]

"LONGINUS," *On the Sublime*

Whoever labors to be Pindar's equal,
Iulus, mounts on wings that are fastened with wax,
Daidalos-fashion, and will give his name to
    glittering water.

As a river roars down a mountain, swollen
by showers of rain, spilling over its banks,
so Pindar rages and the deep of his voice
    pours ever onward,

worthy of the laurel sacred to Apollo,
whither he is tumbling freshly minted words
through frenzied hymns, carried along on meters
    free and unruly . . .

HORACE, *Odes*

Of the nine lyric poets Pindar is by far the greatest,
in virtue of his inspired magnificence, the beauty
of his thoughts and figures, the rich exuberance
of his language and matter and his rolling flood of
eloquence, characteristics which, as Horace rightly
held, make him inimitable.

QUINTILIAN

Pindar lies in the earth, this Pierian trumpet, strong
forger of pure hymns, whose song when heard made
one think a swarm of bees had come from the
Muses to fashion it in the chamber of Kadmos'
bride, Harmony.

ANTIPATROS OF SIDON, *Palatine Anthology*

It was during the quadrennial festival
[Pythian games] with its procession of oxen that,
as a well-loved child, I was first wrapped in
swaddling clothes.

PINDAR, Fragment

A chosen herald of wise speech, I was raised by the
Muses for Hellas. I am proud that my race and
my home are in Thebes, a city of chariots.

PINDAR, Dithyramb for Thebes

❖❖❖❖❖❖❖❖❖❖❖❖❖❖❖❖❖❖❖❖❖❖❖❖❖❖❖❖❖❖

419   ECLIPSE

God has in his power
to make dazzling unmixed light
spring from the somber depths
of evening. He can also
enclose the white explosion of day
under the gloom of black clouds.

420   SINGING DANCE*

Follow the curving line of melody,
and in contest
dance frenetically to imitate
the Amyklian hound or a wild unbroken horse.

And move your body
as a hound flies across the windy plain of Dotia
to kill a horned deer
who, in desperate dance,
bobs her head and neck convulsively
to either side.

---

* Also attributed to Simonides.

[158]

421   OLYMPIAN ODE XII
For Ergoteles of Himera, winner of
the long distance run, 472 B.C., now
exiled from Knossos.

O daughter of liberating Zeus, I beseech you,
O saviour Fortune, guard the strength of Himera.
At sea you pilot our speeding ships,
and on land the erupting wars and assemblies
depend on your will. For men's hopes splash high,
break low as they toss through an ocean of lies.

No man of the earth has ever encountered
a sure sign from God of things to come. The future
is blind to him. It teases
his judgment: as the reversal of delight;
or as after suffering a surge of pain
the sudden turning from gloom to meadows of joy.

Son of Philanor, like a cock who fights only at
         home,
even your legs' splendor might be dull
had civil strife among bitter men
not expelled you from your homeland, Knossos.
Now, Ergoteles, garlanded at Olympia
and twice festooned at Pytho and at the Isthmos,
you honor the Hot Springs of the Nymphs—here
         at your new home, Himera.

422   AFTERLIFE IN ELYSIUM

For them the sun shines at full strength—while we
         here walk in night.
The plains around their city are red with roses
and shaded by incense trees heavy with golden
         fruit.
And some enjoy horses and wrestling, or table
         games and the lyre,
and near them blossoms a flower of perfect joy.
Perfumes always hover above the land

from the frankincense strewn in deep-shining fire
   of the gods' altars.

And across from them the sluggish rivers of black
   night
vomit forth a boundless gloom.

423   OLYMPIAN ODE XI
To the Lokrian boy Agesidamos,
winner in the boxing, 476 B.C.

There is a time when men most need
winds; there is a time for waters from the sky,
for raindrops, daughters of the cloud.
But if by effort a man is victorious, sweet songs
foretell later fame,
and are a pledge for remembrance of great achieve-
   ments.

Abundant is the praise waiting for Olympian
victory, and my lips are pleased
to shepherd these words.
Yet only through God can wisdom blossom in a
   man's soul.
So know this, Agesidamos,
for you, son of Archestratos, for your boxing
triumph I will raise a sweet song to add radiance
to your olive wreath of gold,
and speak of the West Wind Lokrians, your people.
Let us acclaim him here, Muses. I warrant
you will not be received coldly like strangers,
nor find bluntness to lovely things,
but wisdom and excellent spearmen. For neither
the fiery brown fox
nor raucous lion can change his nature given from
   birth.

424   LAMENT
The stars and the rivers
and waves call you back.

425   GLORIOUS ATHENS

O shining city, festooned in violets, draped in song,
you are the marble strength of all Hellas, glorious
  Athens, sacred citadel.

426   OLYMPIAN ODE III

To Theron of Akragas in Sicily,
winner in the chariot race, 466 B.C.

I shall honor glorious Akragas and please the
  Dioskouroi, kind to strangers,
and Helen of the lovely hair,
when I have raised a hymn of Olympic victory for
  Theron and his stallions
of the never-tiring hooves. The Muses were faithful
  as I found a shining virgin mode
to link Dorian rhythms with the speech

of celebration. The olive wreath on his flowing
  locks moves me
to my God-appointed duty
to blend clamoring flutes and the lyre's supple voice
  with my pattern of words,
all for Ainesidamos' son. And Pisa bids me speak
  out. From Pisa
come heavenly songs to man

and to the victor. The upright Aitolian judge of
  Greeks, obeying Herakles' ancient laws,
loops the gray glory of the olive
over the hero's brow and locks. Long ago
  Amphitryon's son carried the silver olive tree
from the shadowy springs of the Danube,
to be the handsomest symbol of the Olympian
  games.

With candid heart he persuaded the Hyperboreans,
  people of Apollo;
he begged them for a tree for Zeus' garden
to bring refreshing shade to all men, and crown
  their valor.

[161]

Already the altars were hallowed for his father;
    and the mid-month moon,
riding in her gold cart, illumined the round eye

of evening. He established the fair judging for the
    great fifth-year games
by the overhanging banks of holy Alpheus River.
But the valley of Kronian Pelops was not yet
    verdant with beauty of trees.
He thought his garden, naked of green, must suffer
    the sun's dagger rays.
So his spirit moved him to journey

to Istrian land. There, Leto's daughter, driver of
    horses,
welcomed him as he came from ridges and mazy
    gullies of Arkadia
when, at Eurysteus' command, his doomed ties with
    Zeus drove him on his mission
to bring back the gold-horned doe that Taygeta
    one day wrote down
to be sacrificed to Artemis Orthosia.

Chasing the doe, he saw the distant land behind
    the cold north wind
and stood in wonder at the trees.
A sweet desire burned in him to plant them at the
    finish-mark of the twelve-lap track
of horses. And now he comes graciously to the
    festival, with the godlike
twin sons of deep-girdled Leda.

At Olympos he had charged those future stars to
    guide the wonderful games
where men's courage and chariot-speed
are tested. My heart impels me to say that glory
    has come to Theron
and the children of Emmenos as a gift from the
    horsemen Dioskouroi. Among all mortals
they drew near the gods through lavish feasts

and true reverence for the mysteries.
If water is best of all things, and gold the dearest
  possession,
then Theron's virtues touch the uttermost realm
  of excellence,
reaching Herakles' pillars. Beyond, the world is
  untracked
by wise or foolish. There I will not venture, being
  no fool.

Bakchylides

*A contemporary, possibly younger, of Pindar,
Bakchylides was born, like his uncle Simonides, on
the island Keos in the Kyklades. He too took part
in the dithyrambic competitions at Athens and
accompanied his uncle to Sicily around 476 B.C. He
was reportedly exiled to the Peloponnesos at some
time in his life. Like Simonides and Pindar, he wrote
for numerous patrons throughout Greece. Until 1896
there survived of Bakchylides only half as many
lyric fragments as those of Simonides. But in that
year a papyrus-find of fourteen epinikia and six
dithyrambs was made in Egypt. Among lyric poets
Bakchylides is now second only to Pindar in state
of preservation. Fragments remain of other genres
of Bakchylides' choral lyrics.*

*The language of Bakchylides is chiefly a combination
of Homeric and Doric—a version of the "standard"
international choral language. His style is on the
whole much more direct and penetrable than
Pindar's, but his diction is distinguished by an
abundance of ornamental compounds, many of them
newly coined.*

Pindar had a feud with Bakchylides,
and compares himself to an eagle and
Bakchylides to a jackdaw.

        SCHOLIAST, *On Pindar*

In this ode (*Pastor cum traheret*)
Horace imitates Bakchylides.

        PORPHYRIO, *On an Ode of Horace*

There are nine Lyric Poets: Alkman,
Alkaios, Sappho, Stesichoros, Ibykos,
Anakreon, Simonides, Bakchylides
and Pindar.

        EUSTATHIOS, *Introduction to Pindar*

It seems that the finest and most famous
works of the ancients were also induced by
exile. The Athenian Thucydides composed his
history of the war between Athens and the
Peloponnesians near Skapte Hyle in Thrace.
Xenophon wrote at Skyllos in Elis. The poet
Bakchylides (from Keos) wrote in the Pelo-
ponnesos.

PLUTARCH, On Exile

❖❖❖❖❖❖❖❖❖❖❖❖❖❖❖❖❖❖❖❖❖❖❖❖❖❖❖❖❖❖

427   PEACE

Only great peace
brings wealth to men
and a flowering of honey-throated song,
and to the gods
ox-thighs burning and long-haired sheep
flaming yellow on the sculpted altars,
and to the young
a love of wrestling and the flute
and Bakchic dance.

In the iron-covered shield
the brown spider hangs his web.
The sharpened spear and double-edge sword
are flaked with rust.
The noise of the brass trumpet is dead,
and the honey of our dawnsleep
is not dried from our eyelids.
Streets clamor with happy outdoor banquets,
and the lovely hymns sung by children
spring like fire up into the bright air.

428   THE WEST WIND

On his farmland Eudemos built this sanctuary
   to the Zephyr,
kind breeze among the harsh gales,

for when the farmer prayed,
the wind awoke briskly
helping him winnow good wheat from the chaff.

429   HERAKLES: A DITHYRAMB
I must not sing of you now,
O Pythian Apollo (though
the lovely-throned Urania
sent me a gold ship from Pieria
cargoed with famous hymns) if you are hunting
far by the flowering bank of the Hebros
or delighting in the soft song
of the long-necked swan.
Before you come to cull
the bloom of paeans
which the Delphian dancers
chant loudly by your shining temple,

we will sing of Amphitryon's
brave son who fled the city
of Oichalia gutted by flames;
who came to that wavewashed cape
(where he was sacrificing nine deep-roaring bulls
to the Kenaian Zeus of the broad clouds,
a pair to the seagod who lifts
salt waters and punishes earth,
and a never-yoked high-horned ox
to chaste Athena of the fierce glance)
when a dread wargod wove
a terrible poisonous weapon of blood

for Deianeira: she had learned
the sorrowful news
that the fearless son of Zeus
was sending white-armed Iole
to his luminous rooms to become his bride.
O doomed insane wife! Why did she plot
disaster! Relentless envy
drove her against

the black veil of future
on that day she took
(on the flowering bank of the Evenos)
the star-cursed gift* from the centaur Nessos.

430   IDAS WINS MARPESSA

One day in spacious Sparta
goldhaired girls
danced to a song
when courageous Idas
led Marpessa of the violet braids
to his own rooms
after eluding death.
Poseidon the sealord
gave him a chariot
and horses equal to the wind,
and sent him to the handsome city of Pleuron
and to the son of Ares of the gold shield.†

431   THESEUS: A DITHYRAMB

A blue-prowed ship was knifing the open sea
off Krete, carrying battle-fierce Theseus
and fourteen glorious
young Ionian men and girls.
The northerly winds slammed into
her white sails glittering far,
by grace of famous Athene of the war-aegis.
But the alarming gifts of Aphrodite,
who wears the headband of desire,
clawed at the heart of Minos,
and he could not keep his hand from a girl
and caressed her white cheek.
But Eriboia screamed
for Theseus the bronze-armored
offspring of Pandion; he looked

---

* The centaur's blood poisoned by Herakles' arrow in which jealous
Deianeira dipped the shirt of her husband, Herakles, thinking it a love
potion; the garment caused Herakles' death and her suicide.
  † Evenos, father of Marpessa.

and his eye rolled black
under his brows, and angry pain
pierced his heart, as he spoke:
"O son of peerless Zeus,
here you are steering
a course of shameful behavior
within your heart.
Hero, control that wanton violence.

Our powerful destiny comes from the gods,
and whichever way the scale of Justice
dips, we shall fulfill
our determined fate—whenever
it comes. So restrain
your heavy hand. Even if true
that you were conceived in the bed of Zeus
under the brow of Mount Ida
from the celebrated daughter
of Phoinix, yet I also came
into being when the daughter
of rich Pittheus lay with the sealord
Poseidon; and the violet-wreathed
daughters of Nereus gave her
a veil of gold. Therefore,
O war-king of the Knossians,
I ask you to hold back insolence
that will bring many tears.
I would never look on sweet light
of ambrosial dawn, were you to force
any of these youths or virgin
girls. Rather, we shall match
the strength of our hands, and the gods will judge."

So spoke the spear-brave hero,
and sailors stood spellbound
before his defiant courage,
but Helios' son-in-law raged in his soul
and concocted new tricks,
and spoke: "Omnipotent Zeus, Father,
hear me. If I am your son by Phoinix' daughter,
your white-armed bride,

now break swiftly from the sky
a fire-haired flash of thunder,
a sign all will know. Theseus, if Aithra
from Troizen really bore you
as son to Poseidon the earth-shaker,
go leap into the deep pelagos,
your father's chambers,
and bring back this shining
gold ornament of my hand,
my ring. Now you will know
if Kronos' son, lord of thunder
and master of all, will hear my prayers."

Zeus, mountain of strength, listened to his pure
prayer and approved; and wishing to honor
his son in great public
display, spilled down
a flash of lightning. Minos, seeing
the welcome portent, raised his arms
to the echoing sky; the battle-fierce
hero spoke: "Theseus, now you see
how shining clear are my gifts
from Zeus. Come, dive into the roar
of the open sea, and your father,
the lord Poseidon, son of Kronos,
will lift you in transcendent glory
over the land of handsome trees."
He spoke, and Theseus did not flinch.
A heart of iron, standing tall
on the solid deck he sprang,
and the deep forest of the sea
took him down kindly. Zeus' son
was inwardly amazed,
and ordered the well-made ship
to sail before the wind.
But Destiny swept them on another course.

Pummeled astern by a northern blast
the rapid vessel shot ahead
and the group of Athenian
youths trembled in fear

as their hero plunged to the water.
Tears formed in their flower-bright
eyes, as they thought of the grave danger.
But dolphins, roamers in the sea,
easily bore great Theseus
to the palace of his horseman father.
He entered the regal hall of gods.
There he looked with fearful wonder
at the beautiful daughters
of rich Nereus. From their
fabled bodies shone a glory
of fire, and ribbons of gold
were twined among their braids
as their nimble feet floated
in happy dance. He saw
in the pleasant palace
the ox-eyed Amphitrite,
his father's true majestic wife,
who wrapped round him a robe of purple linen,

and laid on his heavy mat of hair
an immaculate wreath
that one day at her marriage
cunning Aphrodite in rose garland gave her.
For men of sound mind
no labor by the gods is past belief.
Beside the ship's narrow stern Theseus came up
and how he amazed
the Knossian warlord
when he rose unwet from the sea,
a miracle to all, and on
his limbs gleamed the gift of the gods.
The bright-throned nymphs
shrieked in pristine triumph,
the sea clamored,
and those youths about him
sang a loud perfect paean!
O Lord of Delos, your heart
warmed with Keian chorales,
grant us godly blessings in all we do.

Praxilla

*Poet active about 450 B.C. at
Sikyon in the Argolid. She wrote
dithyrambs, drinking songs and
hymns.*

Praxilla was portrayed in bronze by
Lysippos, although she spoke nonsense
in her poetry.

TATIAN, *Against the Greeks*

Only a simpleton would put
cucumbers and the like on a par
with the sun and the moon.

ZENOBIOS

◇◇◇◇◇◇◇◇◇◇◇◇◇◇◇◇◇◇◇◇◇◇◇◇◇◇◇◇◇◇◇◇◇◇

432   OF THE SENSUAL WORLD

Most beautiful of things I leave is sunlight;
then come glazing stars and the moon's face;
then ripe cucumbers and apples and pears.

433   APPEARANCE

You gaze at me teasingly through the window:
a virgin face—and below—a woman's thighs.

434   ACHILLES

(You understood their words)

but they never reached the heart
buried in your chest.

[171]

435 THE COWARD

Under cover
a coward will strike from any side.
I warn you, friend:
watch out for his sting.
Under every rock is a lurking scorpion.

Parrhasios

A noted painter active at Athens probably in the second half of the fifth century B.C. *His reported skill in details of facial expression and in outline drawing perhaps justified in part the* hybris *of the epigram given below. Parrhasios was represented as discussing painting with Sokrates in Xenophon's* Memorabilia, *and himself wrote on the art.*

Parrhasios so systematized all art that he is known as the lawgiver; the depiction of gods and heroes according to his manner is followed by other painters, as though by necessity.

QUINTILIAN, Elements of Oratory

Euenor was the father and teacher of the great painter Parrhasios.

PLINY, Natural History

❖❖❖❖❖❖❖❖❖❖❖❖❖❖❖❖❖❖❖❖❖❖❖❖❖❖❖❖

436   PERFECTION IN ART

I say, even if those who hear are unbelieving,
I affirm that my hand has discovered the limits
    of art.
Though nothing is flawless in the world of men,
now the mark is fixed and cannot be surpassed.

437   ON A PAINTING OF HERAKLES
FOR WHICH THE GOD POSED

Now you may see the god—exactly as he was,
    coming to me Parrhasios in my dream.

Hippon

Natural philosopher, probably from Samos, was active in the latter half of the fifth century B.C. *He revived and modified the view that water was the source of all things.*

Kratinos also accuses Hippon of impiety.

SCHOLIAST, *On Clement of Alexandria*

Hippon of Rhegium declared that the elements were cold (water) and heat (fire), and that fire, when made from water, overcame the power of its author and formed the world.

HIPPOLYTOS, *Against Heresies*

Because of the impoverished nature of his thinking, Hippon is not worthy of being included with those philosophers who hold water to be an element or first principle.

ARISTOTLE, *Metaphysics*

❖❖❖❖❖❖❖❖❖❖❖❖❖❖❖❖❖❖❖❖❖❖❖❖❖

438   ON THE ATHEIST PHILOSOPHER
FROM RHEGIUM, CALABRIA
Here is the grave of Hippon. When he died
   fate made him equal to the eternal gods.

Melanippides

A famous dithyrambic poet of his time. Born on Melos (and hence a Dorian) he was active during the middle of the fifth century B.C. and died at the court of Perdikkas in Macedonia. A comic poet attributed to Melanippides the first innovations which led to the decadence of choral lyric. One innovation was the introduction of lyric solos into the dithyramb. In addition to dithyrambs, Melanippides wrote epics, elegies and epigrams.

Like his grandafther he was a lyric poet. He made great innovations in the dithyramb and spent part of his life at the court of the Macedonian king Perdikkas, where he died. He wrote lyric poems and dithyrambs.

Suda Lexicon

"Tell me, Aristodemos," he asked, "are there any men whose art you esteem?" "Yes," he said. "Tell us their names," Sokrates asked. "For the epic I especially admire Homer, for the dithyramb Melanippides. . . ."

XENOPHON, *Recollections of Sokrates*

❖❖❖❖❖❖❖❖❖❖❖❖❖❖❖❖❖❖❖❖❖❖❖❖❖❖❖

439   THE DANAÏDS
They were not shaped like handsome men
nor was their voice womanly,
but they trained naked
driving in chariots about the sunny
treelands. Often
they were happy in hunting;
often they sought the holy tear
of the dripping frankincese,
the good smell of dates
or smooth seeds of Syrian cassia.

[175]

Timotheos

*Timotheos was born at Miletos around 450 B.C.
and died around 360 B.C., possibly in Macedon,
whither he (like his friend Euripides) had been
invited by King Archelaos. The most famous lyric
poet of his time, Timotheos was also (according to
some tastes ancient and modern) one of the most
pernicious. His musical innovations were striking,
and carried such weight (with Euripides, for
example) that they contributed mightily to the
decay of the verbal side of the ode. The language
in his surviving fragments is often preposterously
artificial and periphrastic. Yet the long papyrus
fragment on the defeat of the Persians (published
in 1903) includes a jarringly "realistic" imitation
of a Persian speaking in broken Greek. His works
included nomes, dithyrambs, hymns, encomia, etc.*

When Timotheos was hissed because he seemed to
be an innovator and rebel against the laws of
music, Euripides asked him to take heart, for soon
the theater audience would acclaim him.

PLUTARCH, *Should Old Men Govern?*

Here the Spartans hung the lyre of Timotheos of
Miletos, after censuring him for having added four
new strings to the traditional seven in the art
of singing to the lyre.

PAUSANIAS, *On Sparta*

If there had been no Timotheos, we would not
have much of our lyric poetry, and if there had
been no Phrynis there would have been no
Timotheos.

ARISTOTLE, *Metaphysics*

❖❖❖❖❖❖❖❖❖❖❖❖❖❖❖❖❖❖❖❖❖❖❖❖❖❖❖❖❖❖❖

440   TO APOLLO

Sun, your phosphorescent rays pin fire
across the eternal firmament.
Snap a far-hunting arrow against our enemies,
O careering Healer to whom we cry!

Platon (Plato)

*Born about 429 B.C. in Athens and
died in 347. He was a disciple of
Sokrates, later the founder of the
Academy, and in effect the father
of Western philosophy. If he was
in fact the author of the epigrams
attributed to him, his* Phaidros *and*
Symposion *may provide the spirit-
ual link between his amatory epi-
grams and his philosophical works.
"Hesperos" has been called the most
perfect of all epigrams. Shelley
prefixed it to his "Adonais."*

You were the most accomplished
stylist of the fine Attic tongue, and
all Greek literature has no greater
voice than yours. Inspired Plato, you
were the first to contemplate ethics
and life, looking to God and heaven.
You combined the high thinking of
Pythagoras with the cutting spirit of
Sokrates, and were a beautiful
monument of their solemn dissension.

ANONYMOUS, *Palatine Anthology*

If Apollo had not given Plato to
Greece, how could he cure men's
souls by writings? While Apollo's
son Asklepios heals the human body,
Plato heals the immortal soul.

DIOGENES LAERTIOS, *Palatine Anthology*

The golden bough of Plato's poems,
forever divine, and shining with
virtue.

from the *Stephanos of Meleagros, 1st proem*

◆◆◆◆◆◆◆◆◆◆◆◆◆◆◆◆◆◆◆◆◆◆◆◆◆◆◆◆◆◆◆◆◆◆

441 HESPEROS

You were the Morning Star among the living.
In death, O Evening Star, you light the dead.

442 LOVE POEM

My child—Star—you gaze at the stars,
and I wish I were the firmament
that I might watch you with many eyes.

443 THE APPLE

I am an apple, and one who loves you
tossed me before you. O yield to him,
dear Xanthippe! Both you and I decay.

444 LESSON FROM THE ACADEMY

I throw this apple before you.
Take it—if you love me purely,
and give up your virginity.

Yet if you will not love me
keep the apple—and think
how long the beauty lasts.

445 SOKRATES TO HIS LOVER

As I kissed Agathon my soul swelled to my lips,
where it hangs, pitiful, hoping to leap across.

446 THE FAMOUS COURTESAN LAÏS
DEDICATES A MIRROR TO APHRODITE

I Laïs who laughed scornfully at Hellas,
who kept a swarm of young lovers at my door,
I lay my mirror before the Paphian,
for I will not see myself as I am now,
and cannot see myself as once I was.

[179]

447   ON LOVING ALEXIS
       I barely whispered that Alexis was handsome
       and now all the loose hounds goggle at him.
       My heart, why do you show the dogs a bone?
       Soon you'll suffer, as when you lost Phaidros.

448   SOKRATES TO ARCHEANASSA
       My girlfriend was Archeanassa from Kolophon
       and her wrinkles are scars of a sour love.
       Pain, horror. On her first voyage she loved
       a graceful young man, and passed through fire.

449   MODESTY
       Aphrodite cried at Knidos when she saw Aphrodite:
          O Zeus! Where did Praxiteles see me naked?

450   ON TIME
       Time brings everything; and dragging years alter
          names and forms, nature and even destiny.

451   DEATH AT SEA
       Sailors be free of disaster on land and sea,
       for you are passing by a sailor in his grave.

452   PINDAR
       A delight to strangers and loved by friends,
       Pindar labored for the sweet-voiced Muses.

453   SAPPHO
       Some say nine Muses—but count again.
       Behold the tenth: Sappho of Lesbos.

454   IN THE PINE GROVE

Sit below the long needles of the resonant pine
as its branches shudder in the western winds.
A shepherd's piping by the loquacious river
will lay heavy sleep on your spellbound eyelids.

455   PAN

Be still, green cliff of the Dryads. Be still,
springs bubbling among rocks, and confused noisy
bleating of the ewes.
For it is Pan playing on his honey-voiced pipe.
His supple lips race over the clustered reeds,
while all round him
a ring of dancers spring up on joyful feet:
Nymphs of the Water and Nymphs of the Oak
    Forest.

456   ARISTOPHANES

When looking for an inviolable sanctuary,
the Graces found the soul of Aristophanes.

457   ON A DOOMED SETTLEMENT IN MEDIA

We lying here in the open plains of Ekbatana
once heard the throbbing waves of the Aigaian.
Farewell famous Eretria,
                      once our country.
Farewell Athens,
              our neighbor by Euboia.
Farewell beloved sea!

458   CAPTIVITY IN PERSIA

We are Eretrians of Euboia, but we lie in Susa,
    and how remote, now, is our motherland!

459   ON A THIEF

You look upon a shipwrecked man. The sea killed
    me but was ashamed to strip me of my last
    garment.
It took a man's inglorious hands to rob me naked,
    a grave sacrilege for such a shabby
gown. Let the poor wretch wear it down in Hell
    where King Minos may see him in my rags.

460   EQUALITY OF DEATH

I am a sailor's tomb. Beside me lies a farmer.
    Hell is the same, under the land and sea.

461   INSCRIPTION FOR THE TOMB OF DION,
       TYRANT OF SYRACUSE

Tears were fated for Hekabe and Ilium's women
    from the day of their birth,
but Dion, just when you triumphed with famous
    works,
all your wandering hopes were cast down by the
    gods.
Now dead in your spacious city, you are honored
    by patriots—
But I was one who loved you, O Dion!

The
Hellenistic Period

Diphilos

A comic poet of Athens, born before 340 B.C., *died after 289* B.C. *He wrote some one hundred plays. The passage below is in iambics, and was probably taken from one of his plays for inclusion in the* Greek Anthology.

❖❖❖❖❖❖❖❖❖❖❖❖❖❖❖❖❖❖❖❖❖❖❖❖❖

462   ON THE ARGIVES

Argos may be a land of horses
but the inhabitants are wolves.

Anyte

Active about 290 B.C. Poet of Arkadia
in the Peloponnesos, she wrote epigrams,
mock-epitaphs and nature poems in the Doric
dialect.

The many lilies of Anyte.
       from the *Stephanos of Meleagros, 1st proem*

◇◇◇◇◇◇◇◇◇◇◇◇◇◇◇◇◇◇◇◇◇◇◇◇◇◇◇◇◇◇◇◇◇

463   REPOSE
      Lounge in the shade of the luxuriant laurel's
      beautiful foliage. And now drink sweet water
      from the cold spring so that your limbs weary
      with summer toil will find rest in the west wind.

464   EPITAPH OF A SLAVE
      Alive, this man was Manes, a common slave.
      Dead, even great Darius is not his peer.

465   ON A STATUE IN AN ORCHARD
      I am Hermes. I stand in the crossroads by a windy
          belt of trees near the gray shore of the sea
      where the weary traveler may rest: here a fountain
          bubbles forth a cold and stainless water.

Kallimachos

Born about 305 B.C. in Kyrene in
North Africa. He became a school-
master in Alexandria, and then
cataloguer of the royal library (the
most famous library of ancient times).
He produced a systematic catalog
of the library which has been called
"the first scientific literary history."
Kallimachos was the center of a con-
troversy over the proper length of
a poem; he claimed that the long
poem was an anachronism. The
typical "learned" poet composing
for a narrow, sophisticated audience,
he was versatile, experimental and
prolific.

His known works include a long
but episodic narrative-didactic
poem in elegiacs, narrative hymns,
iambics, miniature epics (epyllia),
lyrics (of which little survives),
elegies, dramas (lost) and—most
important for lyric in the modern
sense—epigrams.

The sweet myrtle of Kallimachos
is always full of harsh honey.
>> from the *Stephanos of Meleagros, 1st proem*

Epitaph on Himself

You are walking by the tomb of
   Kallimachos,
who was accomplished in singing
   poems
and knew when to laugh over his wine.
>> KALLIMACHOS, *Palatine Anthology*

❖❖❖❖❖❖❖❖❖❖❖❖❖❖❖❖❖❖❖❖❖❖❖❖❖❖❖❖❖

466   EPITAPH OF A YOUNG BOY
Here Philippos the father buried his son
Nikoteles,
a child of twelve and his dearest hope.

467   TWOFOLD GRIEF
It was morning when we buried Melanippos
and by sundown Basilo his virgin sister
was dead by her own hand.
She could not bear to live
after she had placed him on the funeral pyre.
Their father's home displayed a double sorrow,
its lovely children gone,
and all Kyrene watched with downcast eyes.

468   ON THE DEATH OF A POET
They brought me word of your death,
Herakleitos,
and I wept for you
remembering how often we watched the sun
setting as we talked.

Dear Halikarnassian friend,
you lie elsewhere now
and are mere ashes;
yet your songs—your nightingales—will live,
and never will the underworld,
destroying everything,
touch them with its deadly hand.

469   EPITAPH OF AN ENEMY
Passerby, do not wish me well with your sour
    heart.
Go away. And I shall be well by your being gone.

470   A SAILOR ON THE BEACH

Who are you, O shipwrecked stranger?
Leontichos found your corpse on the beach,
buried you in this grave
and cried thinking of his own hazardous life.
For he knows no rest:
he too roams over the sea like a gull.

Theokritos

*The latest of the major Greek poets. An
approximate contemporary of Kallimachos, he was
born at Syracuse perhaps ca. 310 B.C. Active there,
at Kos (an island in the Dodekanese), and at the
court of Ptolemy II in Alexandria. He died perhaps
ca. 250 B.C. As his best-known genre, the pastoral
mime, suggests, he wrote for an audience of high
sophistication. His Idylls (or "Little Forms") are
for the most part on the borderline or outside the
range of "lyric" poetry. They include works of the
most diverse sort: pastoral and urban mimes (short
quasi-realistic dramatic episodes), epyllia (short
epic narratives), hymns, and love poetry after the
manner of Sappho and Alkaios. Although "literary"
Doric is his predominant dialect, Theokritos also
used the Epic, Ionic and Aiolic dialects with skill.
Some twenty epigrams are included in his surviving
corpus. Pastoral art from Vergil to Picasso and
Ravel is in his debt.*

I am not the other Theokritos from
    Chios.* I am
Theokritos who wrote these poems
    and one of many
Syracusans. Son of Praxagoras and
    noble Philinna,
my muse is from my own native land.
           THEOKRITOS, *Introductory Poem to Idylls*

◇◆◇◆◇◆◇◆◇◆◇◆◇◆◇◆◇◆◇◆◇◆◇◆◇◆◇◆◇

471   TO THE GOATHERD

Goatherd, when you turn the corner by the oaks
you'll see a freshly carved statue in fig wood.
The bark is not peeled off. It is legless, earless,

---

* A fourth-century B.C. orator and sophist.

but strongly equipped with a dynamic phallus
to perform the labor of Aphrodite.
                       A holy hedge
runs around the precinct where a perennnial brook
spills down from upper rocks and feeds a
    luxuriance
of bay, myrtle and fragrant cypress trees.

A grape vine pours its tendrils along a branch,
and spring blackbirds echo in pure transparency
of sound to high nightingales who echo back
with pungent honey.
                 Come, sit down, and beg Priapos
to end my love for Daphnis. Butcher a young goat
in sacrifice. If he will not, I make three vows:
I will slay a young cow, a shaggy goat and a darling
lamb I am raising. May God hear you and assent.

472   DAPHNIS

Daphnis, you lie on the earth on some leaves
resting your tired body.
                    The hunting stakes
are newly set in the hills. Pan
is on your track, and Priapos comes with saffron
    ivy
tied about his forehead. They are heading
for your cave. Hurry!
               Shake off your lethargy and run!

473   OFFERINGS

These are gifts for Pan. And Daphnis
who pays country tunes on a warbling pipe—
he of the milk-white skin—gave them:

his double reed, a staff for hunting hare,
a fawn hide and keen javelin. And a pouch
of leather in which he once carried apples.

[191]

474   SACRIFICIAL GOAT

Morning-wet roses and the redolent thyme
are for ladies of Helikon.
                    But laurel trees
                    with black leaves
that grace the precipice at Delphi
are for you, Apollo: Pythian Healer.

The horned he-goat lowers his white body
as he grazes on the tips of sagging terebinth.
His blood will
soon spill across the altar.

475   LATE SUMMER

Many poplars and many elms shook overhead,
and close by, holy water swashed down noisily
from a cave of the nymphs. Brown grasshoppers
whistled busily through the dark foliage. Far
treetoads gobbled in the heavy thornbrake.

Larks and goldfinch sang, turtledoves were
        moaning,
and bumblebees whizzed over the plashing brook.

The earth smelled of rich summer and autumn
        fruit:
we were ankle-deep in pears, and apples rolled
all about our toes. With dark damson plums
the young sapling branches trailed on the ground.

Leonidas of Tarentum

Early third century B.C. *"One of the greatest
Greek epigrammatists," says Gilbert Highet of
him. Author of about one hundred epigrams in an
elaborate and artificial style, mostly about the life
of the poor, to which class he belonged. Much
admired by the Romans, and imitated by Vergil
and Propertius.*

Far from my Italian soil I lie, far
from my land of Tarentum; and
this is more bitter to me than death.
Such is the intolerable life of a
wanderer. But the Muses loved me,
and I have more honey than bitter
fruits. The name of Leonidas goes
unforgotten. His gifts from the
Muses proclaim it as long as there
is sun.

LEONIDAS OF TARENTUM,
Epitaph on Himself

✧✧✧✧✧✧✧✧✧✧✧✧✧✧✧✧✧✧✧✧✧✧✧✧✧✧✧✧✧✧

476   FAIR WARNING FROM PRIAPOS

The season for sailing. Already the chattering
    swallow
returns with the slender west wind.
Meadows bloom, and the boiling waves of the
    sea,
whipped by gales, are smooth and silent.
Come then, sailor, haul in the anchors and loosen
    the hawsers
and sail with all the canvas flying.
It is Priapos, god of the harbor, who warns you
    now:
set out from this port for foreign cargoes.

[193]

477   SUMMER THIRST

Traveler, do not drink the warm water
from this pool,
all muddy from the quick mountain brook
and the intruding sheep.
Go a little further up the hill
where the heifers are grazing,
and there by a shepherd's pine
                              you will find
bubbling up through the porous rock
a spring colder than northern snow.

Asklepiades

*Active about 270 B.C. in Alexandria.
Asklepiades was the
originator of much of the tradi-
tional imagery of love poetry, in-
cluding Cupid's arrows.*

◇◇◇◇◇◇◇◇◇◇◇◇◇◇◇◇◇◇◇◇◇◇◇◇◇◇◇◇◇◇◇

478   SNOW IN SUMMER

Snow in summer on a dry tongue
    is sweet,
and after winter sweet for the sailor
    to see the spring stars,
but sweetest when one cloak shelters
    two lovers,
and the Kyprian is praised.

479   PRUDENCE

Save your maidenhead? What's the good?
My girl, down in Hades there are no lovers.
The pleasures of Kypris are for the living.
Once past Acheron, river of death,
we shall lie as bones and dust.

480   NEGRESS

Didyme plunders me with her beauty.
When I look at her I am wax over fire.
If she's black, what of it? So are coals.
When kindled, they glow like blooming roses.

481   ON A MAN-DEVOURING WHORE

Voracious Philainion bit me. The bite doesn't show
yet pain crawls in me, creeps to my very fingertips.
Love, I am drained, done in, dead! I fell half-dazed
on a viperous whore, and her embrace was death.

[195]

482   TO ZEUS
Snow, thunder, hail, blaze and blacken the earth,
shake the clouds,
kill me and I will stop,
but let me live
and I shall go on, a slave of love.
And Zeus,
Aphrodite was also your master
when you stormed as gold rain through a bridal
   window
to shower down on lovely Danaë.

Mnasalkas

Of Sikyon, flourished about 250 B.C.

The sharp needles of Mnasalkas' pines.
        from the *Stephanos of Meleagros, 1st proem*

◇◆◇◆◇◆◇◆◇◆◇◆◇◆◇◆◇◆◇◆◇◆◇◆◇◆◇◆◇◆◇◆◇

483   AT THE TEMPLE OF APHRODITE
Let us stand on this low beach by the crashing
        surge
and gaze at the holy groves of the seaborn
Kyprian; at the bubbling spring under shadowy
        poplars
where a shrilling kingfisher dips its bill.

Theodoridas

Syracusan epigrammatist of the second half of the third century B.C.

✧✧✧✧✧✧✧✧✧✧✧✧✧✧✧✧✧✧✧✧✧✧✧✧✧✧✧✧✧

484   EPITAPH OF A SAILOR
I am the tomb of a drowned sailor. Sail on.
Even while we sank, the others sped away.

Moschos

*Of Syracuse, active around 150 B.C. Pastoral poet,
to whom some half-dozen short pieces may be
assigned. The* Rape of Europa *(a short narrative)
and the* Lament for Bion *have also been attributed
to Moschos, but chronology definitely excludes the
latter.*

❖❖❖❖❖❖❖❖❖❖❖❖❖❖❖❖❖❖❖❖❖❖❖❖

485   LANDLOVER

When wind dips calmly over the blue sea
my cowardly soul stirs. My love for land
becomes a craving for the vast salt waters.
But when the ocean bottom roars, and foam boils
spitting skyward on the wild crashing waves,
I gaze at the shore and its forests, and shun
the sea. Then I love black earth and shadowy
woods where even during a blasting gale
a pine tree sings. What a wretched life
the fisherman has—with his berth a home,
the sea his labor and fish his wandering prey!
I prefer to sleep under a leafy plane
and hear the plashing of a bubbling spring
which soothes the soul and never
brings me pain.

Ariston

Lived in time to be included in Meleagros'
anthology.

❖❖❖❖❖❖❖❖❖❖❖❖❖❖❖❖❖❖❖❖❖❖❖❖❖❖❖

486   A POOR SCHOLAR'S WARNING
Mice, if you come for bread, go find another hole;
I live in a humble hut.
Go to some rich man's villa
where you can nibble on fat cheese and dried
    raisins
and make a feast out of scraps.

But if you come to sharpen your teeth on my
    books
your supper will be a dull poison.

Meleagros

Lived about 140-70 B.C., at Tyros and on Kos.
As a philosopher, he wrote Cynic satirical sermons,
now lost. He collected the first serious anthology
of epigrams, and more than 130 of his own epigrams
survive; these are mainly erotic, and written in the
florid and complex "Asian" style.

◇◇◇◇◇◇◇◇◇◇◇◇◇◇◇◇◇◇◇◇◇◇◇◇◇◇◇◇◇

487   SHINING FOE

O morning star, bright enemy of love,
how slowly you turn around the world
while Demos lies warm with another
              under her cloak.
But when my slender love lay on my chest,
how swiftly you came to stand above us,
drenching us with light that seemed to laugh
              at our loss.

488   LOVE'S WAGES

Heavy soul, now you bellow fire,
now recover your cool breathing.
But why cry? When you harbored Eros,
you knew he would rise against you.

So be resigned to fire and snow;
you sheltered him, and this is your pay.
You must suffer now for being a fool,
as you sizzle in boiling honey.

489   MYISKOS

By Love, I swear it!
Tender are the boys whom Tyros nurtures.

[201]

Yet Myiskos is the sun,
and when he illuminates the world
bright stars fade under his light.

490   AFTER CHARYBDIS

Where are you driving me,
foul waves of love,
huge sleepless winds of jealousy,
turbulent sea of orgy?

The rudder of my heart is broken:
I drift.
Will I ever again see
the voluptuous Skylla?

491   FLOWERS FOR HELIODORA

White, white violets
with myrtle and tender narcissus;
I shall weave laughing lilies
and soft crocus and purple hyacinths
with roses, flowers of lovers.
I shall come to decorate her brow
and brighten her perfumed hair
in a fine rain of flowers.

492   LIGHT OF BEAUTY

The flowers looped in Heliodora's hair darken
but she glows brighter as the flowers fade.

493   A THIEVING SKY

Morning Star, herald of dawn: goodbye,
and come back swiftly as the Evening Star;
bring me her, clandestinely, whom you stole.

494   THE WINE CUP
The wine cup is happy. It rubbed against
warm Zenophila's erotic mouth. O bliss!
I wish she would press her lips under my lips
and in one breathless gulp drain down my soul.

495   LOVE ON THE BLUE WATER
Asklepias adores making love. She gazes at a man,
her aquamarine eyes calm like the summer seas,
and persuades him to go boating on the lake of
    love.

496   HELIODORA'S FINGERNAIL
Your fingernail, Heliodora, was grown by Eros
and sharpened by him. How else could
your mere scratching be a claw against my heart?

497   THE KISS
Your eyes are fire, Timarian, your kiss birdlime.
You look at me and I burn. You touch me and I
    stick!

498   SOLE TENURE
Zenophila, my flowering tree, you are asleep.
Though wingless, I would come like Hypnos,
and bury myself under your eyelids—
so that even sleep might not intrude,
and I alone possess you.

499   HOUR OF THE SPRING
Winter squalls are drained out of the sky,
the violet season of flowering spring smiles,
the black earth glitters under a green lawn,
swelling plants pop open with tiny petals,
meadows laugh and suck the dew of morning
while the rose unfolds.

> The shepherd in the hills
> happily blows the top notes of his pipe,
> the goatherd gloats over his white kids.
> Sailors race across the thrashing waves,
> their canvas swollen on the harmless breeze.
> Drinkers acclaim the grape-giver Dionysos,
> capping their hair with flowering ivy.
> Bees from the putrid carcass of a bull
> work with intent care; bunched in their hive
> they spill a limpid honey through the comb's
> perforations.
> All tribes of birds clamor—
> kingfishers on the sea, swallows in rafters,
> swans by river banks, nightingales in groves.
>
> When saplings blossom and dry meadows revive
> or shepherds pipe and shaggy flocks meander
> or fleets scud on the sea and drinkers dance
> or bees labor and birds dazzle the sky with song,
> why can a singer not praise the lovely spring?

500   THE LAST VICTORY

> I'm on the ground, cruel god, so bury your heel
>   in my neck.
>   I feel, God knows! your ponderous weight
> and arrows of fire. Yet you can't burn me any
>   more.
>   Hurl your torches at my heart. All is ashes.

501   I, MELEAGROS

> My nurse was the island of Tyros,
> and Attic land of Syrian Gadara was
> my birthplace. I was sired by Eukrates
> —I, Meleagros, friend of the Muses
> and first to waken to the Graces of
> Menippos. A Syrian? What if I am?
> Stranger, we all live in one country:
>   the world.

The Hellenistic Period

Out of one Chaos were all men born.
In my old age I traced these letters
    on the slab before my grave,
knowing that old men are neighbors
    to death.
Passerby, wish me well, the talkative old man,
and you may also reach a loquacious old age.

Bion

*Born in Asia Minor. Active around 100 B.C.,
mostly in Sicily, where, according to tradition,
he was poisoned by jealous rivals. Classed as a
pastoral poet, though the pastoral element is not
prominent in his surviving seventeen fragments.
The* Lament for Adonis *is sometimes assigned to
him.*

Nightingales mourning in the thick
foliage, carry word to the Sicilian
springs of Arethousa that the cow-
herd Bion is dead. And with him
song and Dorian poetry have like-
wise perished.

UNKNOWN PUPIL OF BION,
from *Lament for Bion*

✧✧✧✧✧✧✧✧✧✧✧✧✧✧✧✧✧✧✧✧✧✧✧✧✧✧✧✧✧✧

502   HESPEROS

Evening Star, gold light of Aphrodite born in the
    foam,
Evening Star, holy diamond of the glassblue night,
you are dimmer than the moon, brighter than
    another star.
Hello, good friend!
            I'm on my way to serenade
my shepherd love. Give me your rays in place of
    moonlight.
There was a new moon today, but quickly set.
I am no thief, no highway man to plague a
    traveler at night.
A lover I am. And those in love must be helped.

503   POLYPHEMOS

What will I do? I'll just go my way
across to that distant hill and down
again to the sandpits on the shore.
And I'll sing quietly to myself
my prayer for Galateia, who doesn't care.
Yet till the shattering end of old age
I will never once abandon sweet hope.

The
Roman Period

Philodemos the Epicurean

Lived about 110-40/35 B.C. A teacher and popularizer of Greek philosophy for the Romans, he was to influence Vergil and Horace. Approximately twenty-five of his epigrams survive in the Anthology.

◇◇◇◇◇◇◇◇◇◇◇◇◇◇◇◇◇◇◇◇◇◇◇◇◇◇◇◇◇◇

504   THE PRIVATE LIFE OF PHILODEMOS

Philenis, fill our silent confidant—
the lamp—with olive dew. Then go,
and lock the stout door behind you,
for love abhors a breathing witness;
and you, sweet Xantho, let us begin . . .

Only my couch, a friend to lovers,
will know the secrets of Aphrodite.

505   AN AGELESS LOVER

Charito is more than sixty
yet her hair is still a dense forest
and no brassiere holds up the marble cones
                of her high-pointed breasts.
Her unwrinkled flesh exhales ambrosia
              and myriads of teasing charms.

Lovers, if you do not run from hot desire,
enjoy Charito
             and forget her many decades.

Diodoros

The poems under this name in the Anthology,
according to highest authority (Wilhelm Schmid),
can be attributed to any of three different men.
At any rate they probably belong to the period
100 B.C.-A.D. *100.*

❖❖❖❖❖❖❖❖❖❖❖❖❖❖❖❖❖❖❖❖❖❖❖❖❖

506   THE FALL
A tiny child in the villa of Diodoros
fell headfirst from a little ladder
and broke his neck bones fatally,
but when he saw his much-loved master
running up,
he suddenly spread out his baby arms to him.

Earth, do not lie heavy on the bones
of a tiny slave child.
Be kind to Korax, who died at two.

Antipatros of Thessaloniki

*Flourished at the beginning of the
Christian era. Some eighty of his
epigrams are in the* Anthology.

◇◇◇◇◇◇◇◇◇◇◇◇◇◇◇◇◇◇◇◇◇◇◇◇◇◇◇◇◇◇◇

507   MORNING GRAY

Morning gray is here, Chrysilla, and long ago
the twilight cock began to herald jealous Dawn
                    and guide her by my window.
Go away, selfish bird!
You drive me out of home to the crowded chatter
   of young men.
Tithonos, you're getting old.
Why else have you chased your bedmate Dawn
so early from her couch?

508   A DOUBLE GRAVE

Neither the sea nor land may claim my body.
In this death they share me in equal parts.
The fish devoured all my flesh in the sea,
but my bones were washed up on this cold beach.

Marcus Argentarius

*Lived at the beginning of the
Christian era. He was probably a
penniless speech teacher. "The
liveliest of the Graeco-Roman
epigrammatists," Gilbert Highet
has said of him.*

◇◇◇◇◇◇◇◇◇◇◇◇◇◇◇◇◇◇◇◇◇◇◇◇◇◇◇◇◇

509   DIALOGUE

"Take a hard look at scrawny Diokleia.
She's a skinny Aphrodite
                   but sweet."

"Then nothing will stand between us;
when I lie on her skinny breasts
I'll be pressing right against her heart."

510   DISCREET WITNESS

As I lay clutching Antigone's body,
my chest throbbed against her bosom,
my lips pressed into her sweet lips—

for the rest you must ask the lamp.

511   OXYMORON*

Melissa, you do everything like a bee:
when you kiss, you drip sweet honey from your
     lips;
when you ask for money,
I feel the savage wound of your sting.

* Melissa is a name and also means honeybee.

[214]

Rufinus

Lived sometime between 50 B.C. and A.D. 50.

◇◇◇◇◇◇◇◇◇◇◇◇◇◇◇◇◇◇◇◇◇◇◇◇◇◇◇◇◇◇

512   A LETTER FROM RUFINUS IN EPHESOS
I Rufinus wish my darling Elpis only pleasure,
    if you are happy away from me.
Yet I swear before you: I am wracked with pain
    without you in my lonely bed.
With moist eyes I go to the hill of Koressos
    or the temple of great Artemis.
Tomorrow when my city receives me, I will fly
    to greet you with a thousand blessings.

513   A NAKED BATHER
A silver-ankled girl was bathing in a brook,
    letting the water flood down
on the gold apples of her milky breasts.

When she walked, her round hips rolled and flowed
    more liquid than the water.
Her arm reached down to shield her swelling belly,
    not all—but all her hand could hide.

514   REMORSE
If women were as enticing after, as before,
no man would be bored with his wife's body.
But after love, all women are distasteful.

Apollonides

Lived sometime between 50 B.C.
and A.D. *50.*

◇◆◇◆◇◆◇◆◇◆◇◆◇◆◇◆◇◆◇◆◇◆◇◆◇◆◇◆◇◆◇

515   THE MESSAGE

If you come to Apollo's harbor at Miletos,
bring Diogenes this desolate word:
off the island of Andros was a shipwreck,
and your son Diphilos, bloated with waves,
lies on the earth bottom of the Aigaian Sea.

Parmenion

Lived sometime between 50 B.C. *and* A.D. *50.*

✧✧✧✧✧✧✧✧✧✧✧✧✧✧✧✧✧✧✧✧✧✧✧✧✧✧✧✧✧

516   A DISCREET PURCHASE
Zeus bought Danaë with golden rain
and I purchase you with a gold coin.
I can't, after all, pay more than Zeus.

Nikarchos

Alexandrian epigrammatist, probably of the first century A.D. About forty of his epigrams are in the Anthology; they are humorous, and often vile.

✧✧✧✧✧✧✧✧✧✧✧✧✧✧✧✧✧✧✧✧✧✧✧✧✧✧✧✧✧✧

517 ON NIKON'S NOSE
Look, I spy Nikon's hooked nose, Menippos,
and the face itself cannot be far removed.
Be patient, friend, and let us wait,
for it stands no more than half a mile behind:
the parabolic snout leads the way
and if we climb a high hill
     we may catch a glimpse of the face.

518 A PHYSICIAN'S TOUCH
Only yesterday the good Dr. Markos
laid his sure hand on a statue of Zeus.
Although he was Zeus and made of marble
          we're burying him today.

519 MISTAKEN IDENTITY
Your mouth and your ass, Theodoros,
smell so alike, only the supple mind
of men of science can tell them apart.
Really, you should label your mouth and your ass,
for when you speak I think you are farting.

520   KISSING*

If you kiss me you hate me; if you hate me
        you kiss me,
but if you don't hate me, my sweet friend,
                    don't kiss me.

521   ENIGMA

Who knows when Diodoros is yawning or farting?
For above and below, his breath is the same.

522   POPULAR SINGER AND A BIRD'S DEATH

Deadly is the singing of the night-raven,
but when you, Demophilos, break into song,
even the night-raven croaks.

523   BIG WOMEN

A plump woman with beautiful limbs
        is always good:
whether she is just ripe or very old.
If young, she takes me in her arms
                    and hugs.
If old and wrinkled, she licks.

* *Kiss* also means here *copulate.*

Lucillius

*Epigrammatist of the middle of
the first century* A.D. *He was expert
at the sharply pointed joke and
lampoon; Nero was his patron.*

✧✧✧✧✧✧✧✧✧✧✧✧✧✧✧✧✧✧✧✧✧✧✧✧✧✧✧✧✧✧✧

524   SHOPPING TIP

Lady, you went to the market
and picked up hair, rouge, honey, wax and teeth.

For a like amount
               you might have bought a face.

525   GOSSIP

Some have passed the word you dye your hair.
They lie, Nikilla,
for in the open market
              you bought it raven black.

526   ON THE HARD LUCK OF DIOPHON

Diophon was being crucified,
but when he saw another near him on a higher
     cross,
he died of envy.

527   LOVE OF LEARNING

Zenonis gives a place in her home to Menandros
             a bearded grammarian,
for she has delivered her son to his instruction;
and the bushy pedant even labors into night,
             with the mother,

practicing their figures, her dangling participles
and his copulative verb.

528   A MONEYLOVER

When miserly Kriton wants to ease his cramping
    stomach
he sniffs not mint
but a copper penny.

529   ON HERMON THE MISER

After spending some money in his sleep,
Hermon the miser was so hopping mad,

he hanged himself.

530   CONTAGION

Demostratis walks in a halo
                of armpit aroma,
but worse,
she makes those who smell her
            exhale the same he-goat fumes.

531   A NIGHT CALL

Diophantos went to bed and dreamed of
                Dr. Hermogenes,
and though he was wearing a good-luck piece,
              he never woke up.

532   ON THE SAME HERMOGENES

The barber is perplexed.
Where can he start to shave the head
of this hairy Hermogenes
who—from head to toe—
seems to be all head?

533   EPITAPH OF A PUGILIST

We his grateful opponents erected this statue
            To Apis a Thoughtful Boxer
who even when clinching never hurt any of us.

534   ON BOXERS

Here you see the ruins of a former Olympic star.
Once he had a real nose, mind you, a chin, forehead,
        ears, and eyes (lids and all),
and then he went pro.

He scrambled everything,
even his share of his father's estate.
For his kid brother showed up
(a spitting image of the former champ)
and the pug
(who looked like an outsider now)
was quietly but sternly ushered away.

535   THE DEVOUT BOXER

Aulos the boxer dedicates his skull to the Lord
        of Pisa,*
having collected the bones one by one.
If he comes out alive from his match at Nemea,
he may, Lord Zeus,
honor you with any surviving ribs.

536   A PRECAUTION

Lazy Markos dreamt he was running, running,
        running. . . .
Out of fear he might run again
Markos never went back to bed.

* Lord of Pisa: Zeus.

537   THE QUEST

We were searching for the giant Eumekios.
We found him sleeping with his arms outstretched,

all under a tiny saucer.

538   A PROSTITUTE BATHING

A girl of a hundred and still in the *métier*,
Heliodora, you spend hours in the bath.
But I know your dream: you pray to grow young,
like old Pelias, by letting them boil you alive.

539   INSIDE AN ATOM

So skinny was the pin-head Markos
that he bore a hole
                          with his own skull
through an atom of Epikouros
                          and slipped inside.

540   FIDELITY IN THE ARTS

Eutychos the portrait painter got twenty sons,
but even among his children—never one likeness.

541   THE POET DESCENDING

Eutychides the lyric poet is dead.
Escape! you who inhabit the underworld,
for he comes with odes,
and orders thirteen lyres and twenty crates of music
to burn beside him on his funeral pyre.
Now Charon has you,
for where can you escape
with Eutychides established in Hell?

542   DECORUM

The miser Asklepiades finding a mouse
one evening in his house, saluted it:
"My very dear mouse, what do you want
    from me?"
With its sweetest smile the mouse replied:
"My dear friend and ceremonious host,
put away your fears,
I did not come for board—merely a bed."

Leonidas of Alexandria

Wrote between A.D. *55 and 85.*
Nero and later emperors were his
patrons. More than forty of his
epigrams are in the Anthology.
Thirty are composed in such a way
that the letters of each couplet in
a poem, if given a numerical
value, produce the same total.

❖◇◇◇◇◇◇◇◇◇◇◇◇◇◇◇◇◇◇◇◇◇◇◇◇◇◇◇◇❖

543 THE PUNISHMENT
The grape-stealer Hekatonymos
       ran all the way down to Hades
            flogged with a stolen vine switch.

Traianus (The Emperor Trajan)

Lived from A.D. *53 to 117. He was*
one of the best of Rome's em-
perors. For the ruling classes at
Rome, Greek was, like French in
modern times, a mark of one's
sophistication.

✧✧✧✧✧✧✧✧✧✧✧✧✧✧✧✧✧✧✧✧✧✧✧✧✧✧✧✧✧✧

544   A NATURAL SUNDIAL

If you point your b i g nose sunward
and open your gaping
                     mouth,
                            all who pass by
will know the time of day.

Ammianus

*Lived at the beginning of the
second century* A.D.

◇◇◇◇◇◇◇◇◇◇◇◇◇◇◇◇◇◇◇◇◇◇◇◇◇◇◇◇

545   ## ON THE AFTERLIFE OF NEARCHOS
May the dust lie lightly on you in your grave,
O wretched Nearchos,
that wild dogs may more easily drag you out.

Loukianos (Lucian)

Born about A.D. *120 in Samosata
in Syria; died sometime after 180.
An itinerant teacher of rhetoric
and Cynic philosophy, he was also
the author of numerous satirical
dialogues and other writings, in-
cluding the fabulous* True History,
*which influenced (among others)
Rabelais and Swift.*

❖❖❖❖❖❖❖❖❖❖❖❖❖❖❖❖❖❖❖❖❖❖❖❖❖❖❖❖

546   ON MAGICAL WHISKERS
If by growing a goatee you hope to come
   upon wisdom,
then, O wise friend, any smelly goat in
       a handsome beard
is at once Plato.

Dionysius Sophistes

One of many poets, sophists, philosophers and miscellaneous writers of the same name who lived in the Roman period.

❖◇❖◇❖◇❖◇❖◇❖◇❖◇❖◇❖◇❖◇❖◇❖◇❖◇❖◇❖

547   A VENDOR OF FLOWERS

You selling roses have a flowery charm.
But rose-girl, what are you selling me?
            your roses? yourself? or both?

Julianus (Julian the Apostate)

A.D. 332-363. The Roman emperor who, among his other reforms, tried belatedly to stem the tide of Christianity and revitalize paganism. He wrote numerous prose works in Greek.

❖❖❖❖❖❖❖❖❖❖❖❖❖❖❖❖❖❖❖❖❖❖❖❖❖❖

548 CALCULATION*

Konon is but two feet tall—his wife four.
When flat in bed
   their feet touching the wall,
imagine where Konon keeps his lips.

* Attribution to Julianus is uncertain.

Aisopos

Ca. fourth century A.D. *(Not the semilegendary fabulist of a thousand years earlier.)*

❖❖❖❖❖❖❖❖❖❖❖❖❖❖❖❖❖❖❖❖❖❖❖❖❖❖❖

549   FUTILITY

How can we escape from you, life, except through
   death?
Our sorrows are endless. Endure? Escape? Neither
   is easy.
Yes, the beauty of nature is sweet—the earth,
      sea, stars,
            the orbit of the moon and sun.
But all else is fear and pain.
One day a bit of luck
and then we wait for inexorable Nemesis.

The
Byzantine Period

Palladas

Active about A.D. *400. An impover-*
ished schoolmaster at Alexandria,
a pagan among Christians, he
wrote more than 150 epigrams,
most of them hopeless and bitter.

◇◇◇◇◇◇◇◇◇◇◇◇◇◇◇◇◇◇◇◇◇◇◇◇◇◇◇◇◇◇◇

550   HER GLORIOUS HOUR
A woman will gnaw at your bile
Yet she has two fine seasons:
        one, in her bridal bed;
        two, when she is dead.*

551   HERITAGE
A grammarian's daughter made love with a man,
and the poor creature gave birth to a child
who was, in orderly sequence:
        masculine, feminine, & neuter.

552   ON THE RHETOR MAUROS
I was thunderstruck
on beholding Mauros, Professor of Rhetoric,
raise his elephantine snout
and spew murder in a voice
made from lips weighing one pound apiece.

553   ON MONKS
If solitary, how can they be so many?
If many, how again are they solitary?
O crowd of solitaries feigning solitude!

---

* Occasionally, in Greek, such an example of internal rhyme as *thalamo*
and *thanato* is used, especially for humor and satire.

554   THE SLAUGHTERHOUSE
We all are watched over and foddered for death
  like a herd of pigs absurdly butchered.

555   A PAGAN IN ALEXANDRIA CONSIDERS
LIFE UNDER CHRISTIAN MOBS WHO
ARE DESTROYING ANTIQUITY
Is it true that we Greeks are really dead
and only seem alive—in our fallen state
where we imagine that a dream is life?
Or are we truly alive and is life dead?

556   GRAVE WARNING
Sir, you talk a lot, and after a short span
  are laid out in the earth.
Keep silent
and while you are alive, meditate on death.

Julianus (Julian the Prefect of Egypt)

Active during the sixth century A.D.

❖❖❖❖❖❖❖❖❖❖❖❖❖❖❖❖❖❖❖❖❖❖❖❖❖❖❖❖❖❖

557   ON A YOUNG WIFE

      O black winter of savage death
that froze the spring of your unnumbered charms.
The tomb tore you from brilliant day
in this, your bitter sixteenth year.
      Your husband and father—blind with grief—
Think of you, Anastasia, who were our sun.

558   GIFT FROM THE DEAD

Your dear husband, Rhodo, erects a monument
    of shining marble to redeem your soul;
he gives money to the poor—for, kindest of wives,
    you died early and gladdened him with
        freedom.

559   AT ANAKREON'S TOMB

I often sang this, and even from the grave I shout:
drink, for soon you must put on this garment of
    dust.

560   ON ANAKREON

A. You died from filling your paunch with wine,
Anakreon.
B. But I enjoyed it, and you who do not drink will
also find yourself in Hades.

Paulus Silentiarius

*An official at the court of Justinian
ca. A.D. 560. He wrote about eighty
epigrams in the* Anthology, *in-
cluding some of the liveliest love
poems.*

◇◆◇◆◇◆◇◆◇◆◇◆◇◆◇◆◇◆◇◆◇◆◇◆◇◆◇◆◇◆◇◆◇◆◇

561   VISIONS

A man bitten by a mad hound, they say,
sees an image of the beast in the water.

Is Eros then wild with rabies?
Did he gash me with his bitter tooth
and ravage my spirit with his heat?

For now I see your darling form mirrored
in winecup, river whirlpool and the sea.

562   TABOO

My fingers on her breasts, our mouths joined;
I graze with deep fury on her silver neck;
yet though I labor over Aphrogeneia
this virgin lets me go so far—and denies
me her bed.
              Her upper body she allows
to Aphrodite, but her under parts she commits
to chaste Athena. I waste away between.

563   PURITY

Beautiful girl, let us cast off these garments.
Let our naked limbs be knotted
so that no space is left between.

To me the clothes you wear are as strong
as the great wall of Babylon.*
Let us press chest against chest,
mouth into mouth,
and plunge the rest into silence.
I cannot bear trivial chatter.

* Wall erected by Semiramis.

Agathias Scholastikos

Lived from A.D. *536 to 582. He was a lawyer of Byzantium, and compiler of the epigram-anthology which was the basis for the existing* Greek Anthology. *Agathias was a friend of Paulus Silentiarius but not his poetic equal.*

◇◆◇◆◇◆◇◆◇◆◇◆◇◆◇◆◇◆◇◆◇◆◇◆◇◆◇◆◇◆◇◆◇◆◇

564   INTIMATE DIALOG

A. What are you mooning about?
B. I am in love.
A. With whom?
B. A virgin.
A. Is she good looking?
B. Perfectly exquisite.
A. Where did you meet her?
B. At a dinner party. I found her lying on the same couch with me.
A. You think you'll get in?
B. Yes, yes, my friend, but I don't wish to broadcast it. Actually I want it to be nice and discreet.
A. You mean you want to avoid marriage.
B. My friend, I found out she isn't worth a dime.
A. You know this already. You are not in love, dear friend. You are lying. How can your heart be madly in love when it calculates so well?

Damaskios

Ca. fifth-sixth centuries A.D.

✧✧✧✧✧✧✧✧✧✧✧✧✧✧✧✧✧✧✧✧✧✧✧✧✧✧✧

565   EPITAPH OF A SLAVE GIRL

Zozime, you were a slave girl only in body
and now find freedom for your body too.

Julianus (Julian Antecessor)

Sixth century A.D.?

◇◇◇◇◇◇◇◇◇◇◇◇◇◇◇◇◇◇◇◇◇◇◇◇◇◇◇

566   WINNING CHARM

Your face is the face of an ostrich.

Was it Circe in her island sanctuary
who made you drink her secret potion
to turn your sourpuss into a birdhead?

567   HARVESTING

Tall and wavy are the crops
                         on your hairy face.
Scissors?
         Never.
Throw them away and bring out a plow.

Authors and Anonymous
Works of Indefinite Period

Glykon

Little is known of Glykon. He is credited by Hephaistion with the invention of the Glykonic meter, but the Glykon of the Greek Anthology, where this single poem appears under that name, may be a later poet of the same name.

❖❖❖❖❖❖❖❖❖❖❖❖❖❖❖❖❖❖❖❖❖❖❖❖❖❖❖❖❖❖❖❖

568   LIFE WITHOUT MEANING
All is laughter and dust. And all is nothing,
   since out of unreason comes all that is.

Kallikteros

A poet known only through his poems in the
Palatine Anthology.

◇◇◇◇◇◇◇◇◇◇◇◇◇◇◇◇◇◇◇◇◇◇◇◇◇◇◇◇◇◇◇

569   A SKILLFUL THIEF
Rhodo removes leprosy and scrofula by drugs
   and removes the rest with agile fingers.

570   BARTERED VIRTUE
The unpurchased wheat in your home may inform
     you
   that your dear wife has been a horn of plenty.

Ammonides

Known only through the Palatine Anthology.

◇◇◇◇◇◇◇◇◇◇◇◇◇◇◇◇◇◇◇◇◇◇◇◇◇◇◇◇◇◇◇◇

571   A WAR PLAN
Show off Antipatra naked to the Parthians,
and the enemy will flee beyond the horizon,
yes, beyond the pillars of Herakles.

Diophanes of Myrina

Known only through the Palatine Anthology.

✧✧✧✧✧✧✧✧✧✧✧✧✧✧✧✧✧✧✧✧✧✧✧✧✧✧✧✧✧

572   FOR A STATUE OF EROS

Love is really a highway robber:
  1) He waits in ambush through the night,
  2) He is a desperado,
  3) and in the end he strips us naked.

The Anakreonteia

*These imitations, long attributed
to Anakreon, were written between
the first century B.C. and the sixth
century A.D.*

◇◇◇◇◇◇◇◇◇◇◇◇◇◇◇◇◇◇◇◇◇◇◇◇◇◇◇

573   THE OLD MAN

Anakreon, singer of Teos,
came to me in a dream
and laughingly called me.
And I ran up to him
and kissed and hugged him.
He was old but handsome
and wild over wine.
His lips smelled of grape.
Though old and tottery
he fed on love. He slipped
the wreath from his head
and offered it to me.
It smelled of Anakreon.
I stupidly took it
and stuck it in my hair,
and ever since, I can't
keep myself from loving.

574   THE WELL-TEMPERED PARTY

Bring Homer's lyre but mute
the chords of savage war.
Bring winecups and the laws
of proper revelry.
I shall get drunk and dance
at our party, and even
roar on my tanging lyre,

[249]

yet with a tempered fury.
Bring Homer's lyre but mute
the chords of savage war.

575 THE RUB OF LOVE

Once while plaiting a wreath
I found Eros among the roses.
I grabbed him by the wings
and dipped him in the wine
and drank him down.
Now inside my limbs
he tickles me with his wings.

576 PLAY BEFORE DEATH

"Anakreon, you are old,"
the women say to me.
"Look in the mirror, you
haven't one lonely patch
on your abandoned temples
or desolate pate." Yes,
I cannot boast about
my hair, but I know this:
an old man must have love
the closer he is to death.

577 TODAY

I don't care for Gyges' gold,
the king of fabled Sardis,
for money is repugnant.
I don't envy the despots.
I live to soak my beard
in perfume, and twine my hair
in roses. Day is my gold.
Who can tell the future?
So while sun is sweet, drink,
shoot dice and offer a toast
to Bakchos. Tomorrow
disease may cut your wine.

578 A NUISANCE

What can I do to you,
verbose swallow? Shall I
clip your agile wings
or slit your sharp tongue
like a heartless Tereus?
Why do your morning cries
rip me from my dreams
of my tender Bathyllos?

579 BARGAIN

A young peddler was hawking
a wax replica of Eros.
I went to him and said:
"How much is the statue?"
He answered me in Doric.
"You name it. Just so
I can get rid of him.
I'm no sculptor in wax
and I am sick of living
with this grubby Eros."
Now Eros, make me burn
or I'll melt you in fire.

580 ARITHMETIC

If you can count the leaves
of trees, waves in the ocean,
I shall make you the sole
accountant of my loves.
Mark down 20 from Athens,
and throw in 15 more.
From Corinth a small army
(Greek women are splendid!)
From Lesbos and Ionia,
Karia and Rhodes: 2,000
satisfying affairs.
Do my numbers overwhelm you?
I haven't mentioned Syria

or love in Egypt and Krete
where in the cities love
is both refined and wild.
And shall I count up those
from Cadiz and from far
Afghanistan and India?

581   A WOMAN

Nature gave the bull horns
and nimble hooves to horses,
springing legs to the hare,
a chasm of teeth to lions.
She furnished fins to fish
and speckled wings to birds.
To man she offered wisdom.
Was nothing left for woman?
Yes, she gave her beauty
in place of shields and swords,
and beauty glides in victory
over virile swords and fire.

582   STRATAGEM

You chant of Theban battles
or the slaughter before Troy.
I tell of my disaster,
It was no horse or hoplite,
no black vessel in the port.
A new weapon hobbled me:
two eyes stuck me to the bone.

583   THE TEST

Eros came and struck me
with his hyacinth rod
and ordered me to come.
We crossed uncrossable
torrents; forests, cliffs.
We raced, dripping sweat:
my heart was in my mouth,

my body nearly dead.
Then Eros touched my forehead
with his deft wing, and spoke:
"Are you unable to love?"

584 BEFORE THE SHADOWS

Lying on a soft bed
of myrtle and lotus
I want to drink.
Eros, put your apron on
with the papyrus ribbon,
and pour my dark wine.
Like a swift wheel
our life speeds past
and soon we will lie:
dust of scattered bones.
Why waste those perfumes
on the soil by my grave?
While I live, bring flowers
and my lovely mistress.
Before my somber climb
down to death's choir,
I would forget my grief.

585 THE MIDNIGHT GUEST

Once in the frozen hours of night
While the Great Bear circled Arktouros
and mortals lay drugged with sleep,
Eros stood at my gate, knocking.
"Who is pounding on my door?" I said.
"You are splitting my dreams."
"Open up. I'm only a child.
Don't be alarmed," Eros called in.
"I'm dripping wet and lost
and the night is black and moonless."
Hearing his words I pitied him
and quickly lit a candle.
Opening a door I saw a boy

with bow, wings and quiver.
I sat him down by the fire
and warmed his hands with my own,
and squeezed water from his hair.
When he recovered from the cold
he said, "Let's test this bow.
Rain has weakened the string."
He drew and struck me square
in the groin like a gadfly.
He leapt up laughing with scorn:
"Stranger, let us be happy.
My bow is unharmed, but you
will have trouble in your heart."

586   CICADA
We bless you, cicada,
high in the branches.
You sip a dew drop
and whistle like a king.
What you see is yours:
all the soft meadows
and furry mountains.
Yet you do no harm
in the farmer's field,
and men exalt you
as the voice of summer.
You are loved by Muses
and Apollo himself
who gave you clear song.
Wise child of the earth,
old age doesn't waste you.
Unfeeling and bloodless
you are like a god.

587   GOLD, DEATH, WINE
If gold could buy life,
I would guard my wealth
with jealous desire,

and when death came
he would take some
and leave me alone.
Yet being mortal
I cannot prolong
my life, so why
should I cry or moan?
If we must die,
what good is gold?
So bring sweet wine,
and when I've drunk
bring my good friends.
I'll lie on a soft bed
and be lost in love.

588　REFLECTION

How good it is to roam
on the ripe grassy meadows
where the sweet wind drifts;
look at the grapevines,
and lie under the leaves
with a soft girl in my arms
who is willing and warm.

589　SPRING

Spring comes: see where
Graces leave the rose,
how the ruffled sea
smooths into peace,
the water-duck dives,
how the crane soars.
The hot sun burns up
the somber clouds;
fields shine with crops
and olive trees bud.
Everywhere the flood
of swollen grapes
flowers in the vineyard.

590   ADAPTABILITY

Once the daughter of Tantalos*
became a stone on the Phrygian hills,
and the daughter of Pandion
flew into the sky as a swallow.
I wish I were a mirror
so you would look at me.
I wish I were a tunic
so you would always wear me.
I should like to be water
so I could bathe your body.
I would become myrrh
so I could anoint you.
I would gladly be a scarf
for your breasts, a pearl
for your throat, a sandal—
if you would be sure to step on me.

591   DRUNKARD

The black earth drinks
and trees suck rain.
The seas drink brooks
and sun the sea
and moon the sun.
Why do you rage, friends,
when I want to drink?

---

* The daughter of Tantalos was Niobe.

Miscellaneous

❖✦❖✦❖✦❖✦❖✦❖✦❖✦❖✦❖✦❖✦❖✦❖✦❖✦❖

592   ON A DROWNED SAILOR

Do not ask, mariner, whose tomb I am,
but chance your life upon a kinder sea.

593   PLEASURE*

To praise is the highest good, and censure
is the beginning of hatred,
yet to speak maliciously of one's neighbor
is, after all, Attic honey.

594   A BITTER TALE

After eating little and drinking less,
I suffered the pains of lingering disease.
I have lived long and now am dead. I say:
a curse on you all!

595   METAMORPHOSIS

I wish I were a scarlet rose
so you might lift me in your hands
and pull me to your snowy breasts.

596   BY THE SEA

If I were the wind
you might walk slowly along the shore
and remove your dress
and, as I blow, take me to your naked breasts.

---

* Sometimes attributed to Palladas.

597   A PRIVATE BATH

Delicious girl of the bath,
why do you rub so fiercely
                    when you bathe me?
Before I am fully undressed
I feel the fire.

598   PRAYER TO APHRODITE

Kypris, if you save those from the pelagos,
save me: I founder shipwrecked on the land.

599   DREAMS

Sthenelais (who is an expensive whore and burns
                    up the town, breathing a smell of gold
                        on all those who desire her)
lay naked with me and came and came
                    through my dreamy night,
all for nothing until the pleasant dawn.

Nor more will I crawl before that barbarous girl
nor sink into the sticky juice of self-pity,
for sleep gives me gratuit
                    my fill of sweet flesh.

600   ON GORGIOS

I am the head of the Cynic Gorgios—
no longer spitting or blowing my nose.

601   FOREST MUSIC*

Come, sit under my pine tree which is shaking
pleasantly as it plays with the mild west wind,
and hear the gossipy riverlets where I finger
my lonely reeds—and merge into soft sleep.

* Similar to a poem ascribed to Plato, 454 B.C.

602　HIS PATIENCE

You denied me your green grape.
When ripe, you sent me on my way.
Do you now begrudge me
a small bite of your dry raisin?

603　PROKLOS

Proklos cannot wipe his nose with his hand,
his arms being shorter than the wild snout,
and when the poor thing sneezes, he won't even
say,
　　　　　Zeus preserve us!
　　　　　　　　　He cannot hear his nose,
his ears being O so far away.

604　AT THE TOMB OF ANAKREON

Stranger, passing near the tomb of Anakreon,
pour me a libation as you approach,
for in life I was a drunkard.

605　ON PLATO'S TOMB

Apollo had two sons, Asklepios and Plato:
one to save the body; the other the soul.

606　EPITAPH OF THE PHILOSOPHER EPIKTETOS

I was a slave: crippled in body and poor
as the beggar Iros—yet loved by the gods.

607　HER UNIQUE VIRTUE

Under this slab I rest, famous among women,
　　having opened my legs for one man alone.

608　ON DIONYSIOS OF TARSOS

At sixty I, Dionysios, lie in my grave.
I was from Tarsos,
I never married and wish my father had not.

609   THE EXPECTATION
I no longer mourn those gone from the sweet light
   but those who live ever waiting for death.

610   BREVITY
The rose blooms for a brief season. It fades,
and when one looks again—the rose is briar.

Folksongs

◇◇◇◇◇◇◇◇◇◇◇◇◇◇◇◇◇◇◇◇◇◇◇◇◇◇◇◇◇◇

611   THE OWL
Send the screaming owl of night
away from our land, away
from our people. Send
the contemptible bird
to our enemy's fleet of quick ships.

612   AGING LOVER'S APPEAL*
Please—keep old age
away a while longer,
O beautiful Aphrodite.

613   DAWN
What happened to you? Don't betray me,
I beg you.
Before he comes, get up from the bed
so you won't hurt yourself or me.
I am unhappy!
It is already day.
Don't you see the light in the window?

614   THE SUN
Shine on us,
friendly sun.

* Diehl attributes this song to Alkman.

Sappho

❖❖❖❖❖❖❖❖❖❖❖❖❖❖❖❖❖❖❖❖❖❖❖❖❖❖❖❖❖❖❖❖❖❖❖❖

Additional Poems

❖❖❖❖❖❖❖❖❖❖❖❖❖❖❖❖❖❖❖❖❖❖❖❖❖❖❖❖❖❖

615   APOLLO

Apollo, son of Leto and Zeus,
come to your mysteries,

leaving the oracle at woody Gryneia
and your sister Artemis.

Descendants of Polyanax,
I want to expose the mad one.

616   APHRODITE

For Aphrodite,
speaking beautiful words,
tosses out something
and sits.
Then dew.

617   CHANGES

Far from them,
yet we became
like the goddesses
sinful
and Andromeda
blessed.
No longer unstained,
twin star sons of Tyndareos,
graceful
but no longer honest.

618   PRAYER

Silent
aegis-carrying Zeus,
I pray.
With kindness
hear my prayer,
if ever you have.
She left me.
Severity.

619   DECISION

Now I leave harmony
and more,
beauty
of the clear-voiced
dance choir.

620   ALLY

As it happens
I want all my plans
to turn out.
I call. Suddenly
my heart demands
all you dream about
having. Fight
alongside me,
obeying
the haughty one.
You know.

621   IN THE CHAMBER

In the chamber is the bride
with her beautiful feet.

622   STRANGE SPIRIT
And this
destructive daemon,
we didn't love it much.
We couldn't find
its source.
Maybe it was nothing.

623   PLECTRUM MUSIC
After a short while come
the descendants of Polyanax.

Striking the strings come
women wearing the dildo.

It kindly
quivers.

624   I SAY
You would want
few
to be carried away.
Sweeter.
You yourself know
but someone forgot.

Some might say
I will love
as long as there is breath
in me.
I'll care.
I say I've been a firm friend.

Things grievous,
bitter,
but know
I will love.

Sappho: Her Life and Poems

In Sappho we hear for the first time in the Western world the direct words of an individual woman. It is the lyric voice in solitude. "I begin with words of air / and they are good to hear." It cannot be said that her song has ever been surpassed.

The first woman poet wrote with candid passion, power, and simplicity, and with singular individuality. As a woman she wrote from her dubiously privileged position as a minor outsider in a busy male society. Outside the main business of the world — of war, politics, remunerative work — Sappho could speak with feeling of her own world: her apprehension of stars and orchards, the experience of love, and herself. She wrote giving the impression of complete involvement, though even in her most intensely self-revealing poems her words have the jarring strength of detachment and accuracy. She wrote as one might speak, if one could speak in ordinary but perfectly metrical speech. It is both overheard internal speech of "I convulse greener than grass / and feel my mind slip" and conversation in which she, Sappho, is one of the speakers:

> Honestly I wish I were dead!
> Although she too cried bitterly
>
> when she left, and said to me,
> "Ah, what a nightmare it is now.
> Sappho, I swear I go unwillingly." (143)

At times, as in George Herbert, we overhear an internal dialogue: she talks with her friend Atthis or, in the famous ode to Aphrodite, with her ally the Cypriote. In each case she uses the device of speech in poetry to achieve both intimacy and objectifying distance. We overhear Sappho as a wholly distinctive personality as opposed to a voice construed by thematic and prosodic convention. Her contemporary could be Cavafy, for time does not separate their use of conversation and the recollection of past happiness, or the objective and overpowering confessional intimacy of these two poets of modernity. Line by line, with relentless and sly candor, they construct the biography of a voice.

By contrast, Homer, the first man in Western literary history, is but a shadow in his own poetry. By some he is considered two Homers, one of the *Iliad*, and one of the *Odyssey* and, by others, merely a combined voice made from elements of a bardic tradition. Sappho, despite scanty and semimythical biographical tradition, emerges as a realized figure through her poems. Homer was of the epic-heroic tradition, but it took a lyric age to produce the first woman poet and one of the earliest individual voices.[1] Or more justly, we can say that Sappho herself created the lyric age of antiquity. She talks, laughs, insults, speaks with irony or despair. As "Longinus" tells us, she knows how to assemble details from true life to give us the lightning force of sublimity.[2] We will find such ecstatic transcendence in later poets, notably in the mystico-erotic poems of Saint John of the Cross. But Sappho also conveys another joy—easy, spare, and piercing—as in the meeting and vision of two lovers:

1. Archilochos had preceded Sappho by some fifty years as the man to whom we can attribute a significant body of extant lyric poetry and is the very first individual voice in the Western lyric tradition. The earliest poet whose texts we know, and even possess in cuneiforms from the third millennum, is the Sumerian woman poet Enheduanna, from about 2300 B.C.

2. "Longinus," *On the Sublime*, 10.

Sappho

I barely heard you,
my darling;

You came in your
trim garments,

and suddenly: beauty
of your garments.   (238)

Sappho was born in Lesbos, an island in the Aegean, a few miles off the coast of Asia Minor. Lesbos was—as it is today—an island of wheat, grapes, redolent orchards, and salt flats, spotted with five coastal cities that commanded their harbors from a rocky acropolis. Greece is a country of light and sea rock—its source of beauty and poverty—and shows off its few precious bits of fertile land almost as rare tanagra. Lesbos was unusual in having a large part of its terrain tillable, along with its salt flats, dry hills, then wooded, and a 3,000-foot mountain called Olympos, after the traditional abode of the gods in Thessaly. It was known in ancient times for its grain, fruit trees, and, above all, the large valleys of olive groves. In 2,500 years the island has probably changed very little in its village architecture and landscape. As one should know Baeza and Soria to understand Antonio Machado, or Vermont to know Robert Frost, so there is no better way to know the images of Sappho's poetry than to see today the light, sea, and land of Mytilene.

The biographical tradition of Sappho begins after her death and is a mixture of possible fact, contradiction, gossip, and myth. Virtually all the *testimonia* are found in much later grammarians, commentators, and historians, such as Strabon, Athenaios, Herodotos, and Suidas (*Suda Lexicon*). From all this at least some statements of probable truth may be made. Sappho's birthplace in Lesbos was Eresos or Mytilene; in any case, it was in Mytilene, capital of Lesbos, that she spent most of her life. She was born c. 630 B.C. Her name in Attic Greek was Sappho (Σαπφώ), by which she is known, but in her native Aiolic she called herself Psappho ($\Psi\alpha\pi\phi\omega$).[3] She wrote as she spoke, and the speech of Lesbos was Aiolic Greek.[4]

Her father's name was given by Herodotos as Skamandronymos; but it also appears as Skamandros, Skamon, Eunominos, Eurygyos, Euarchos, Ekrytos, Semos, and Simon. Her mother's name was Kleïs. Some suggest—and some deny—that she married a rich merchant from Andros named Kerkolas or Kerkylas, who may have been the father of her daughter Kleïs. She had two brothers, perhaps three: Charaxos, Larichos and possibly the more shadowy Eurygyos. Several poems speak disapprovingly of Charaxos, a young man who paid for voyages abroad by trading wine off his estates and who had spent large sums of family money to buy the freedom in Egypt of a courtesan named Doricha. Larichos was a public cup-bearer in Mytilene. We know nothing of Eurygyos, if he indeed existed.

As for her personal appearance, there were no statues, coins or vase paintings until long after her death. But she was frequently referred to as the "lovely Sappho," and with the same authority she was described as short, dark and ugly, "like a nightingale with misshapen wings enfolding a tiny body." These are the words of the Scholiast on Lucian's *Portraits*. Yet the same Lucian, referring to her person, calls Sappho "the delicious glory of the Lesbians." In a poem ascribed to Plato from the *Palatine Anthology*, she is called the "tenth muse." What are certainly Plato's words are in the *Phaidros*, in which he has Sokrates speak of her as "the beautiful Sappho." In this, Plato was reflecting at least one contemporary belief in her feminine beauty; and in the existing statues and coins the "nightingale with misshapen wings" is depicted with the idealized features and beauty of Aphrodite.

3. The name also appears less correctly as Sáppho ($\Sigma\acute{\alpha}\pi\phi\omega$), Saphphó ($\Sigma\alpha\phi\phi\acute{\omega}$), and Saphó ($\Sigma\alpha\phi\acute{\omega}$).

4. This dialect differed from Attic, for example, in preserving the original long *a* and the digamma *F*, shifting the accent near the beginning of a word and resisting the change of *p* into *t*.

The evidence of her activities is not more conclusive. Sappho lived during the reigns of three tyrants in Lesbos: Melanchros, Myrsilos, and Pittakos, the Sage. When she was young, it appears that she and her family went, for political reasons while under Myrsilos, to the Lesbian hill city of Pyrrha, and later, about 600 B.C., to Syracuse in Sicily, probably in the time of Pittakos. To have left for political reasons implies that her family was important in city affairs. As for her own social position, there is no question that her wealth and class distinction gave her privilege and immunity from male domination. And she writes with no trace of rebellion against the chauvinist sex. In this attitude she differs from her aesthetic cousin, the Shulamite of the Song of Songs, who is one of the earliest voices to speak eloquently and powerfully from a woman's vantage. The Shulamite celebrates erotic love and protests against the night guards who have beaten her, "those guardians of the walls." Sappho is at least free from the bullying of such "night guards," but nevertheless confined by her sex to a parallel world of aristocratic women.

This should not suggest, however, that Sappho and other women were viewed, or viewed themselves, as equals. Although the Greeks did honor nine male poets—Pindar being first among them—we find Aristotle stating superciliously in the *Rhetoric* (1398b): "The Mytileneans honored Sappho although she was a woman."

The women mentioned in Sappho's poems as companions are Anaktoria, Atthis, and Gongyla; she loved them passionately and shared catalogues of happiness with them, which she recalls with pain and pleasure after they have left her. Other friends are Mika and Telesippa and Anagora; she was angry with Gorgo and Andromeda, who had left her to become rivals. But the widely held theory of Wilamowitz that her relationship to all these women was that of high priestess in a cult-association *(thiasos)*, or a young lady's academy of manners, has no basis in the ancient biographical tradition and no support in the existing remains of her poems.

The ancient commentators have also told us that there were really two Sapphos, one a poet and one a prostitute who also wrote poems; or that Sappho herself was a prostitute; and Ovid recounts the legend that she threw herself from the Leukadian cliffs out of love for the ferryman Phaon. It should be remembered when considering these more extravagant tales that there were at least six plays dealing with Sappho in later Attic comedy[5] and that by then she had become a stock figure on the Athenian stage. It was on the stage, her modern apologists contend, that the black legend of Sappho originated.

Sappho is credited with certain technical innovations. She is said to have been the first to use the *pectis* (a kind of harp), and to have invented the Mixolydian mode and the Sapphic stanza, which was imitated by Horace and Catullus.[6] A Sapphic stanza, as in the ode to Aphrodite (147), reads:

$$
\begin{array}{l}
- \; \smile \; - \; x \; - \; \smile \; \smile \; - \; \smile \; - \; - \\
- \; \smile \; - \; x \; - \; \smile \; \smile \; - \; \smile \; - \; - \\
- \; \smile \; - \; x \; - \; \smile \; \smile \; - \; \smile \; - \; - \\
- \; \smile \; \smile \; - \; - \; \smile \; \smile
\end{array}
$$

We have good reason to believe that Sappho was a prolific writer. We do not know how she recorded her work—whether on papyrus, on wooden tablets overlaid with wax, or orally through song—but centuries later, when the Alexandrian grammarians arranged her work according to meter into nine books, the first book contained 1,320 lines (330 four-line stanzas in Sapphics); judging from this, we

5. Plays by Ameipsias, Amphis, Antiphanes, Diphilos, Ephippos, and Timokles.

6. Sappho was not the first Lesbian to contribute innovations to Greek poetry. Before her were the semilegendary poets Arion and Lesches and then Terpandros, who invented and wrote poetry for the seven-string lyre, of whom we have four small and doubtful fragments, the earliest examples of lyric poetry in Greece. Her contemporary Alkaios wrote Alcaics, which were also imitated by Horace and other latin poets.

may suppose that the nine books contained a very extensive opus. Her work was well known and well preserved in antiquity. We have Athenaios' claim in the third century A.D. that he knew all of Sappho's lyrics by heart. But the best indication, perhaps, of the general availability of her works in the Classical Age is in the number of quotations from her poems by grammarians, even late into Roman times, which suggests that both commentator and reader had ready access to the corpus of the work being quoted.

Of the more than five hundred poems by Sappho, we have today about seven hundred intelligible lines, and these come from no single collected copy but are pieced together from many sources: from the scholia of ancient grammarians to the mummy wrappings in Egyptian tombs. Plato's entire work has survived virtually intact, having been both popular with and approved by pagan and Christian alike. Sappho's work did not lack popularity, but as one who, in Ovid's words, "taught how to love girls" (*Lesbia quid docuit Sappho nisi amare puellas?*), her popularity did not always win approval.

To the Church mind Sappho represented the culmination of moral laxity, and her work was treated with zealous disapproval. About A.D. 380 Saint Gregory of Nazianzos, Bishop of Constantinople, ordered the burning of Sappho's writings wherever found. She had already been violently attacked as early as A.D. 180 by the Assyrian ascetic Tatian: "Sappho was a whorish woman, love-crazy, who sang about her own licentiousness."

Σαπφὼ γύναιον πορνικὸν ἐρωτομανὲς καὶ
τὴν ἑαυτῆς ἀσέλγειαν ἄδει.

(*Orat. ad Graec.*, 53)

Then in 391 a mob of Christian zealots partially destroyed Ptolemy Soter's Classical library in Alexandria. The often repeated story of the final destruction of this famous library by the Arab general Amr and Caliph Omar is now rejected by historians. Again we hear that in 1073 Sappho's writings were publicly burned in Rome and Constantinople by order of Pope Gregory VII. Until late in the eleventh century, however, quotations from Sappho still appeared in the works of grammarians, suggesting that copies of her poems were still preserved. We shall never know how many poems by Sappho were destroyed in April 1204 during the terrible pillage of Constantinople by the Venetian knights of the Fourth Crusade, or by the Ottoman Turks at the fall of Byzantium in 1453.

But apart from official hostility, Sappho's works suffered equally from the general decline of learning in the early Middle Ages and the consequent ravages of time upon neglected manuscripts. It is probably that some of her work was lost in about the ninth century when Classical texts, preserved in uncial script, were selected and recopied in modern letters. No single collection of her poems, in whole or in part, survived the medieval period. Nevertheless, in the Renaissance, Sappho came back into light. Italian scholars found the essay *On the Sublime* by "Longinus" and *On Literary Composition* by Dionysios of Halikarnassos, which contain two of her most important poems: "To me he seems like a god" ($\phi\alpha\acute{\iota}\nu\epsilon\tau\alpha\acute{\iota}$ $\mu o\iota$) and the complete ode to Aphrodite (Lobel and Page, 1). Every stanza, line, and isolated word by Sappho that appeared in the works of other Greek and Latin writers was assembled.

Very few fragments of eight original papyrus manuscripts have survived in continental Greece,[7] but in parts of rainless Egypt in the Fayum, an oasis semidetached from the Nile valley near Crocodilopolis, important papyrus manuscripts with poems by Sappho were discovered in 1879. The Egyptian expeditions by the English scholars Grenfell and Hunt, beginning in 1897,

---

7. In 1961, for the first time, original papyrus was found in continental Greece, at Dervani (Lagada). See Herbert Hunger, "Papyrusfund in Griechenland," *Chronique d'Egypte* 37, no. 74 (July 1962), Brussels.

yielded a wealth of material. In addition to important poems by Sappho, parts of four plays of Menandros were found in a refuse heap near Aphroditopolis; at Oxyrhynchos, Alkman's maiden-song choral ode, the first in Greek literature, and twenty odes by Bakchylides were discovered. Bakchylides ceased to be simply a name and became again a major poet of antiquity, rivaling Pindar.

But above all, the range of Sappho's work was dramatically expanded. The precious papyri were used as Papier-mâché in mummy wrappings; unfortunately, many were torn in vertical strips, and as a result the Sappho fragments are mutilated at the beginning or end of lines, if not in the middle. The mummy-makers of Egypt transformed much of Sappho into columns of words, syllables, or single letters, and so made her poems look, at least typographically, like Apollinaire's or e.e. cummings' shaped poems.

$$'.]\delta\eta[$$
$$'.]\kappa\omega\sigma\alpha[$$
$$]\nu.\sigma o\iota[$$
$$].\delta\eta\kappa.[$$
$$]\epsilon\sigma\iota\pi\pi[$$
$$].\alpha\lambda.[$$
$$].\epsilon\sigma\sigma\alpha[$$
$$].[.].[\quad {}^{8}$$

But the price of this unwitting modernization was the loss of intelligibility of many fragments. The cost was also high to the English and German scholars who undertook the labor of unraveling the documents (both literally and

---

8. Ezra Pound goes back full circle when he "antiques" the form of a poem in order to make it resemble a vertical strip of a Sappho papyrus. His brief poem "Papyrus," addressed to Gongyla, reads:

Spring...
Too long...
Gongyla...

figuratively): The German scholar Friedrich Blass, who first deciphered important poems by Sappho in the Fayum manuscript, lost the use of his eyes, and Grenfell, for a while, lost his mind. It has been the modern commentators, however, who, in their enthusiasm for Sappho, quite lost their perspective of the poet and have hopelessly muddled the poet's life with the poems.

While a thousand years of bigotry destroyed the greater part of Sappho's poetry, the zeal of her later defenders, from Anna Le Fevée Dacier in 1682 to Wilamowitz, Snell and Bowra,[9] to rehabilitate her moral character has not helped the poet's cause, nor has it contributed to our understanding of her work. It is no less than astonishing how otherwise temperate scholars become outraged and imaginatively unobjective at the slightest suggestions by others of moral frivolity on Sappho's part. Not Sappho's poems but Middle and New Comedy and Horace and Ovid are accused of incepting the black legend.

Several arguments are offered and reiterated to justify her love poems to other women: Sappho was a priestess and head of a *thiasos,* a circle of young women, and these poems did not mean literally what they say; her love poems to women were epithalamia written for ceremonial purposes; the poems castigating her brother Charaxos for his affair with Doricha prove her own high virtue; Alkaios once addressed her as ἄγνα (holy or chaste); she came from a noble and highly respectable Lesbian family. The arguments read like a brief—in an unnecessary trial.

Denys Page was the first modern scholar to oppose all this. Page, who with Lobel has produced the most authoritative edition of Sappho's works, chose to look at the texts and found that the poems gave no support whatsoever to the arguments; moreover, Page contends: Sappho was not a high priestess, only a small portion of her poems might be considered epithalamia, and Sappho

9. Bowra modifies his defense in the 1962 edition of *Greek Lyric Poetry.*

herself, far from being a woman of unfailingly noble sentiments, was a common mortal concerned with common matters of love and jealousy. In deflating the contentions of her supporters, Page also deflates Sappho herself—not without a note of moral reproach.

I have spent some time reviewing the history of Sappho's usually violent encounter with the world, not because one must necessarily know something or anything about an author to appreciate the work, but because in Sappho's case the world has known—or assumed—too much, and this knowledge interferes with any fair appraisal of her poems. The question has been whether or not Sappho was indeed a Lesbian in the sexual, as well as in the geographical, sense of the word.

First, it should be stated that whatever Sappho was in her life has very little to do with the content of her poetry; whether she was indeed bisexual or merely ascetic like her contemporaries Jeremiah and Gautama Siddhartha will not change the meaning of her poems. It is not that an author's intention must be discounted, nor need we puristically fear the heresy of intentional fallacy or other critical sins; but if the author's intention is meaningful, it must be seen through the text, through the lyrical speaker in the poem, and not merely from outside sources. In Sappho's case the problem is more rudimentary; for even if we could accept outside authority, there is, in fact, no reliable authority outside the poems themselves to explain the author's intended meaning in her many poems dealing with love.

To find Sappho, then—the Sappho of the poems—we must look at the poems themselves. One fragment is addressed to her daughter Kleïs. A few of them may have been addressed to men. The majority are love poems to women. They are passionate poems, self-critical, self-revealing, detached, and intense. If we are to believe what they say, we will conclude that the speaker in the poems experienced a physical passion for her beloved, with all the sexual implications that similar poems between men and women normally imply.[10] To give the poems meanings that the texts do not support, for whatever moral motive, is to dilute her language and to weaken and falsify her work. Even though the remains of her oeuvre are scant, the poems should be allowed a plain reading of unimaginative literalness. "Uninterpreted" they speak for Sappho more directly and eloquently than the countertexts of her defenders.

In the fragments we have left, only a few lines give details of physical love: "May you find sleep / on a soft girlfriend's breast" (165). Many speak of her desire for her friends:

> O Gongyla, my darling rose,
> put on your milk-white gown. I want
> you to come back quickly. For my
> desire feeds on
>
> your beauty. Each time I see your gown
> I am made weak and happy. I too
> blamed the Kyprian. Now I pray
> she will not seek
>
> revenge, but may she soon allow
> you, Gongyla, to come to me
> again: you whom of all women
> I most desire.   (203)

Sappho's best-known love poem, "To me he seems like a god," imitated by Catullus, is an example of her precision, objectivity, and cumulative power. The poem is direct, self-revealing, yet detached and calmly accurate at the moment of highest fever. She begins with a poised statement of her jealousy of the man sitting near the woman she loves, who, because of his envied position, appears godlike to her; she

10. This will not seem so unusual when we recall that the majority of Greek love poems by male poets, from Ibykos to Pindar, are addressed to other men.

recounts the physical symptoms of her passion for the woman; and with full intensity but without exaggeration she uses the metaphor of green turning greener than grass to show her suffering, verging on death, because of a love not returned:

To me he seems like a god
as he sits facing you and
hears you near as you speak
softly and laugh

in a sweet echo that jolts
the heart in my ribs. For now
as I look at you my voice
is empty and

can say nothing as my tongue
cracks and slender fire is quick
under my skin. My eyes are dead
to light, my ears

pound, and sweat pours over me.
I convulse, greener than grass,
and feel my mind slip as I
go close to death,

yet, being poor, must suffer
everything.   (128)

The poem states a love relationship, but more, it states the poet's agony when, consumed by love, she is unable to compete with the rival—a man, a species with powers inaccessible to her as a woman, and who therefore appears equal to a god. She cannot reach the woman she loves, yet the woman affects her with paralyzing force, and she can in no way escape—except through words—from the solitude in which she is suddenly enclosed. Her senses are violently agitated and fail her. She can no longer see, speak, or hear. As her bodily functions weaken, she moves close to death, her analogue of the *via negativa*. The mystics would describe this state as dying away from space and time. In Taoist terminology, she is moving to the open country of emptiness. There, as in Saint John of the Cross's dark sensory night of aridities, she reaches momentary detachment from bodily senses, which permits her to speak objectively of the symptoms of her passion. She too is "dying from love"; and, like those who have had intense physical pain, at a certain threshold she becomes a distant observer of herself. Unlike Saint John, however, the night of purgation is not, at least in this fragment, the moment before the joyful night (*la noche dichosa*) of illumination and union.

Sappho's desire is conveyed as a loss of self. She is exiled, as it were, from her desire, and remains in a darkness before death. In Saint John this darkness is described as "withdrawal ecstasy."[11] In Sappho the movement from the self into an extraordinary condition of void and separation results in a violent failure of the senses, a seizure, the ekstasis of negative ecstasy. For the mystics the second stage is illumination, the discovery of a new self, but in Sappho this second stage is blackness, the discovery of the loss of self. The catalogue of symptoms of her seizure is a universal condition that finds expression in varying diction and metaphors, secular or religious, from Santa Teresa's interior castles and Marvell's entrapment in the garden to Marghanita Laski's medical analyses and Jorge Guillén's passionate merging in the circle of light. Hers, however, is love's lightless inferno, without union and without the peace that follows union.

Unable to reach the object of her love, there is no fulfillment and no release except in the objectification of

---

11. For an interesting and full examination of the condition of transport, see Marghanita Laski, *Ecstasy: A Study of Some Secular and Religious Experiences* (Bloomington: Indiana University Press, 1962).

her passion in the poem. Yet in her poetry she does indeed reach the world, if not her beloved. Her words, used masterfully, make the reader one with the poet, to share her vision of herself. There is no veil between poet and reader. Here, as elsewhere in her art, Sappho makes the lyric poem a refined and precise instrument for revealing her intensely personal experience. As always, through the poems themselves, we construct the true biography of voice. In a poem in the *Palatine Anthology*, Plato speaks of Sappho as the "tenth Muse." The ascription of the epigram to Plato, as of all thirty-seven poems ascribed to him, is shaky. What is certain is that these words reflect ancient opinion. Sappho's own expression of the continuity of her word appears in an astonishing line, which contains neither silly phrases "worthy of a Muse" nor betrays any of the ambitious glitter and bay leaves in Petrarch's notion of fame. Rather, the intimate voice, serenely ascertaining its future, is prophetic:

> Someone, I tell you,
> will remember us.   (256)

Sappho is remembered despite the multiple violations of time. The fragments of her poems contain the first Western examples of ecstasy, including the sublime, which "Longinus" recognized and preserved for us. They also include varieties of ekstasis briefly alluded to in these pages: the bliss of Edenic companionship, dancing under the moon, breakfasts in the grass; the whirlwind blast of love; the desolation and rage of betrayal; the seizure and paralysis before impossible love; and, as all her ordinary senses fail, the movement near death—the ultimate negative ecstasy.

Sources and Notes

❖❖❖❖❖❖❖❖❖❖❖❖❖❖❖❖❖❖❖❖❖❖❖❖❖❖❖❖❖❖

For more information about the poems, see *Glossary*.
Many lines of Sappho have been saved in the ancient
commentaries: those remarks that immediately precede or
follow Sappho's lines are given below except where they
are purely linguistic in nature. The poem number, in
brackets, precedes each entry.

[120] Hermogenes, *On Kinds of Oratory*, 3.317 Walz. The
grammarian Orion in *Etymologicum*, 28.15, also cites the
word χέλυννα, tortoise or lyre, and the word is
probably from this same fragment cited by Hermogenes.

[121] From a vase painting of the middle of the fifth
century B.C. *Museo Italiano* vol. 2, pl. 6. This introductory
poem may have stood at the beginning of Sappho's
poems. Haines reads ἀνα[ι]τίων where Edmonds reads
ὀνάτων.

[122] From a third-century papyrus, in Copenhagen, first
published by Vogliano in a booklet entitled *Sappho: una
nuova della poetessa* (Milan, 1941). In this intimate domestic
poem addressed to her daughter Kleïs, Sappho contrasts
an artificial adornment with the natural, inexpensive
adornment of a wreath of fresh flowers, which is, in any
case, more appropriate for one with fair hair. Another
reference to Kleïs' blond hair is suggested in 231. Another
reason for a natural adornment, however, is implied in the
fragment that follows in Greek, 232, where Sappho seems
to speak of poverty, possibly during exile, when an
elaborate headband was probably more than she could af-
ford.

[123] *Etymologicum Magnum*, 2.43. This may be addressed
to one of her rivals, to Gorgo or to Andromeda.

[124] From a second century papyrus, *Oxyrhynchus Papyri*, 1231; Lobel and Page, 120. The last four fragmentary lines, 21–24, which Edmonds restores largely by conjecture, are omitted. Sappho begins the poem with a paratactic trope, found also in Tyrtaios, fr. 9 Diehl, and Pindar, *Olympian Odes*, 1, to compare the apparent splendor of military spectacles with the power of love. While she does not dull the public sparkle of the masculine world of war, to her all this bright clutter of history cannot match the illumination of love and physical beauty in her personal world. See *Glossary* for Anaktoria.

[125] Hephaistion, *Handbook on Meters*. Although this is one of the two or three best-known poems attributed to Sappho, her authorship is now denied by recent editors. The poem is Lesbian, however, and a simple yet impeccable example of her imagery and ideas.

[126] Apollonios Dyskolos, *On Pronouns*, 127a.

[127] Maximus of Tyre, *Orations*, 18.9, writes: "Sokrates says Eros is a sophist, Sappho calls him a weaver of tales. Eros makes Sokrates mad for Phaidros, and eros shatters Sappho's heart like a mountain whirlwind punishing the oak trees."

[128] "Longinus," *On the Sublime*, 10. Catullus' fifty-first ode to Lesbia—Lesbia for the Lesbian Sappho—is an imitation of Sappho's poem:

> Ille mi par esse deo videtur,
> ille, si fas est, superare divos,
> qui sedens adversus identidem te
>   spectat et audit
>
> dulce ridentem, misero quod omnis
> cripit sensus mihi: nam simul te,
> Lesbia, aspexi, nihil est super mi
>   . . .
>
> lingua sed torpet, tenuis sub artus
> flamma demanat, sonitu suopte
> tintinant aures, gemina teguntur
>   lumina nocte.

A recent tradition of scholarship holds this poem to be a wedding song to be sung before a bride and groom. There is no internal evidence of this, and these verses of violent personal passion would be inappropriate at the ceremony. The poem is a marvel of candor and power in which Sappho states her jealousy of the calm godlike man and describes with striking objectivity and detachment the physical symptoms of her passionate love for the girl.

Some years before, Archilochos, the first poet to speak of passions of the outsider and individual, had written:

> I lie here miserable and broken with desire,
> pierced through to the bones by the bitterness
> of this god-given painful love.

> O comrade, this passion makes my limbs limp
> and tramples over me. (fr. 104 Diehl).

[129] Herodianos, *On Anomalous Words*, 7 (2.912 Lentz). Horace wrote: "Sublimi feriam sidera vertice." (*Odes*, 1.1.36).

[130] Athenaios, *Scholars at Dinner*, 2.54f.

[131] Scholiast on Apollonios of Rhodes, *Argonautika*, 1.1123.

[132] Athenaios, *Scholars at Dinner*, 13.571d, writes: "Free women and girls call a friend or acquaintance *hetaira* as Sappho does: [poem follows]." The verse shows that hetaira, as used by Sappho, signified *comrade*, not *courtesan*.

[133] Julian (the Apostate), *Letters*, 194, 387a. Julian writes: "Sappho says the moon is silver and so conceals all other stars from view." Eustathios writes: "In the expression, 'around the shining moon' one should not interpret this as the full moon, for then the stars would be outshone and appear dim, as Sappho says."

[134] Ammonios, *Words that Differ*, 75. The word *thief* is not in the Greek text.

[135] Demetrios, *On Style*, 142. This fragment is also attributed to Alkaios (Lobel and Page, 347b). Alkaios' poem begins:

Wash your gullet with wine for the dog-star returns
with the heat of summer searing a thirsting earth.
Cicadas cry softly under high leaves, and pour down
shrill song incessantly from under their wings.

Alkaios' poem is itself a version of lines by Hesiod in *Works and Days.*

[136] Scholiast on Pindar, *Pythian Odes*, 1.10, writes: "He [Pindar] has described a picture of an eagle perched on Zeus' scepter and lulled to sleep by music, letting both wings lie still. . . . On the other hand Sappho says of pigeons: [poem follows]."

[137] Scholiast on Sophokles, *Elektra*, 149, writes: "The phrase messenger or herald of Zeus is used of the nightingale because it is a sign of the coming of spring. Sappho writes: [poem follows]." Ben Jonson took from this fragment his line in *The Sad Shepherd*, act 2: "The dear good angel of the Spring, The Nightingale." He gave Sappho's word ἄγγελος, *herald,* or *messenger,* its later Biblical meaning of *angel.*

[138] Himerios, *Declamations,* 46.8. Himerius cites this fragment from an "Ode to Hesperos" by Sappho.

[139] Demetrios, *On Style,* 164, writes: "Charm and also elegant effects occur when the most beautiful words are used as in: [poem follows]".

[140] Pollux, *Vocabulary,* 10.124.

[141] From a seventh-century parchment, *Papyri Berlinenses,* 9722, fol. 5; Lobel and Page, 96, 11.1–20. It is presumed that this poem is addressed to Atthis.

[142] From a sixth-century parchment, *Papyri Berlinenses,* 9722, fol. 1; Lobel and Page, 92. This translation, unlike other substantial fragments which are derived from Lobel and Page or in some cases from Denys Page alone or from C. M. Bowra, is derived from Edmonds' restoration and invention. Edmonds was a major classicist who served a generation of scholars and readers of the Loeb Library. I include this translation with pleasure, as it is a fine poem — but with misgivings since it is largely Edmonds' words.

The fragmentary state of Sappho's poems have led many translators to seek support in Edmonds' restorations — Mary Barnard's brilliant and pioneer translations are based exclusively on them. In my *Sappho: Lyrics in the Original Greek with Translations* (New York: NYU Press, 1965), I resorted to Edmonds on a few occasions when the alternative seemed no poem at all. Here, however, this poem 142 represents the only major piece where Edmonds' voice is heard, and I offer it as representative not of Sappho's, but of the English classicist's masterful hand.

[143] From a sixth-century parchment, *Papyri Berlinenses*, 9722, fol. 1; Lobel and Page, 94.

[144] Hephaistion, *Handbook on Meters*, 7.7. Also, Plutarch, *Dialogue on Love*, 751d.

[145] Terentianus Maurus, *On Meters*, 6.390 Keil, writes: "[Sappho]... sings that Atthis was small in those days when her own girlhood was blossoming."

[146] From a second-century papyrus, *Oxyrhynchus Papyri*, 1231; Lobel and Page, 24a.

[147] Dionysios of Halikarnassos, *On Literary Composition*, 23. The Page text is used, as it appears in *Sappho and Alcaeus*. Page has not included the brackets in this edition. He does use brackets in the Lobel-Page text of the same poem, but his brackets do not mean a conjectural supplement, as they do in Edmonds' texts, but merely doubt or obvious restoration. This poem to Aphrodite is usually considered the one complete poem that has survived of Sappho. There are fragments of other poems, however, which have more lines than this complete poem. Despite the tone of intimate friendship and even gay camaraderie, the poem has the formal structure of a prayer with the expected invocation, sanction, and entreaty.

[148] From the third century B.C. ostracon, ed. by Norsa, *Annali della reale Scuola normale superiore de Pisa, Lettere, Storia e Filosofia*, series 2, 6 (1937). The text is from Bowra's *Greek Lyric Poetry*, but I reproduced Diehl's reading of line 10, substituting Diehl's πφρινίνοισιν for Bowra

and Page's ἠρίνοισιν. Krete was thought to be the original seat of worship of Aphrodite, or so its inhabitants claimed. While the scene described appears real and particular, the elements are relevant to the worship of Aphrodite. Apples and horses were symbols of Aphrodite, who was known as Aphrodite of the Apples as well as Aphrodite of the Horses. The prayer for epiphany in the poem is by no means proof that Sappho was a priestess or a poet of cult songs. Her concern with Aphrodite was with a figure that represented beauty and love.

[149] From a second-century papyrus, *Oxyrhynchus Papyri*; Lobel and Page, 120. The text is from Page's *Sappho and Alcaeus*. Page makes helpful supplements and restorations. Sappho's poem suggests that the Atreidai, Agamemnon and Menelaos, left Troy together and reached Lesbos together. This Lesbian version differs from Homer's *(Odyssey,* 3), in which Menelaos leaves Agamemnon at Troy and reaches Lesbos alone.

[150] Hephaistion, *Handbook on Meters,* 10.5.

[151] Aristotle, *Nikomachean Ethics,* 1149b.15, writes: "For desire is cunning, as is said about Aphrodite: [poem follows]." The title and words "For I am" are added to indicate the speaker.

[152] Maximus of Tyre, *Orations,* 18.9g, writes: "Diotima [in Plato's *Symposium*] tells Sokrates that Eros is not the son but the attendant and servant of Aphrodite, and in a poem Aphrodite says to Sappho: [poem follows]."

[153] Scholiast on Apollonius of Rhodes, *Argonautika,* 3.26, writes: "Apollonios makes Eros the son of Aphrodite, but Sappho makes him the child of Gaia [Earth] and Ouranos [Sky]."

Scholiast on Theokritos, 13.2, writes: "He is uncertain of whom to make Eros the son. Hesiod . . . and Sappho make him the son of Gaia [Earth] and Ouranos [Sky]."

Pausanias, *Description of Greece,* 9.27.2, writes: "It is written that Hesiod made Chaos the first creation, then Gaia [Earth] and Tartaros and Eros. And in the poems of Sappho the Lesbian there are many mutually inconsistent statements about Eros: [poems follows]." The text used here has been restored by Edmonds.

[154] Hephaistion, *Handbook on Meters*, 64 (see *Testimonia*).

[155] Athenaios, *Scholars at Dinner*, 9.410 e, writes: "When Sappho in her Fifth Book of Lyric Poems says to Aphrodite [poem follows] she means the handkerchief as an adornment for the head, as indicated also by Hekataios, or some other writer, in the book entitled *Guide to Asia* where he writes: 'Women wear handkerchiefs on their heads.' " The reading is difficult. Edmonds inserts Timas, gratuitously; Diehl finds Mnasis in the poem; Page finds no distinct lady at all. David A. Campbell also finds Mnasis, which reading I have followed.

[156] Hephaistion, *Handbook on Meters*, 12.4.

[157] Apollonios Dyskolos, *Pronouns*, 104. Other readings of the fragment interpret the first and last phrase as "I will bring to the altar" and "I shall pour a libation for you."

[158] Apollonios Dyskolos, *Syntax*, 3.247.

[159] Philodemos, *Piety*, 42 Gomperz. Lobel and Page place these lines in the *Incertum utrius auctoris fragmenta* section of the poems of Sappho and Alkaios.

[160] Scholiast on Hesiod, *Works and Days*, 73, writes: "Sappho calls Peitho [Persuasion] the daughter of Aphrodite." Edmonds restores the Greek line.

[161] *Argument to Theokritos*, 28.

[162] Hephaistion, *Handbook on Meters*, 9.2.

[163] Hephaistion, *Handbook on Meters*. "Your gold house" is probably the house of Zeus.

[164] Apollonios Dyskolos, *Pronouns*, 144a.

[165] *Etymologicum Magnum*, 250.10s.

[166] Hephaistion, *Handbook on Meters*, 14.7. In place of "Why do you condemn?" other read "Why honor?"

[167] Herodianos, *On the Declension of Nouns;* Aldus, *Cornucopia*, 268.

[168] Syrianos on Hermogenes, *Kinds of Style*, 1.1, writes: "Some kinds of style have to do with one kind of thought only.... Others... express things pleasing to the senses

Sappho

of sight, hearing, smell, taste, touch, such as Homer's *Iliad*, 347f., or Sappho's: [Like a sweet apple, etc]." Demetrios, *On Style*, 106, writes: "The epiphonema, as it is called, may be considered as a phrase that adds adornment, and elevates style. . . . For example, the sense is intensified by such a phrase as 'like a hyachinth' . . . while it is adorned by the succeeding words 'on the earth yet blooming purple.' " Himerios, *Declamations*, 9–16, writes: "Sappho compared a virgin to an apple, allowing those who would pluck it before its time not even to touch it with their fingertips, but he who would pick it in the right season might watch its beauty grow; compared the bridegroom to Achilles and his deeds to the hero's." Sappho's words also occur in Theokritos, *Idylls*, 18.38; Catullus, 11.21–24; and Vergil, *Aeneid*, 9.435.

[169] Philostratos, *Pictures*, 2.1, and Aristainetos, *Letters*, 1.10. Philostratos refers to the phrase "honey-voiced," and Aristainetos refers to the phrase "gentle-voiced" as "Sappho's most delightful epithet."

[170] Scholiast on Aristophanes, *Thesmophoriazusae*, 401, writes: "Garlands were woven by young people and lovers. This refers to the custom where among the people of antiquity the women wove garlands: [poem follows]."

[171] Hephaistion, *Handbook on Meters*, 7.6.

[172] From a second-century papyrus, *Oxyrhynchus Papyri*, Lobel and Page, 30. This text is from Bowra's *Greek Lyric Poetry*. Bowra adds a few letters to Page's text. This song sung by girls outside the window of the newlyweds humorously tells the groom to awaken and go out and join his old friends. the taunting tone goes well with the happiness of the occasion.

[173] From a second-century papyrus, *Oxyrhynchus Papyri*, 1231; Lobel and Page, 54.

[174] Himerios, *Epithalamy of Severus*, 1.20, writes: "And if an ode were needed, I would give a song such as this: [paraphrase of poem follows]." The Greek text is the prose paraphrase.

[175] Dionysios of Halikarnassos, *On Literary Composition*, 25.

[176] Hephaistion, *Handbook on Meters*, 15.26, and Choricius, *Epithalamy of Zachary*, 97. Catullus has phrases reminiscent of these lines: *mellitos oculos* (48.1) and *Pulcher es, neque to Venus neglegit* (61.194).

[177] Hephaistion, *On Poems*, 7.1. Demetrios, *On Style*, 148, writes: "There is a charm peculiarly Sapphic in its way when having said something, she changes her mind, as [poem follows], as if interrupting herself because she has resorted to an impossible hyperbole, for no one really is as tall as Ares."

[178] Athenaios, *Scholars at Dinner*, 10.425d, writes: "According to some versions the wine-bearer of the gods was Harmonia. Alkaios makes Hermes also the wine-bearer, as does Sappho in the following: [poem follows]."

[179] Hephaistion, *Handbook on Meters*, 4.2, and Servius on Vergil, *Georgics*, 1.31.

[180] Hephaistion, *Handbook on Meters*, 7.6. Synesios in *Letters*, 3.158d, writes: "The man who is wronged is Harmonios, the father of the Head Doorkeeper, who, as Sappho would say, though in other respects he lived soberly and honestly, he claimed to be better born than Kekrops himself."

[181] Chrysippos, *Negatives*, 23.

[182] Libanios, *Orations*, 1.12.99, writes: "If nothing prevented Sappho the Lesbian from wishing that the length of her night be doubled, then I may make a similar prayer." From this Edmonds suggests Sappho's words.

[183] Hephaistion, *Handbook on Meters*, 11.3.

[184] Himerios, *Epithalamy of Severus*, 1, writes: "Come then, we will lead our discourse into the bridal chamber and introduce it to the beauty of the bride. O beautiful and charming, these are the Lesbian's praises for you. Your playmates are the roseate-ankled Graces and golden Aphrodite, and the seasons make the meadows bloom." Edmonds construes the Greek text from these words of Himerios.

[185] Demetrios, *On Style*, 140.

[186] Apollonios Dyskolos, *Conjunctions*, 490.

[187] From a third-century papyrus, *Oxyrhynchus Papyri*, 1232; Lobel and Page, 44. The poem ends with Σαπφοῦς μελῶν β′ "End of the Second Book of Sappho's Poems." This hymeneal song, from the book of epithalamia, is more narratively epic and Homeric in word and idea than any other existing fragment of Sappho. Because of these qualities not normally found in Sappho, Page casts some doubt as to her authorship. David A. Campbell and most scholars affirm her authorship. Campbell observes, "Sappho's authorship is confirmed by quotations in Athenaeus, Bekker's *Anecdota Graeca* and Ammonius.

[188] From a sixth-century parchment, *Papyri Berlinenses*, 9722, fol. 5; Lobel and Page, 96, 11.21–37. The text is very fragmentary.

[189] Julian, *Letter to Iamblichus*, 183.

[190] Maximus of Tyre, *Orations*, 18.9d.

[191] Hephaistion, *Handbook on Meters*, 14.7.

[192] Athenaios, *Scholars at Dinner*, 1.21b,c.

[193] Herodianos, *On Anomalous Words*, 26 (2.932 Lentz).

[194] Herodianos, *On the Declension of Nouns*; Aldus, *Cornucopia*, 286b.

[195] Priscian, *Grammar*, 6.92 (2.77. Keil). Bergk and Edmonds assign this fragment to Sappho; Diehl and Lobel and Page to Alkaios.

[196] Athenaios, *Scholars at Dinner*, 13.571d (see *Niobe* in *Glossary*).

[197] Hephaistion, *Handbook on Meters*, 12.2. Where Edmonds has ὄρραννα, Diehl has Ὦ<ι>ραν<ν>α and Page Ὦιρανα, both proper nouns.

[198] Scholiast on Pindar, *Olympian Odes*, 2.96f. The second line of text is uncertain and may not be Sappho, although the Scholiast's commentary suggests that it is. "The meaning. Wealth when not by itself but embellished by virtue in its own time enjoys its own good and that of virtue [arete] and has a wise concern for the pursuit of the good. Neither of these on its own is welcome."

[199] Stobaios, *Anthology*, 3.4.12, writes: "Sappho to a woman of no education."

[200] Athenaios, *Scholars at Dinner*, 13.56d, writes: "And Sappho also says to the man who is excessively admired for his beauty: [poem follows]."

[201] Hephaistion, *Handbook on Meters*, 44. Aristotle, *Rhetoric*, 1367a, writes: "We are ashamed of what is shameful, whether it is said, done or intended; compare Sappho's answer when Alkaios said: 'I want to speak to you but shame disarms me.'" Edmonds assigns part one to Alkaios and part two to Sappho. Diehl and Page assign the first line of part one to Alkaios and the remaining lines to Sappho. The text in all cases is substantially the same.

[202] Galenos, *Exhortation to Learning*, 8.16s, writes: "Since we know that the time of youth is like spring flowers and its pleasures do not last long, it is better to praise the Lesbian poet: [poem follows]."

[203] From a second-century papyrus, *Oxyrhynchus Papyri*, 1231; Lobel and Page, 22.

[204] *Etymologicum Magnum*, 485.41.

[205] From a second-century papyrus, *Oxyrhynchus Papyri*, 1231; Lobel and Page, 28. The text is very fragmentary. David A. Campbell's accurate translation in *Greek Lyric* reads: " ... brightness ... with the help of good fortune ... to gain (the harbour?) ... beach (earth?) ... the sailors (are unwilling?) ... great gusts ... and on dry land ... sail ... the cargo ... since ... flowing (?) many ... (receive?) ... tasks ... dry land. ... "

[206] Chrysippos, *Negatives*, col. 8, fr. 13.

[207] Scholiast on Pindar, *Pythian Odes*, 4.410c, writes: "Gold [the Golden Fleece] is immortal [indestructible]. And Sappho says ... and Pindar says that gold is the child of Zeus." The lines in brackets are derived from the above context.

[208] Scholiast on Aristophanes, Peace, 1174, writes: "For the Lydian dyes differ ... and Sappho states: [her lines follow]."

[209] Pollux, *Vocabulary*, 7.73.

[210] Scholiast on Apollonios of Rhodes, *Argonautika*, 1.727.

[211] Herodianos, *On Anomalous Words*, 39 (2.945 Lentz).

[212] Gregorios on Hermogenes, 7.1236 Walz (Edmonds, 61).

Demetrios, *On Style*, 161s, writes: "The charm of comedy lies especially in hyperbole, and each hyperbole is an impossibility... such as Sappho's: [phrases follow]."

Athenaios, *Scholars at Dinner*, 2.57d (Edmonds, 62).

[213] Demetrios, *On Style*, 146.

[214] Athenaios, *Scholars at Dinner*, 15.674e, writes: "Sappho gives a more simple reason for wearing garlands: [her lines follow] in which she urges all who offer sacrifice to wreathe their heads, since being adorned with flowers makes them more pleasing to the gods."

[215] Hephaistion, *Handbook on Meters*, 11.5.

[216] Herodianos, *On Anomalous Words*, 26 (2.932 Lentz).

[217] Plutarch, *On Restraining Anger*, 7.456e, writes: "A man who is silent over his wine is boring and vulgar, and in anger there is nothing more dignified than tranquility, as Sappho advises [her lines follow]." Sappho gives her advice in the second person imperative. In this translation the advice is given in the first person singular.

[218] Philon, *On Punishment*, in a third-century papyrus, *Oxyrhynchus Papyri*, 1356; Lobel and Page, 139, writes: "... yielding to the good counsel of the woman poet Sappho." The poem follows.

[219] Aristides, *Orations*, 1.425, writes: "The glow which is upon the whole city, not as Sappho said, blinding the eyes, but... nor indeed as she said, like a hyacinth, but..." The city may also be Mytilene.

[220] Herodianos, *On Theokritos*, 1.55b.

[221] Apollonios Dyskolos, *Pronouns*, 66.3; Lobel and Page, 129a, b.

[222] Julian, *Letter to Eugenius*, 193, writes: "I would fly to the very foot of your mountains to embrace you, my

darling, as Sappho says." The lines enclosed in brackets are derived from Julian's letter.

[223] *Etymologicum Magnum*, 576.23ff.

[224] Klearchos, in Athenaios, *Scholars at Dinner*, 12.554b, writes: "All lovers ripe with passion are attracted to beautiful things. For it is natural that those who believe themselves to be beautiful and blooming find it natural to gather flowers. That is why Persephone's companions are described as gathering flowers and Sappho says that she saw a very beautiful girl picking flowers."

[225] Herodianos, *On Anomalous Words*, (2.932 Lentz). There are many variant readings of this fragment.

[226] From a second-century papyrus, *Oxyrhynchus Papyri*, 1231; Lobel and Page, 26.

[227] Tryphon, *Figures of Speech*, 25, writes: "[Sappho's lines], said of those who are unwilling to take the sour with the sweet."

[228] Apollonios Dyskolos, *Pronouns*, 126b; *Etymologicum Magnum*, 117.14ff.

[229] From a second-century papyrus, *Oxyrhynchus Papyri*, 1231; Lobel and Page, 27.

[230] From a second-century papyrus, *Oxyrhynchus Papyri*, 1231; Lobel and Page, 22. Hermione was Helen's daughter.

[231] Hephaistion, *Handbook on Meters*, 15.18.

[232] From the oldest extant papyrus of Sappho and Alkaios, of the third century B.C., or a little later. The fragment is in Milan and was first published by Vogliano in *Philologus*, 93 (1939): 277ff. For the material on the first part of the papyrus (a), see poem 122 and notes for 122. The free translation of the second stanza is based on Page's interpretation, *Sappho and Alcaeus*, p. 102. He suggests that line 6 refers to the tyrant Myrsilos.

[233] From a third-century papyrus, *Oxyrhynchus Papyri*, 1787; Lobel and Page, 71. Mika may be a shortened form for her friend Mnasidika. The house of Penthilos may refer to a rival school (*thiasos*) or, more likely, a rival political

party. Pittakos, the tyrant of Lesbos, married the sister of a former leader, Drakon, who was the son of Penthilos.

[234] From a third-century papyrus, *Oxyrhynchus Papyri*, 2289; Lobel and Page, 5. Our text is from Page's *Sappho and Alcaeus*. This version differs from Lobel and Page in the partial restoration of line 7. The poem is to her brother Charaxos. The black torment is presumably his Egyptian mistress, Doricha, on whom Charaxos was "wasting" his fortune. In the very mutilated lines that follow (not included here), Sappho seems to broaden her attack on Doricha.

[235] From a second-century papyrus, *Oxyrhynchus Papyri*, 1231; Lobel and Page, 15.

[236] From a third-century papyrus, *Oxyrhynchus Papyri*, 1787; Lobel and Page, 58. Commenting on the last lines of the poem, Athenaios in *Scholars at Dinner*, 15.687a, writes: "So you think that refinement without virtue is desirable? But Sappho, who was a real woman and poet, was loath to separate good from refinement, saying: 'Yet I love refinement, and beauty and light / are for me the same as desire for the sun.' It thus is clear that the desire to live included for Sappho both the bright and the good, and these belong to virtue."

[237] From a third-century papyrus, *Oxyrhynchus Papyri*, 1787; Lobel and Page, 63.

[238] From a third-century papyrus, *Oxyrhynchus Papyuri*, 1787; Lobel and Page, 62.

[239] *Palatine Anthology*, 7.505. Ascription to Sappho is unlikely.

[240] Hephaiston, *Handbook on Meters*, 11.5. Where Edmonds reads *peace*, Diehl and other editors read a name, Irana, or some variation of such a name.

[241] From a first-century papyrus, *Oxyrhynchus Papyri*, 220.9; Lobel and Page, insert 18.

[242] Aristotle, *Rhetoric*, 2.23. Edmonds' text contains his metrical version. The Lobel and Page text, used here, records Aristotle's paraphrase.

[243] *Palatine Anthology*, 7.489. The ascription of this well-known poem to Sappho is not accepted by most recent scholars.

[244] R. Ranier, 29.777a. The text is from Max Treu's edition of Sappho. Treu restores a few letters not found in Lobel-Page text. Here the Atreidai is probably Menalaos.

[245] From a second- or third-century papyrus, *Les Papyrus Fouad*, 239; Lobel and Page, 44a, also Lobel and Page (Alcaeus), 304. Lobel and Page assign the poem hesitantly to Alkaios, but Treu strongly defends it as Sappho's. He cites the line "I shall always be a virgin" as Sappho's speech and rejects as insufficient the Page argument based on recurring forms. The single unintelligible words of the first and last lines of the Greek text are omitted here.

[246] Athenaios, *Scholars at Dinner*, 257d. It is uncertain what flower the hyacinth was to the Greeks.

[247] Stobaios, *Anthology*, 4.22.112, writes: "In marriage it is best to consider the ages of the people concerned. Sappho writes: [her lines follow]."

[248] Maximus of Tyre, *Orations*, 18.9b, writes: "Diotima says [in Plato's *Symposium*] that love flowers in prosperity and dies in want." Sappho put these together and called it bittersweet [see poem 144] and giver of pain. While Sokrates calls love sophistical, Sappho calls it a weaver of tales.

[249] Apollonios Dyskolos, *Pronouns*, 83b, c. In Lobel and Page, this fragment, 129a, precedes 129b (poem 221).

[250] Apollonios Dyskolos, *Pronouns*, 124c.

[251] Demetrios, *On Style*, 141, writes: "Sappho also creates charm from the use of anaphora, as in this passage about the Evening Star: [her lines follow]. Here the charm lies in the repetition of the word *bring*." In *Don Juan*, canto 3, stanza 107, Byron imitated Sappho.

> O Hesperus, thou bringest all good things—
> Home to the weary, to the hungry cheer,
> To the young bird the parent's brooding wings,
> The welcome stall to the o'erlaboured steer;

Whate'er of peace about our hearthstone clings,
  Whate'er our household gods protect of dear,
Are gathered round us by thy look of rest;
Thou bring'st the child too to its mother's breast.

[252] From a sixth-century parchment, *Papyri Berlinenses,* 9722, fol. 4; Lobel and Page, 95. In this fragmentary papyrus The subject of verbs is in question. Sappho is probably responding to Gongyla, whose name appears as the only word in line 1 of the extant papyrus. It is uncertain whom (or what) the sign may refer to in line 1 of the translation. The remaining lines of the fragment hang together.

[253] From a second-century papyrus, *Oxyrhynchus Papyri,* 1231; Lobel and Page, 21. The text is very fragmentary. David A. Campbell's accurate translation in *Greek Lyric* reads: ". . . (in possession of?) . . . pity . . . trembling . . . old age now . . . (my) sky . . . covers . . . (Love?) flies pursuing (the young?) . . . glorious . . . taking* (your lyre?) sing to us of the violet-robed one† . . . especially wanders . . ."

[254] Maximus of Tyre, *Orations,* 18.9, writes: "Sokrates reproves Xanthippe for crying when she is near death as Sappho does her daughter: [her lines follow]."

[255] Aristides, *On the Extemporised Addition,* 2.508, writes: "Sappho too once boasted to some women who were thought to be wealthy that the Muses had given her true happiness and good fortune and that when dead she would not be forgotten." Edmonds devises his text from Aristides' prose paraphrase of Sappho's words.

[256] Dio Chrysostom, *Discourses,* 37.47, has: " 'Someone I tell you, will remember us,' as Sappho has well said, '. . . for we are oppressed by fears of oblivion, but always saved by judgment of good men.' " The lines in brackets derive from Dio Chrysostom's summary of Sappho's words.

* Addressed to a girl or woman.

† Aphrodite?

[257] Scholiast on Sophokles' *Electra*. This fragment, included in Edmonds' *Lyra Graeca* (1940), vol. 3, is ascribed to Sappho or Alkaios.

[258] From a seventh-century parchment, *Papyri Berlinenses*, 5006, fol. 4; Lobel and Page, 4. The Lobel - Page text is followed except for line 7 where]λον is amended to read κά]λον. The text is obviously fragmentary, scarcely more than a column of words, yet the words are intelligible; The syntax and connective words present the main difficulty. Ezra Pound's early poem, imitating Sappho, suggest a similar scrap of papyrus:

PAPYRUS
Spring...
Too long...
Gongula...

[259] From a third- century papyrus, *Oxyrhynchus Papyri*, 1787; Lobel and Page, 65. No new word in the translation has been added apart from the connective *as* in line 9. Where the Greek text has *Acheron*, the river of death running through Hades, I have used *Hades*.

[260] *Etymologicum Magnum*, 174.42ff.

[615] From a third-century papyrus, *Oxyrhynchus Papyri*, 2291; Lobel and Page, 99b.

[616] From a third-century papyrus, *Oxyrhynchus Papyri*, 1787; Lobel and Page, 73a. The text is very fragmentary. No basic nouns, verbs, or adjectives are added, but what remains uncertain is who is the speaker, who is the subject of each verb.

[617] From a third-century papyrus, *Oxyrhynchus Papyri*, 1787; Lobel and Page, 68a. The text is very fragmentary and the same uncertainties persist as in 616.

[618] From a third-century papyrus, *Oxyrhynchus Papyri*, 1787; Lobel and Page, 86. Fragmentary text.

[619] From a third-century papyrus, *Oxyrhynchus Papyri*, 1787; Lobel and Page, 70. Fragmentary text.

[620] From a third-century papyrus, *Oxyrhynchus Papyri*,

1787; Lobel and Page, 60. Fragmentary text is from the right column.

[621] From a late second- or early third-century papyrus, *Oxyrhynchus Papyri*, 2308; Lobel and Page, 103b.

[622] From a third-century papyrus, *Oxyrhynchus Papyri*, 1787; Lobel and Page, 67a.

[623] From a third-century papyrus, *Oxyrhynchus Papyri*, 2291; Lobel and Page, 99a. The lines may be by Alkaios. Very fragmentary.

[624] From a late second- or early third-century papyrus, *Oxyrhynchus Papyri*, 2291; Lobel and Page, 88. The text is from the long, narrow right-hand column of the papyrus.

Glossary
and Index

◇✕✕✕✕✕✕✕✕✕✕✕✕✕✕✕✕✕✕✕✕✕✕✕✕✕✕✕✕✕✕✕✕✕✕✕✕✕✕◇

"In." followed by poet's name refers to the headnotes on the poet; "Te." followed by poet's name refers to testimonia on the poet; numbers refer to poems in which the cited word occurs.

Abdera—Greek city in Thrace founded by Herakles in memory of his attendant Abderos. Superstition held that the air of the city caused its inhabitants to be stupid and "Abderite" became a term of reproach. 339, In. Anakreon

Academy—A grove of olive trees near Athens held sacred to the hero Akademos. Here Plato and his successors taught, hence the name "Academic philosophy." 452

Acheloodoros—Father of the Boiotian poet Korinna. Te. Korinna

Acheron—One of the five rivers of the Underworld that dead souls must cross. 119, 252, 417

Achilles—Son of Peleus and the sea nymph Thetis, he is the tragic hero of the *Iliad*. 106, 244

Admetos—King of Pherai in Thessaly. 291

Adonis—A beautiful youth loved by Aphrodite and lamented by the goddess after he was killed by a boar. His death was celebrated by women in a yearly festival. 154, 188

Adrianos—Of Tyros, Sophist, pupil, and successor of Attikos Herodes at Athens. Te. Archilochos

Aelianus Claudius—Author of *Historical Miscellanies*, a fourteen-volume book in Greek about political and literary celebrities, written in the second century A.D. Te. Xenophanes, Te. Korinna

Agamemnon—King of Mykenai, son of Atreus and brother of Menelaos. Leader of the Greek forces against Troy. 289

Agathokles—Teacher of Apollodoros. Te. Apollodoros, Te. Lamprokles

Agathon—Proper name. 339, 445

Agesidamos—Lokrian boxer celebrated by Pindar in his "Olympian Ode XI." 423

Agido—Proper name. 72

Aiakos—Son of Zeus, father of Peleus and grandfather of Achilles, he was known as a just man and a judge in the underworld. 106

Aietes—King of Kolchis and father of Medeia. 278

Aigaian (Aegean) Sea—That part of the Mediterranean Sea between Greece and Asia Minor. 2, 457, 515

Aigialos—A city of Amorgos founded by the poet Semonides. Te. Semonides.

Aigisthos (Aegisthus)—Surviving son of Thyestes and lover of Agamemnon's wife, Klytaimnestra. 289

Ainesidamos—Father of Theron. 426

Ainesimbrota—Proper name. 72

Ainos—Aiolic city at mouth of Hebros River. 105

Aiolic/Aiolia—Dialect of eastern Greece (Aiolia) in which Sappho and Alkaios wrote. In. Alkman, In. Alkaios, In. Sappho, 283, 390, In. Theokritos

Aiolos—Father of Sisyphos. 119

Aischylides—Proper name. 43

Aischylos (Aeschylus)—Greek tragic poet generally regarded as the founder of Greek tragedy. In. Simonides

Aisimides—Proper name. 41

Aithra—Daughter of Pittheus, King of Troizen, and mother of Theseus. 431

Aitolia—A division of Greece celebrated in mythology as the home of the Kalydonian boar hunt. 426

Akragas (Agrigentum)—A city on the southern coast of Sicily known for its splendor. In. Stesichoros, In. Simonides, In. Pindaros, 426

Alexandria/Alexandrian—The capital of Egypt, founded by Alexander the Great, and the center of learning and culture during the Hellenistic period. The Library of Alexandria is said to have contained over half a million volumes. In. Mimnermos, In. Stesichoros, In. Kallimachos, In. Theokritos, In. Asklepiades, In. Nikarchos, In. Palladas, 555

Alexis—Proper name. 447

Alkaios—Lyric poet of Mytilene of Lesbos (fl. ca. 611-580 B.C.). In. Alkaios, In. Terpandros, 107, In. Sappho, Te. Sappho, 201, In. Ibykos, Te. Ibykos, 245, 257, In. Anakreon, Te. Bakchylides, In. Theokritos

Alkestis (Alcestis)—Daughter of Pelias and wife of Admetos. 291

Alkibia—Proper name. 33

Alkman—Lyric poet of the second half of the seventh century B.C. His work is concerned mainly with Spartan feasts and festivals. In. Alkman, In. Terpandros, 67, 77, 79, In. Stesichoros, Te. Bakchylides, 612

Alkmena—Daughter of Elektryon, King of Mykenai, and wife of Amphitryon. Mother of Herakles by Zeus. 378

Alpheus—One of the largest rivers in Greece. As a hunter, Alpheus pursued the nymph Arethosia; he was transformed into a river, she into a spring. See *Arethosia*. 415, 426

Ammianus Marcellinus—Last of the great Roman historians, he wrote a history of the Roman Empire from A.D. 353 to 378. Te. Stesichoros

Amorgos—An island of the Aigaian Sea and the birthplace of Semonides. In. Semonides, Te. Semonides, 209

Amphiptolemos—Father of Asios. Te. Asios

Amphitrite—Daughter of Nereus and wife of Poseidon. 431

Amphitryon—Son of Alkaios, grandson of Perseus and husband of Alkmena. Amphitryon's son refers to Herakles. 426, 429

Amyklian—Of Amyklai, an ancient town in Lakonia. 420

Anakreon—Lyric poet of Teos (ca. 560 B.C.). In. Anakreon, In. Ibykos, Te. Ibykos, In. Simonides, Te. Hipparchos, Te. Bakchylides, In. Anakreonteia, 559, 560, 572, 576, 604

Anaktoria—One of Sappho's friends. One theory is that she left Sappho in order to marry a soldier stationed in Sardis. In. Sappho, 124

Anastasia—Proper name. 557

Anatolia—The peninsula of Asia Minor. In. Mimnermos

Andromache—Daughter of Eetion, King of Thebes, and wife of Hektor. Her husband was killed by Achilles during the Trojan War, her son Astyanax was put to death, and she herself was taken prisoner by the Greeks. 187

Andromeda—A rival of Sappho, perhaps a poet. In. Sappho, 144, 190, 191, 192, 259, 617

Andros—The most northerly island of the Kyklades. 515, In. Sappho

Anthology— See PALATINE ANTHOLOGY. In. Philodemos, In. Diodoros, In. Antipatros of Thessalonike, In. Nikarchos, In. Leonidas, In. Paulus Silentiarius

Antigone—Proper name. 510

Antimenidas—Brother of the poet Alkaios, who fought with the Babylonian army under Nebuchadnezzar in the early 6th century B.C. 101

Antipatros of Sidon—Greek epigrammatist who influenced Catullus and other Republican poets (fl. 1st century B.C.). Te. Pindaros

Antipatros of Thessalonike—Greek epigrammatist of the

Augustan Age whose work closely resembles that of Ovid. In. Antipatros of Thessalonike, Te. Alkman

Aphrodite (Kyprian, Kypris, Kythereia, Paphian)—Goddess of love, beauty, and the sea. She was born in the seafoam (*aphros*) off the shore of Paphos in Kypros (Cyprus) or near the island of Kythera. 28, 78, 86, 87, In. Sappho, 147, 148, 152, 155, 157, 158, 159, 160, 166, 176, 184, 188, 234, 299, Te. Telesilla, 431, 446, 449, 471, 482, 483, 502, 504, 509, 562, 598, 612, 616

Aphrogeneia—Proper name. 562

Apis—Proper name. 533

Apollo—Son of Zeus and Leto, and twin brother of Artemis, he was the ideal of young manly beauty and of civilized Greek man. God of medicine, music, the sun, archery and prophecy. 50, 65, 107, 187, 245, 295, 370, 416, Te. Pindaros, 426, 440, 474, Te. Platon, 515, 586, 605

Archeanassa—The girlfriend of Sokrates. 448

Archedike—Daughter of the Athenian despot Hippias. 387

Archelaos—King of Macedonia from 413 to 399 B.C. He obtained the throne by murdering his half-brother; he took a keen interest in Greek culture, and the poets Euripides, Agathon and Timotheos frequented his court. In. Timotheos

Archestratos—Father of Agesidamos. 423

Archilochos—Iambic and elegiac poet of Paros; lived in the seventh century B.C. In. Archilochos, 49, In. Semonides, Te. Semonides, In. Hipponax, Te. Phokylides

Archon—The name given to the nine rulers of Athens after the abolition of royalty. In. Solon

Areiopagos—A hill at Athens where Ares was tried for the murder of Poseidon's son, the lover of Ares' daughter. Here the Council of State held its meetings. In. Solon

Areistogeiton—Athenian tyrannicide. See HARMODIOS. In. Hipparchos, Te. Hipparchos

Ares (Enyalios)—The god of war. 27, 177, 195, 336, 339, 360, 430

Areta—Proper name. 72

Arete—Girlfriend of Hipponax. In. Hipponax

Arethosia—In order to escape the river god Alphaios, the nymph Arethosia was transformed into a fountain in Ortygia, which then bore her name. Te. Bion

Argives—People of Argos. 462

Argos/Argolid—Argos is a city in Thessaly and the Argolid is the region around the city. In. Telesilla, Te. Telesilla, 462, In. Praxilla, In. Lasos

Ariphantos—Proper name. 43

Aristarchos—Grammarian and great critic of antiquity. The founder of scientific scholarship. Te. Archilochos

Aristodemos—Pupil of Sokrates, one of the Seven Sages. 104, Te. Melanippides

Aristogeiton—Assassin, along with Harmodios, of the tyrant Hipparchos in 511 B.C. In. Hipparchos, Te. Hipparchos

Aristophanes—Greatest playwright of comedy in antiquity (ca. 450-ca. 385 B.C.). 456

Aristophon—Proper name. 46

Aristotle—Great Greek philosopher (384-322 B.C.). Te. Solon, Te. Xenophanes, Te. Simonides, Te. Hipparchos, Te. Hippon, Te. Timotheos, 376

Aristoxenos—Philosopher and musician (fl. ca. 318 B.C.). Te. Lamprokles

Arkadia—A country in the middle of the Peloponnesos. The Arkadians regarded themselves as the most ancient people of Greece. 426, In. Anyte

Arkesime—A city of Amorgos founded by Semonides. Te. Semonides

Arktouros—A bright star near the constellation of the Great Bear. 585

Artemis—The twin sister of Apollo, daughter of Zeus and Leto. She was the goddess of chastity, the hunt, the moon and childbirth. 88, 245, 318, 415, 512, 615

Artemis Orthosia—Artemis was frequently identified with the Dorian goddess, Orthia, who was worshiped at Sparta as Artemis Orthosia. 426

Artemon—Proper name. 329

Asimides—Proper name. 41

Asklepiades—Proper name. 542

Asklepias—Proper name. 495

Asklepios—The god of the art of medicine. The son of Apollo and the pupil of Chiron, Asklepios was killed by Zeus because he could raise the dead. Te. Platon, 605

Astaphis—Proper name. 72

Astypalaia—Sister of Europa. Te. Asios

Athena (Athene, Pallas)—Goddess of wisdom, war, arts and sciences. The daughter of Zeus. 10, In. Stesichoros, 280, 337, 418, 429, 431, 562

Athenaios—Greek grammarian (ca. A.D. 230). Te. Tyrtaios, Te. Asios, Te. Timokreon

Athenis—A Chian sculptor satirized by Hipponax.

Athens—The capital of Attica. In. Tyrtaios, In. Hipponax, Te. Tyrtaios, In. Solon, 261, In. Anakreon, In. Simonides, Te. Apollodoros, In. Hipparchos, Te. Hippa, In. Lamprokles,

Te. Lamprokles, 364, 366, 371, 387, In. Pindaros, 425, In. Bakchylides, Te. Bakchylides, 431, In. Parrhasios, In. Platon, 457, In. Diphilos, 580, In. Alkaios

Atreidai—Sons or descendants of Atreus, usually referring to Agamemnon or Menelaos. 149, 244

Atreus—King of Mykenai, son of Pelops and grandson of Tantalos. The gods cursed Atreus and his house because he dared to serve them the flesh of his brother's children. 118

Attales—Brother of Alyattes, King of Persia, whose tomb still exists. 309

Attalyda—Founder of city of the same name. 309

Atthis—One of Sappho's friends who is treated with great affection. Like Anaktoria, she leaves Sappho. In. Sappho, 140, 141, 142, 143, 144, 145

Attica/Attic—A division of central Greece where Attic Greek was spoken. Its capital city was Athens. 261, 262, Te. Hipparchos, Te. Platon, 501, 593

Atys—Mythical lover of Kybeles. 309

Bakchos (Bacchus, Bacchis)—See Dionysos. 96, 427, 577

Bakchylides—One of the nine great Greek lyric poets. In. Bakchylides, In. Pindaros, Te. Pindaros

Basilo—Sister of Melanippos. 467

Bathyllos—A beautiful youth loved by the poet Anakreon. 578

Battos—Father of Kallimachos. Te. Kallinos

Boiotia—A district in Greece north of Attica. Boiotians were considered to be dull-witted despite the fact that Pindar, Hesiod, Korinna and Plutarch were Boiotians. In. Korinna, In. Pindaros

Boupalos—Sculptor suitor of Hipponax's girlfriend, Arete. In. Hipponax, Te. Hipponax, 308

Brotachos—Proper name. 382

Byzantium—A town of the Thracian Bosporos later renamed Constantinople. In. Sappho, In. Agathias, In. Scholastikos

Calabria—A region in southern Italy. 438

Catullus—Outstanding Roman lyric poet (84-54? B.C.). In. Archilochos, In. Sappho

Centaurs—A mythological race of creatures with the heads and torsos of men on the bodies of horses. 345

Chalkis—Chief town in Euboia. 27, 110

Chaos—The infinite space that existed before the creation of the world. 501

Charaxos—Brother of Sappho. In. Sappho

Charito—Proper name.

Charon—The boatman who ferried the dead across the rivers of the underworld. Also means "underworld." 541

Charon—Proper name. 31

Charybdis—A giant whirlpool opposite the cave of Skylla off the coast of Sicily. 314, 490

Cheiron—The wisest of the Centaurs, known for his skills in medicine, music, art, hunting and gymnastics. He was accidentally killed by Herakles and later placed among the stars as Sagittarius. 106

Chian/Chios (Scio)—Of Chios, a large island south of Lesbos, near Asia Minor. Celebrated for its wine and marble, Chios was reputed to be the birthplace of Homer. 63, 142, 317, Te. Pindaros, Te. Theokritos

Chrysilla—Proper name.

Cicero—Great Roman orator, statesman and essayist (106-43 B.C.). Te. Ibykos, Te. Anakreon

Cimmerian incursions—Invasions of Assyria and Asia Minor in the eighth and seventh centuries B.C. by barbarians from southern Russia. In. Kallinos, 55

Circe—A beautiful witch famous for her magical powers, who held Odysseus captive on her island. Daughter of the sun-god Helios. 566

Clement of Alexandria—One of the early Greek Fathers, important because of his extensive knowledge of Greek literature and philosophy (ca. A.D. 160-215). In. Archilochos

Cupid—See Eros. In. Asklepiades

Cynic—Member of a school of philosophy founded at Athens by Antisthenes, pupil of Sokrates. The name is taken from the Kynosarges gymnasium where the school was established. In. Meleagros, In. Loukianos

Daidalos—Legendary Athenian craftsman who with his son Ikaros escaped from their prison tower with wings made of wax and feathers. Ikaros flew too near the sun and fell into the sea, hence the name Ikarian Sea. Te. Pindaros

Damareta—Proper name. 72

Damon of Athens—Celebrated musician and Sophist, teacher of Perikles and Sokrates. Te. Lamprokles

Danaë—A girl of Argos, whose father prophesied that her son would kill him. To prevent the conception of a son her father enclosed her in a chamber. Zeus penetrated the chamber in a shower of gold and begot Perseus. 374, 482, 516

Danaids—The daughters of Danaos. 439

Daphnis—A Sicilian shepherd, son of Hermes, and regarded as the inventor of bucolic poetry. 471, 472, 473

Darius—King of Persia (521-485 B.C.). During his reign the great war between the Persians and the Greeks began. 464

Deianeira—Wife of Herakles. 429

Delos—The center island of the Kyklades in the Aigaian Sea. The birthplace of Apollo and Artemis and an important center for their worship. 431

Delphi—An ancient oracular shrine of Apollo in Phokis, and also a center for theatrical and athletic events. 107, 370, Te. Hipparchos, 429, 474

Demeter—Daughter of Kronos and Rhea and the mother of Persephone. She was the goddess of corn and a patroness of agriculture. 390

Demophilos—Proper name. 522

Demos—Proper name. 487

Demostratis—Proper name. 530

Denthiades—A town of Lakonia. 82

Diagorases—Famous boxer of Rhodes praised in Pindar's "Olympic Ode VII. " 421

Diagoras—Poet and philosopher, known for his atheism. Te. Xenophanes

Didyme—Proper name. 480

Didymos—Of Alexandria, nicknamed "brazen-guts" because of his great industry. This author of the first century B.C. wrote a commentary on Homer. Te. Anakreon

Dika—Probably short for MNASIDIKA, one of Sappho's friends. 214

Diodoros—Poet of the *Greek Anthology*. In. Diodoros, 506

Diodoros—Proper name. 527

Diogenes—Proper name. 515

Diogenes—A Cynic philosopher (ca. 400 B.C.) known in Athens for his pithy sayings. Te. Ibykos

Diogenes Laertios—Author of *Lives and Opinions of Eminent Philosophers*, an account of the principal Greek thinkers of his day (fl. A.D. 150). Te. Solon, Te. Xenophanes, Te. Platon

Diokleia—Proper name. 509

Dion—Son of Hipparinos and son-in-law of the Syracusian tyrant Dionysios the Elder, Dion was a disciple of Plato and a statesman in Sicily. 461

Dionysios—Proper name. 608

Dionysos (Bakchos)—Greek god of wine and fertility. The son of Zeus and Semele, Dionysos was the god of natural vitality also. 149, 344, 499

Diophantos—Proper name. 531

Dioskouri—From the Greek "Dios Kouri," literally "sons of Zeus," or Kastor and Polydeukes. These twin sons of Zeus and Leda were regarded as both courageous gods and mortals and were later identified with the constellation Gemini. 75, 95, 426

Diphilos—Proper name. 515

Dirphian/Dirphys. Central mountain range of Euboia. 362

Doric/Dorian—Dialect of Greek used in Sparta. In. Alkman, In. Stesichoros, In. Ibykos, In. Simonides, 426, In. Bakchylides, In. Anyte, In. Melanippides, In. Theokritos, Te. Bion

Dodekanese—Twelve islands in the southeast Aigaian Sea. In. Theokritos

Doricha—Egyptian courtesan and lover of Sappho's brother, Charaxos. 235

Dotian Plain—Part of Pelasgiotis in Thessaly. 420

Dryads (Hamadryads)—The nymphs of the trees. 455

Ekbatana—The capital of Media, a country of Asia above Persia. 457

Elea—A town on the west coast of Lakonia. Here Parmenides founded the Eleatic school of philosophy. In. Xenophanes

Elis—A state in the northwest of the Peloponnesos, which included the important site of Olympia. Te. Bakchylides

Elpiniki—Proper name. 48

Elpis—Proper name. 512

Elysium—In mythology, the residence of the blessed after death. 422

Emmenos—Children of Emmenos refers to the family of Theron. 426

Empedokles—Philosopher and scientist of Akragas (fl. ca. 460 B.C.). The inventor of the art of rhetoric. Te. Theognis

Enyalios—Epithet of the god Ares and later a different god of war. 25

Ephesos—One of the principal Ionian cities on the coast of Asia Minor. In. Kallinos, Te. Kallinos, In. Hipponax, In. Xenophanes, 512

Epikouros (Epicurus)—Greek philosopher (341-270 B.C.) and founder of the Epicurean school of philosophy. Te. Xenophanes, 539

Epiktetos—Stoic philosopher of first century A.D. 606

Epinikion—A victory ode, a form used by Pindar, Bakchylides and Simonides. In. Pindaros

Eretria—A town of Euboia situated on the Euripos Strait. It was destroyed by the Persians in 490 B.C. 27, 412, 457, 460

Ergoteles—A political exile from Krete and a victor in the Olympian games; Krete enjoyed a reputation for its runners. 421

Eriboia—Wife of Telamon and mother of Aias (Ajax). 431

Eros (Cupid)—The god of all striving toward union, particularly of sexual love. Usually regarded as the son of Aphrodite. 87, 126, 153, 258, 297, 299, 321, 324, 488, 496, 561, 575, 579, 583

Erysiche—A city of Arkanania. 77

Erytheia—Birthplace of the monster Geryon, slain by Herakles. It was either Cádiz (Gades), the Balearic Islands, or islands off the coast of Epiros. 292

Euboia—The largest island of the Aigaian Sea and near the mainland. 27, 402, 457, 460

Eudemos—Proper name. 428

Euenor—Father and teacher of Parrhasios. Te. Parrhasios

Eukrates—Father of Meleagros. 501

Eumekios—Proper name. 537

Euripides—One of the three great Attic tragedians (480-406 B.C.). In. Timotheos, Te. Timotheos

Euripos—The strait between Euboia and the mainland. 362

Europa—In mythology, Europa was kidnapped by Zeus in the disguise of a bull and carried off to Krete where she became the mother of Minos. Te. Asios, In. Stesichoros

Eurotas—The chief river in Lakonia. 402

Eurymedon—Proper name. 314

Eurymedon—A river in Pamphylia. 360

Euryalos—A young man loved by Ibykos. 302

Eurysteus—King of Argos for whom Herakles performed his twelve labors. 426

Eurytion—The Centaur whom Herakles slew. 292

Eustathios—Grammarian and historian of the eleventh century A.D. Te. Apollodoros

Eutychides—Proper name of a poet. 541

Eutychos—Proper name of a portrait painter. 540

Evenos (Euenos)—A river of Aitolia taking its name from Evenos, whose daughter was kidnapped by Marpessa. Evenos, being unable to rescue his daughter, threw himself into the river. 429

Examyes—Proper name. Te. Mimnermos

Five Hills—A town in Lakonia. 82

Gadara—A city in Syria.

Galateia—Sea nymph, daughter of Nereus and Doris, and loved by Polyphemos. 503

Geraneia—The mountain range between the territories of Megara and Corinth. 373

Geryon—A monster with three heads and three bodies joined together, living on the island of Erytheia. 293

Giants—The sons of Ge produced from the blood of the mutilated Uranus. Beings of great size with serpent feet, the Giants were eventually destroyed by Herakles and the other gods and were buried beneath volcanoes. 345

Glaukos—Proper name. 6, 32, 377, 378

Gongyla—One of Sappho's intimate friends. 203, 252

Gorgios—Sicilian rhetorician and orator of the fifth century B.C. A leading Sophist, his writings influenced much of Attic prose, especially the writings of Isokrates. 601

Gorgo—A rival of Sappho's; perhaps a poet. In. Sappho, 167

Gorgo—Proper name. 380

Gortyn—An ancient city in Krete famous for two groups of inscriptions about social institutions written on the interior wall of the courthouse. 382

Graces—Goddesses of grace and charm, associated with the Muses. 161, 162, 184, 214, 296, 302, 456, 501, In. Diphilos, In. Agathias Scholastikos, In. Glykon, 589

Greek Anthology—See PALATINE ANTHOLOGY

Gyara—An island of the Kyklades in the Aigaian Sea. 194

Gyges—King of Lydia whose wealth became proverbial. 31, 309, 577

Gyrai—Some rocks off the island of Mykonos. 6

Gyrinno—One of Sappho's companions. 215

Hades—God of the underworld, or sometimes a name for the underworld itself. 109, 258, 259, 265, 295, Te. Hipponax, 479, 543, 560

Hagesichora—Leader of Alkman's chorus of girls. 72

Halikarnassos—Birthplace of Herodotos. This city of Asia Minor stood in the southwestern part of Karia, opposite the island of Keos. 468

Harmodios—Assassin, along with Aristogeiton, of the tyrant Hipparchos in 511 B.C. In. Hipparchos, Te. Hipparchos

Harmony—Daughter of Ares and Aphrodite, the wife of Kadmus. Te. Pindaros

Hebros—Chief river in Thrace. It is frequently mentioned in the worship of Dionysos. 105, 429

Hekabe (Hekuba)—The wife of Priam and mother of Hektor. 461

Hekate—Earth goddess associated with sorcery, magic and ghosts, and worshiped by night at crossroads. 159

Hekatonymos—Proper name. 543

Hektor—Son of Priam and husband of Andromache, Hektor was the hero of the defense of Troy. He was killed by Achilles in Homer's *Iliad*. 187

Helen—Daughter of Zeus and Leda, a goddess of extraordinary beauty. As wife of Menelaos, she was seduced and taken to Troy by Paris and so became the overt cause of the Trojan War. 106, 124, 230, In. Stesichoros, 288, 290, 426

Helikon—Mountain in Boiotia named after a legendary man. 410, 474

Heliodora—Girlfriend of Meleagros. 491, 492, 496

Heliodora—Proper name. 538

Helios—God of the sun. 281, 293, 431

Hellas/Hellenes—The Greeks called their country Hellas and themselves Hellenes. 2, 107, In. Hipponax, Te. Pindaros, 425, 446

Hephaistion—A writer on prosody in the second century A.D. In. Glykon

Hephaistos—God of fire and metalwork. 12, 195, 281

Hera—Sister and wife of Zeus; the goddess of marriage. 33, 76, 149, 174

Herakleitos—Proper name. 468

Herakles—Son of Zeus and Alkmena (whose husband was Amphitryon). Herakles was a strongman and the performer of the Twelve Labors. In. Stesichoros, 293, 305, 378, 426, 429, 437, 571

Hermes—Herald of the gods. Patron of heralds, travelers and thieves. Also guide of the souls to the underworld. 178, 252, 312, Te. Hipparchos, 407, 408, 410, 411, 412, 465

Hermesianax—Greek elegiac poet of the fourth century B.C. In. Photius, Te. Mimnermos

Hermione—Daughter of Menelaos and Helen. Hermione's beauty, as a demigod, did not match the beauty of her mother, Helen. 230

Hermione—Birthplace of Lasos in the Argolid of the Peloponnesos. 309, Te. Mimnermos, In. Lasos, Te. Lasos

Hermobios—Proper name. Te. Mimnermos

Hermogenes—Proper name. 531, 532

Hermon—Proper name. 529

Hermos—A river of Asia Minor. 280

Hero—One of Sappho's friends. 194

Herodotos—The "Father of History," according to Cicero. Herodotos (fifth century B.C.) was the first author to make the events of the past the subject of research and verification. Te. Solon

Herondas—A writer of mimes and a native of Kos or Miletos (ca. 300-250 B.C.). In. Hipponax

Hesiod—Early Greek poet of the eighth century B.C., and author of *Works and Days* and the *Theogony*. Te. Phokylides, 356

Hesperides—Divine maidens, guardians of the golden apples in the garden of the gods. Islands in "distant" west. 281

Hesperos—The evening star, the son of Astraios or Kephalos or Atlas and Eos (Dawn) and father of the Hesperides. 138, 251, 441, 502

Hesychios—Greek grammarian of Alexandria whose chief literary work was a Greek lexicon. He lived in the fourth century A.D. Te. Lasos, Te. Simonides

Hieron—Tyrant of Syracuse and victor in the Olympic and Pythian games. In. Pindaros

Himera—A Greek city on the north coast of Sicily. Probably the birthplace of the poet Stesichoros. 421

Hipparchos—Brother of the Athenian despot Hippias. He was murdered in 514 B.C. In. Anakreon, In. Simonides, In. Lasos, 407, 408

Hippias—Son of the despot Peisistratos, Hippias was despot of Athens from 527 to 510 B.C. In. Anakreon, 387, In. Hipparchos, Te. Hipparchos

Hippokrateia—Mother of the poet Korinna and wife of Acheloodoros. Te. Korinna

Hippolytos—A Christian writer (fl. A.D. 200). Te. Hippon

Hipponax—Of Ephesos, a Greek iambic poet (fl. 546-520 B.C.). In. Hipponax, Te. Semonides, 312, 313

Hippon—A physical philosopher (fl. 430 B.C.). Te. Xenophanes

Homer—First epic poet of Greece. His poems were the basis of Greek literature and education. The author of the *Iliad* and the *Odyssey*. Te. Archilochos, In. Kallinos, In. Tyrtaios, 63, In. Alkman, Te. Alkaios, In. Sappho, In. Stesichoros, 314, 356, In. Bakchylides, 574

Horace—One of the main Roman lyric poets (65-8 B.C.). In. Archilochos, In. Alkaios, Te. Mimnermos, Te. Pindaros, Te. Bakchylides, In. Philodemos

Hymen—God of marriage. 177

Hyperboreans—A fabulous people living in a land of perpetual sunshine somewhere beyond the North Wind. Poets use "Hyperborean" to mean most northerly. 107, 426

Hyperion—A Titan, son of Uranus (Heaven) and Ge (Earth), and father of Helios (Sun), Selene (Moon) and Eos (Dawn). Sometimes refers to Helios himself. 293

Hypnos—God of sleep. 498

Ianthemis—Proper name. 72

Ibykos—Greek lyric poet of Rhegium, Ibykos lived at the court of Polykrates at Samos. In. Ibykos, In. Stesichoros, In. Anakreon

Ida—In Homer, Ida is the summit from which the gods watched the battle of Troy. 187

Ida—Zeus was said to have been brought up in a cave in Mt. Ida, in central Krete. 431

Idas—The kidnapper of Apollo's beloved Marpessa. 430

Idyl, Idyll—"A little picture," or a short poem depicting a pastoral scene. In Theokritos

Ilios—Son of Tros and founder of Ilium (Troy). 187

Ilium—Another name for Troy. 106, 149, 187, 461

Iole—Daughter of King Eurytos. Herakles sought to marry her. 429

Ion—Poet and playwright of fifth century B.C. Te. Pindaros

Ionia—A district on and off the west coast of Asia Minor, colonized by the Ionians. This is the region where early Greek literature and philosophy developed. 143, In. Stesichoros, In. Mimnermos, In. Anakreon, 431

Ionic—The Greek dialect of Ionia. In. Archilochos, In. Anakreon, In. Theokritos

Iphimenes—Proper name. 373

Irana—Proper name. 197, 240

Iris (Thaumantias)—The goddess of the rainbow and a messenger of the gods. She is the wife of Zephyros, the West Wind. 353

Iros—A beggar in the house of Odysseus. 606

Ismarian—Of Ismaros, a town in Thrace which produced excellent wine. Poets use the term "Ismarian" as equivalent to "Thracian." 26

Isokrates—Fourth of the "Ten Attic Orators," he was a great teacher of rhetoric. Te. Phokylides

Isthmos—The isthmus at Corinth separating the mainland from the Peloponnesos. 364, 421

Istrian—The Istrian land was by the Istros or Danube River. 426

Iulus (Ascanius)—Son of Aeneas. Te. Pindaros

Jason—Leader of the Argonauts who set sail in the *Argo* to find the Golden Fleece. 210, 278

Justinian—Roman emperor at Constantinople (A.D. 527-565). In. Paulus Silentiarius

Kadmos—Son of Agenor and founder of the Greek city of Thebes. Te. Pindaros

Kallia—Father of Megakles. 369

Kallimachos—Alexandrian grammarian and poet of the third century A.D. In. Kallimachos, In. Archilochos, In. Hipponax, In. Theokritos

Kallinos—Of Ephesos. The earliest Greek elegiac poet (fl. 700 B.C.?). In. Tyrtaios

Karia—A district of western Asia Minor. 580

Karystos—A town of Lakonia. 82

Kastalia—A nymph who, when pursued by Apollo, threw herself into a spring on Mount Parnassos. The spring was henceforward held sacred to Apollo and to the Muses. The latter were often called Kastalides. 107

Kastor—See Dioskouri. 75, 95

Kean—Of the island of Keos. 431

Kenaian Zeus—Of the temple to Zeus in Kenaion. 429

Keos—An island of the Kyklades and birthplace of Simonides. In. Simonides, In. Bakchylides

Keres—Spirits of death. 282

Kerkidas—Greek poet of an uncertain date. Wrote in lyric meters on ethical subjects. In. Hipponax

Kerkylas—Husband of Sappho. In. Sappho

Kephissos—Chief river in the Athenian plain. 107

Kithairon—A mountain in Boiotia named after a legendary man. 375, 410

Klazomenai—City of Asia Minor. The birthplace of Anaxagoras. In. Hipponax

Kleësisera—Proper name. 72

Kleinorides—Proper name. 340

Kleïs—Name of Sappho's daughter, also her mother, and perhaps a friend. In. Sappho, 142, 231, 232

Kleomenes—King of Sparta, 520-489 B.C. Te. Telesilla

Klymenos—A god of the nether world. 390

Klytaimnestra—Wife and murderess of Agamemnon and mistress of Aigisthos. Murdered in turn by her son Orestes. 289

Knidos—City of Asia Minor and the home of the famous astronomer Eudoxos. 449

Knossos—An ancient town in Krete. "Knossian" is the equivalent of "Kretan." 148, 421, 431

Koios—Father of Leto, the mother of Apollo. 245

Kolophon—One of the twelve Ionian cities of Asia Minor and said to be the birthplace of Homer; the site of the oracle of Apollo Klarios. Te. Kallinos, In. Mimnermos, 283, In. Xenophanes, 346

Konon—Proper name. 548

Korax—Proper name. 506

Koressos—A hill. 512

Korinna—Greek lyric poetess (fl. ca. 500 B.C.). Believed to have been the instructor of Pindaros. In. Korinna, 409, 414

Kos—One of the islands called Sporades, home of Hippokrates and a favorite place for men of letters. Theokritos lived there at one time. Te. Kallinos, In. Theokritos, In. Meleagros

Kratinos—Athenian poet of the Old Comedy. Te. Hippon

Krete (Crete)—A large island in the Mediterranean where Minoan civilization flourished. 148, 183, 382, 431, 580

Krines—Father of Semonides. Te. Semonides

Kritias—Proper name. 317

Kriton—Rich citizen of Athens and friend of Sokrates. 528

Kroisos—The last king of Lydia. His wealth and power attracted the poet Solon to his court. Te. Solon

Kronian Pelops—Pelops was the great-grandson of Kronos. 426

Kronos—Father of Zeus. 119, 410, 431

Kyklades—A group of islands in the Aigaian Sea lying in a circle around the sacred island of Delos. In. Bakchylides

Kyllene—The highest mountain in the Peloponnesos, sacred to Hermes, who had a temple on the summit. Hermes is sometimes called "Kyllenios." 312

Kynoskephalai—"Dog Heads," two hills in Thessaly where Flaminius defeated Philip of Macedonia (197 B.C.). In. Pindaros

Kyprian/Kypris/Kytherea—See APHRODITE. 150, 154, 203, 234, 235, 294, 297, 302, 478, 479, 483, 598

Kypros—An island in the Mediterranean and one of the chief seats of worship of the goddess Aphrodite. 86, 151, 156, 187, 259, Te. Solon.

Kyrene—A Greek city of North Africa between Carthage and Alexandria. In. Kallimachos, 467

Kyrnos—Friend of the poet Theognis; also the Greek name for Corsica. Poems which specifically mention Kyrnos by name are considered authentic poems of Theognis. In. Theognis, 392, 393, 394, 396, 405

Laïs—A famous courtesan of Corinth, known for her beauty. 446

Lakedaimonians—Spartans. In mythology Lakedaimon, a son of Zeus and Taygete, married Sparta and named his city after her. 359

Lakonia—A region of the Peloponnesos. Sparta was its capital. Te. Alkman, 82

Lampsakos—City of Asia Minor celebrated for its wine. The chief seat of worship for Priapos. 387

Lasos—A poet and teacher of Pindar. Te. Apollodoros

Leda—Mother of Helen and Klytaimnestra, Kastor and Polydeukes. Wooed by Zeus in the disguise of a swan. 95, 246, 426

Lelantine War—A war between Chalkis and Eretria for possession of the plain watered by the Lelantos (ca. 690 B.C.). 27

Leonidas—King of Sparta, 487-480 B.C., died heroically at Thermopylai, fighting against the invading Persians. 340, 362, 367

Leontichos—Proper name. 470

Lesbos—An island in the Aigaian Sea off the coast of Mysia in Asia Minor. Birthplace of the poets Terpandros, Sappho, and Alkaios. Te. Terpandros, In. Alkaios, 116, In. Sappho, Te. Sappho, 213, 231, 321, 453, 580

Lethaios—A small tributary of the Maiandros River in Asia Minor. 318

Leto—Mother of Apollo and Artemis. Leto was worshiped in connection with her children. 65, 196, 426, 615

Leukadian Rock—Promontory on the island of Leukas from which suspected criminals were cast into the sea. Birds were attached to them in order to break their fall. This rock gave rise to the story that lovers leapt from it to escape the pangs of love. See PHAON. In. Sappho

Lokria—Greek city in southern Italy, known for its laws. 423

Longinus—Greek philosopher, literary critic and grammarian of the third century A.D. Teacher of Zenobia. Te. Pindaros

Loukianos/Lucian—Greek writer of the second century A.D. In. Loukianos, Te. Semonides

Lydia—A district in Asia Minor between Mysia and Karia. An early seat of Asian civilization, exerting an important influence on the Greeks. 31, In. Alkman, Te. Alkman, 72, 112, 124, 141, 208, 231, 280, 309, 316, 346, 379

Lykambes—Nobleman, father of Neoboule, loved by Archilochos. In. Archilochos, 34, 52

Lykas—Proper name. 375

Lysippos—Famous Greek sculptor, contemporary of Alexander. Te. Praxilla

Lysis—Pythagorean philosopher and teacher of Epaminondas. Te. Lamprokles

Macedon/Macedonia—A region of northern Greece; birthplace of Alexander the Great. In. Malanippides, Te. Melanippides, In. Timotheos

Maia—Daughter of Atlas and Pleione. The eldest and most beautiful of the Pleiades. Mother of Hermes. 312

Manes—Proper name. 464

Marathon—Village in Attica and the site of the crucial battle between the Persians and the Athenians in 490 B.C. In. Simonides, 366

Mauros—Proper name. 552

Marpessa—Daughter of Evenos and wife of Idas. 430

Media—North of Persia, its inhabitants were the Medes. When Media was conquered by Persia, Mede and Media became synonymous in Greek for Persian and Persia. 457

Megakles—Proper name. 369

Megalostrata—Loved by Alkman. 78

Megara—Capital of Megaris, a district of Greece. One of the four divisions of Attica. In. Theognis, Te. Theognis

Megastrys—Lover of King Gyges. 309

Megatimos—Proper name. 46

Megistes—Proper name. 342

Megistias—An Akarnanian seer who at Thermopylai refused to return to the rear and died in battle. 368

Melanchros—Tyrant of Lesbos in 610 B.C. Overthrown by Pittakos. In. Alkaios

Melanippos—Friend of Alkaios. 119

Melanippos—Proper name. 467

Meles—Proper name. 286

Melissa—Nymph, discoverer of honey, and from whom bees received their name. Here used as a proper name. 511

Melos—An island in the Aigaian and the most westerly of the Sporades. In. Melanippides

Menandros—Proper name. 527

Menelaos—Son of Atreus and younger brother of Agamemnon. The rape of his wife, Helen, by Paris, caused the Trojan War. 290

Menippos—Cynic philosopher of Gadara in Syria (fl. 250 B.C.). 501

Menippos—Proper name. 517

Meniskos—Father of Pelagon. 239

Messene—Country in Peloponnesos. Defeated three different times by Sparta in the Messenian Wars (seventh century B.C.).

Mika—Probably a shortened form of "Mnasidika," a rival who had gone over to the rival house of Penthilos, ruling nobles of Mytilene. 233

Miletos—A great city of Asia Minor. Birthplace of Anaximandros, Anaximenes and Thales. In. Phokylides, In. Timotheos, Te. Timotheos, 515

Mimnermos—Greek elegiac poet and contemporary of Solon. In. Mimnermos, Te. Kallinos, In. Phokylides

Mimnes—Proper name. 311

Minoa—City in Amorgos founded by Semonides. Te. Semonides

Minos—Son of Zeus and Europa, Minos was a mythical king of Krete, ruling at Knossos. Later he was one of the judges of the underworld. 431, 459

Mnasidika—A friend of Sappho's who appears to have deserted her. "Mika" is probably a shortened form of "Mnasidika." 215

Molione—The twins of Molione were the Aktoridai; they were killed by Herakles. 305

Molouris—A rock on the coast near Megara, from which Ino and Melikertes threw themselves into the sea. 373

Muses—Daughters of Zeus, the nine Muses lived on Mount Helikon where they presided over the arts and sciences. Te. Archilochos, 65, 66, Te. Alkman, 78, 91, Te. Sappho, 162, 163, 164, 255, 302, 314, 396, 410, Te. Pindaros, 423, 426, 452, 453, Te. Theokritos, Te. Leonidas of Tarentum, 501, 586

Myiskos—Proper name. 489

Mykonians/Mykonos—Of Mykonos, an island in the Aigaian Sea. The place where Herakles defeated the Giants. 6, 40

Myrsilos—Tyrant of Mytilene who probably caused the exile of Sappho and Alkaios. In. Alkaios, 118, 232

Myrtis—Teacher of Korinna. 413

Mysians—Of Mysia, a district in the northwest corner of Asia Minor. 333

Mytilene—Chief city of Lesbos. 112, 116, In. Alkaios, In. Sappho, 142, 232

Nanno—A flute-girl to whom Mimnermos addressed his elegies. 72, In. Mimnermos, Te. Mimnermos

Naxos—An island in the Aigaian. 26, 46

Nearchos—Proper name. 545

Nebuchadnezzar—King of Babylon from 605 to 562 B.C., who captured Jerusalem. In. Alkaios

Neleian Pylos—Neleus of Pylos, son of Poseidon and king of Pylos in the western Peloponnesos. Brother of Pelias. 283

Nemea—Valley in Argolis where Herakles slew the Nemean lion, and where the Nemean games were held. 535

Nemesis—The Greek goddess of retribution for sinful excess; also of compensation for good fortune. 549

Neoboule—Daughter of Lykambes, loved by Archilochos. In. Archilochos, 34

Nereids—Sea nymphs. Fifty in number, they were the daughters of Nereus. 234

Nereus—The god of the sea. His empire is the Aigaian Sea. Sometimes he is called the Aigaian. 106, 431

Nero—Emperor of Rome (A.D. 54-68). In. Lucillius, In. Leonidas

Nessos—A Centaur who tried to seduce Herakles' wife Deianeira. 429

Nikilla—Proper name. 525

Nikon—Proper name. 517

Nikoteles—Proper name. 466

Niobe—Daughter of Tantalos, wife of Amphion. Niobe once boasted that her family was larger than Leto's. To avenge this insult Leto killed twelve of Niobe's children. Niobe is a stock figure of bereavement. 196

Nymphs—Female divinities of a lower rank represented as beautiful girls living in the mountains, forests, meadows and waters. 421, 455

Oichalia—City of Euboia. 429

Oineos—Father of Perimede. Te. Asios

Oinos—Town of Lakonia. 82

Olympia/Olympians—A plain in Elis where the Olympian Games were held. This plain was sacred to Zeus. 13, 261, 377, 421

Olympian Games—Athletic events celebrated at Olympia from earliest times in Greece every four years. 426, 534

Olympos—A range of mountains separating Thessaly and Macedon. The home of the gods. 229, 320, 426

Onogla—A town in Lakonia. 82

Orestes—Son of Agamemnon and Klytaimnestra and avenger of his father's murder by Klytaimnestra and Aigisthos. In. Stesichoros

Orthria (Orthia)—A goddess. Later Artemis Orthia. 72

Ortygia—An island near Syracuse, claimed as birthplace of Artemis. Ortygia was also a name associated with Artemis, and hence another name for Delos, where Artemis, according to most accounts, was born. 307

Ossa—A mountain in the north of Thessaly associated with the war of the Giants. 375

Ovid—Roman poet (fl. ca. 23 B.C.). In. Sappho

Palatine Anthology (Greek Anthology)—Collection of Greek epigrams started by Constantine Cephalas and finished by

Planudes. Te. Hipponax, Te. Platon, Te. Kallimachos, In. Kallikteros, In. Ammonides, In. Diophones

Pan—Goat-footed god of shepherds and flocks. 455, 472, 473

Pandion—Father of Prokne, who became a swallow, and Philomela, who became a nightingale. Reputed grandfather of Theseus. 197, 431

Paphian—Of Paphos, and therefore of Aphrodite. Aphrodite was born in the foam near the city of Paphos in Kypros. 84, 174, 446

Parrhasios—Painter and poet, second century B.C. In. Parrhasios, 437

Parmenides—Philosopher of Elea and founder of the Eleatic school of philosophy. Born ca. 510 B.C. Te. Phokylides, Te. Theognis

Parnassos—A mountain in central Greece thought to be the dwelling place of Apollo and the Muses. Also sacred to Dionysos. 107

Paros—An island in the Aigaian Sea. Birthplace of Archilochos. In. Archilochos, Te. Archilochos, 4

Parthians—Of Parthia, a country of Asia. The Parthians were a warlike people and their savagery became proverbial. 571

Pasiphile—Proper name meaning literally "lover of everybody." 16

Paulus Silentiarius (Paul the Silentiary)—An officer of the Justinian household (fl. A.D. 540) and a Greek poet of epigrams. In. Silentiarius, In. Agathias Scholastikos

Pausanias—Greek travel writer of the second century A.D. Author of *Hellados Periegetes*, a guide to the cities and monuments of Greece. Te. Asios, Te. Telesilla, Te. Timotheos

Peisistratos—Despot of Athens, 561-527 B.C., with intervals of exile. In. Simonides, In. Hipparchos

Peitho—Personification of persuasion, the goddess of seductive charm. 160, 188, 302

Pelagon—A fisherman. 239

Peleus—King of the Myrmidons at Phthia in Thessaly. The father of Achilles and the husband of the Nereid Thetis. 106

Pelias—Son of Poseidon and Tyro. Ordered Jason to search for the Golden Fleece and was later butchered by his own daughters, and boiled. 538

Pelion—A mountain of Thessaly. 375

Peloponnesos—The southernmost part of Greece, connected with the central region by the Isthmus of Corinth. In. Lasos, In. Bakchylides, Te. Bakchylides, In. Anyte

Pelops—Son of Tantalos. When he was a child his father killed him and served him as food for the gods. He was later restored to life by the gods and Tantalos was punished in Hell. Pelops murdered his wife's suitor, Myrtilos, and brought about a curse on his two sons, Atreus and Thyestes. 95

Penthilos—A rival family of ruling nobles in Mytilene. The tyrant Pittakos was the son of Penthilos. 233

Perdikkas—King of Macedonia (454?-413 B.C.). In. Melanippides, Te. Melanippides

Perikles—Great Athenian statesman. Under his direction the Parthenon and Propylaea were constructed. In. Anakreon

Perikles—Proper name. 11, 40, 48

Perimede—Wife of Phoinix and daughter of Oineos. Te. Asios

Persephone (Kore)—Wife of Hades and queen of the underworld. Daughter of Zeus and Demeter. 243, 390

Perseus—Son of Danaë and Zeus. He was cast away with his mother so as not to fulfill the prophecy that he would kill his grandfather, Akrisios, whom he actually killed later. 374

Phaidros—Proper name. 447

Phalaris—Tyrant of Akragas in Sicily in the first half of the sixth century B.C. He commissioned the "brazen bull," a torture device, whose inventor was the first to be put to death by it. In. Stesichoros

Phaon—Legend says that Sappho leaped from the Leukadian rock out of love for Phaon, but there is no evidence for this story. In. Sappho

Pherekles—Proper name. In. Mimnermos

Philainion—Proper name. 481

Philanor—Father of Ergoteles. 421

Philetas—Greek grammarian and poet of the Alexandrian Age. His amatory poems were imitated by Ovid. Te. Kallinos

Philinna—Mother of Theokritos. Te. Theokritos

Philippos—Poet of the *Greek Anthology* (second century A.D.). Te. Hipponax

Phillipos—Proper name. 466

Philochoros. Greek historian of Athens (fl. third century B.C.). Te. Tyrtaios

Philodemos—Epicurean philosopher and an epigrammatic poet. A contemporary of Cicero. In. Philodemos, 504

Philon—Son of Glaukos, and champion in boxing for two years at the Olympian Games. 377

Philylla—Proper name. 72

Polydeukes—See DIOSKOURI. 75, 95, 378

Polykrates—Tyrant of Samos in the second half of the sixth century B.C. He maintained a sumptuous court at Samos where Anakreon and Ibykos lived. In. Ibykos, In. Anakreon

Polypas—Proper name. 397

Polyphemos—A Cyclops and son of Poseidon. 503

Porphyrio—Neoplatonic philosopher (fl. A.D. 270). Te. Bakchylides

Poseidon—The brother of Zeus and the lord of the sea and of earthquakes and horses. 53, 335, 430, 431

Praxagoras—Father of Theokritos. Te. Theokritos

Praxinoa—Friend of Sappho. 142

Praxiteles—A famous Greek sculptor of the fourth century B.C. 444

Priam—King of Troy at the time of the Trojan War and husband of Hekuba. The father of fifty sons and daughters, including Paris. 106, 187

Priapos—God of fertility and of the herds. Son of Aphrodite and Dionysos, he is represented as a grotesque character with a phallic symbol. It was customary to inscribe short poems on his statues. 471, 472, 476

Priene—A city of Ionia near Mount Mykale. 19

Proklos—Proper name. 603

Propertius—Roman poet of the first century B.C., rivaled only by Catullus as a love poet. In. Leonidas

Ptolemy II—King of Egypt in the second century B.C. Patron of literature and science. The Holy Scriptures were translated into Greek by his command. In. Theokritos

Pygelia—A city in Ionia near Ephesos. 316

Pyrrha—A town of Lesbos. In. Alkaios

Pythagoras—Celebrated Greek philosopher and mathematician. 349, Te. Lamprokles, Te. Platon

Pythia/Pythian Healer—A surname for Apollo. 429, 474, Te. Pindaros

Pytho—Older name for Delphi, where the Pythian priestess gave her ambiguous answers and where Pythian games were held. The Apollo of Delphi was the Pythian Apollo. 421

Pythokleides—A Pythagorian musician of the sixth century B.C. Te. Lamprokles

Python—Proper name. 337

Quintilian—Roman rhetorician. His greatest achievement was a complete system of rhetoric. Te. Archilochos, Te. Alkaios, Te. Simonides, Te. Pindaros, Te. Parrhasios

Rhegium—A Greek town on the coast of Bruttium in the south of Italy. This was the cross-over point for Sicily. In. Ibykos, Te. Ibykos, Te. Hippon, 438

Rheia (Rhea)—Greek earth goddess, daughter of Ge and Uranus, wife of Kronos and mother of Demeter, Hestia, Zeus, Hera, Hades, Poseidon. 410

Rhipé—A legendary mountain range in northern Greece. 74

Rhodes—The most easterly of the islands of the Aigaian. In. Timokreon, Te. Timokreon, 580

Rhodo—Proper name. 558, 569

Rome—Capital of modern and ancient Italy. In. Mimnermos

Salamis—An island off the coast of Attica, where the Greeks defeated the Persian fleet of Xerxes in 480 B.C. In. Solon, Te. Solon, 267

Salmydessos—A town in Thrace on the coast of Euxine. The name originally referred to the whole coast. 3

Samos—An Ionian island off the southwest coast of Asia Minor. Birthplace of Pythagoras. In. Asios, Te. Asios, In. Ibykos, In. Semonides, Te. Semonides, In. Anakreon, In. Hippon

Samosata—Capital of the province of Commagene, north of Syria. Birthplace of Loukianos. In. Loukianos

Sappho—Lyric poet of Eresos or Mytilene in Lesbos. In. Sappho, In. Terpandros, 109, 142, 143, 147, 152, 166, 169, 201, 245, 259, In. Ibykos, Te. Bakchylides, In. Theokritos, In. Anakreon, Te. Anakreon

Sardis—Ancient city of Asia Minor, capital of Lydia. In. Alkman, 77, 122, 141, In. Anakreon, 577

Scholiast—Refers to an ancient commentator whose scholia, marginal commentaries of a Greek text, have been preserved. Te. Lamprokles, Te. Bakchylides, Te. Hippon

Semele—Mother of Dionysos. 98

Semiramis—Assyrian queen known for her beauty, reputed founder of Babylon. 563

Seneca (Lucius Annaeus)—Roman philosopher and playwright born in the first century B.C. Convicted in a conspiracy to assassinate Nero, Seneca was ordered to commit suicide. Te. Anakreon

Seven Against Thebes—Polyneikes and six other warriors in a force against Eteokles in Thebes. In. Korinna

Sicily—A large island separated from Italy by the Straits of Messina. Birthplace of Stesichoros and Theokritos, it was one of the principal points of contact between Roman and Hellenistic cultures. 1, In. Sappho, In. Stesichoros, In.

Simonides, Te. Theognis, 402, In. Pindaros, 426, In. Bakchylides, In. Bion, Te. Bion

Sigeion—Promontory near Troy, commanding the mouth of the Hellespont. In. Alkaios

Simonides—Greek elegiac poet of the seventh century B.C. The uncle of Bakchylides, he is famous for his heroic epigrams. In. Simonides, In. Stesichoros, In. Lasos, Te. Hipparchos, In. Timokreon, Te. Bakchylides

Sirens—Fabulous creatures of the sea that drove men to destruction by their song. Often represented as birds with the heads and torsos of women. 72

Sirios—The Dog Star in the constellation of the Great Dog. 23, 72, 97, 304

Siris—A river in southern Italy. 1

Sisyphos—A mortal who persuaded Hades to release him from Hell for a time. When he failed to return, he was forcibly retrieved by Hermes. He was punished by being forced to roll a stone up a hill, only to find it ever rolling back again into the valley. 119

Skamandronymos—Father of Sappho. In. Sappho

Skapte Hyle—A town of Thrace. Te. Bakchylides

Skopelinos—Flute teacher of Pindar. Te. Lasos

Skylla—A fearful monster with twelve feet and six heads. Once the lover of Poseidon, Skylla was turned into a monster by her rival Amphitrite. 490

Skythia—Region of southern Russia. 72, 373

Smyrna—City on the Ionian coast. 56, In. Mimnermos, 283, 309

Smyrneid—A long poem on the history of Smyrna. In. Mimnermos

Sokrates—The most famous of Greek philosophers. Left no writings and is chiefly known through the works of Plato and Xenophon. In. Parrhasios, Te. Melanippides, Te. Stesichoros, 445, 448, In. Platon

Solon—Athenian poet and statesman (ca. 640-559 B.C.). He was one of the "Seven Wise Men." In. Solon, 267, In. Phokylides

Sophokles—Athenian tragic poet of the fifth century B.C. Te. Pindaros

Sparta—The capital of Lakonia and the most important city of the Peloponnesos in historical times. In. Tyrtaios, In. Alkman, Te. Tyrtaios, 57, In. Terpandros, Te. Terpandros, 66, 104, 303, 362, 365, 367, 368, 402, Te. Telesilla, 430, Te. Timotheos

Spercheios—A river in the southern part of Thessaly, named after the river god Spercheios. 368

Sporades—A group of scattered islands in the Aigaian Sea, off the island of Krete and on the west coast of Asia Minor. Te. Simonides

Stathmi—Town of Lakonia. 82

Stephanos of Meleagros—The wreath or anthology of poems of Meleagros, forming part of the *Palatine Anthology.* In. Anyte, Te. Kallimachos, Te. Mnasalkas

Stesichoros—His name means literally "setter or arranger of the chorus." Contemporary with Sappho, Stesichoros was one of the "nine great Greek lyric poets." In. Stesichoros, In. Ibykos, Te. Bakchylides

Stobaios—Compiler of a small anthology ot excerpts from Greek writers. His work preserved many valuable fragments. Te. Theognis

Strabon—Geographer of first century A.D. Te. Semonides, Te. Sappho

Suda Lexicon—A Greek lexicon (ca. A.D. 970) of unknown authorship, formerly attributed to Suidas. It is valuable for its quotations, explanations of words, and biographical information. Te. Tyrtaios, Te. Semonides, Te. Terpandros, Te. Ibykos, Te. Theognis, Te. Korinna, Te. Melanippides

Susa—The winter residence of the Persian kings, in the province of Susi and of the Persian Empire. 460

Syracuse—A city in Sicily. 307, In. Simonides, In. Pindaros, 461, In. Theokritos, In. Theodoridas, In. Moschos

Syria—A general name for the country north of Palestine. 439, 501, In. Loukianos, 580

Tanagra—A town in Boiotia famous for its statuettes. Te. Korinna, 409, 412

Tanais—The Don River. 373

Tantalos—Father of Pelops and Niobe. For the sin of serving his son's flesh to the gods as a test, Tantalos was punished in Hades by being set thirsty in a pool of water that always receded when he tried to drink. 5, 85, 590

Tarentum—An important city and harbor on the southeast coast of Calabria. Te. Leonidas of Tarentum

Tarsos—The chief city of Cilicia. Birthplace of the apostle Paul. 608

Tartaros—A place of torment in the underworld. 417

Tartessos—Ancient town in Spain settled by the Phoenicians; river near town. 292

Tatian—Christian writer (fl. A.D. 160). Te. Praxilla

Taygeta—A nymph sacred to Artemis. 426

Tegea—An ancient city of Arkadia and capital of the district of Tegeatis. 358

Telephos—Father of Philetas. Te. Kallinos

Telesikles—Father of Archilochos. In. Archilochos

Teos—An Ionian city on the coast of Asia Minor. The birthplace of Anakreon. In. Anakreon, 573

Tereus—The son of Ares and king of the Thracians. Husband of the sisters Prokne and Philomela. He deprived Philomela of her tongue. 578

Thasos—A rocky island off the coast of Thrace. In. Archilochos, 1, 2

Thebe—A city of Mysia, in the northwest of Asia Minor. 187

Thebes—Principal city of Boiotia. Birthplace of Pindar and Korinna. Te. Korinna, Te. Pindaros, 58, 582

Themistokles—A celebrated Athenian statesman and archon in 493 B.C. Important for his role in the second Persian War. In. Simonides

Theognis—Elegiac poet (fl. second half of sixth century B.C.). He is the best preserved of the Greek elegists. In. Theognis, In. Alkaios, Te. Phokylides

Thermopylai—A narrow pass between the spurs of Mount Oita and the sea, the gate of eastern Greece, where the Spartans delayed the Persians in a famous battle in 486 B.C. In. Simonides, 361, 365, 368

Theron—Tyrant of Akragas, victor in the Olympian Games. See dedication of "Olympian Ode III." In. Pindaros, 426

Theseus—Attic hero who went to Krete to slay the Minotaur. In. Bakchylides he is represented as a son of Poseidon. 431

Thessaly—The largest division of Greece. The mythological home of the Centaurs and also a country of magicians. 77, In. Anakreon, In. Simonides, 375

Thetis—A Nereid, daughter of Nereus and Doris. The mother of Achilles. 106

Thrace—The northern part of the Greek peninsula. 3, 29, 297, In. Anakreon, 322, 351

Thucydides—Greek historian who started a history of the Peloponnesian War. Te. Bakchylides

Thylakis—Proper name. 72

Thyone—Semele, mother of Dionysos, was raised to the sky, deified as a star, and known as Thyone. 149

Timas—One of Sappho's companions. 243

Timokritos—Celebrated Greek lyric poet of Rhodes (fl. fifth century B.C.). 336

Titans—Monstrous children of the primeval couple of Uranus and Ge. 345

Tithonos—Lover of Eos (Dawn), who left him each morning. Through the prayers of Eos he became immortal but he did

Bibliography

✦✦

Texts in Greek

Andrados, Francisco R. *Líricos griegos: elegiacos y yambógraphos arcaicos*, 2 vols. Barcelona, 1956. (Includes translation and notes in Spanish.)

Bowra, C. M. *Pindari carmina.* Oxford, 1947.

Diehl, Ernst, et al. *Anthologia Lyrica Graeca.* 3d ed. Leipzig, 1949–84.

Garzya, A. *Alcmane, I Frammenti* (with commentary). Naples, 1954.

Gentili, B. *Anacreon.* Rome, 1958.

Gow, A. S. F. *Bucolici Graeci.* Oxford, 1952.

Heitsch, Ernst. *Die griechischen Dichterfragmente der Römischen Kaiserzeit.* Göttingen, 1961.

Lobel, Edgar, and Denys Page. *Poetarum Lesbiorum Fragmenta.* Oxford, 1955.

Masson, O. *Les fragments du poète Hipponax* (with commentary). Paris, 1962.

Moore, J. A. *Selections from the Greek Elegiac, Iambic, and Lyric Poets* (with English commentary). Cambridge, Mass., 1947.

Murray, Gilbert, et al. *The Oxford Book of Greek Verse.* Oxford, 1930.

Page, Denys. *Poetae Melici Graeci.* Oxford, 1962.

———.*Supplementum Lyricis Graecis.* Oxford, 1974.

———.*Epigrammata Graeca.* Oxford, 1975.

Powell, John U. *Collectanea Alexandrina.* Oxford, 1925.

Prato, C. *Tyrtaeus* (with commentary). Rome, 1968.

Smyth, Herbert Weir. *Greek Melic Poets* (with English commentary). London and New York, 1900; rep., 1963.

Bibliography

Snell, Bruno, and H. Maehler. *Pindarus.* 2 vols. Leipzig, 1971, 1975.

_____.*Pindari carmina cum fragmentis,* Leipzig, 1980.

_____.*Bacchylidis carmina cum fragmentis.* Leipzig, 1970

Tarditi, I. *Archilochus.* Rome, 1968.

Turyn, A. *Pindari carmina.* Oxford, 1947.

Untersteiner, M., *Senofane* (with commentary). Florence, 1955.

Voigt, E.-M. *Sappho et Alcaeus.* Amsterdam, 1971.

West, Martin L. *Iambi et Elegi Graeci.* 2 vols. Oxford, 1971–72.

Young, D. *Theognis.* Leipzig, 1971.

Texts in Greek with English Translations

Barnstone, Willis. *Sappho: Lyrics in the Original Greek with Translations.* Foreword by Andrew R. Burn. New York, 1965.

Campbell, David A. *Greek Lyric with an English Translation.* 4 vols. Cambridge, Mass., and London, 1982.

Edmonds, J. M. *Elegy and Iambus: Anacreontea.* 2 vols. London and New York, 1931.

_____.*The Greek Bucolic Poets.* Rev. ed. London and New York, 1928.

_____.*Lyra Graeca.* 3 vols. 2d ed. London and New York, 1928.

Farnell, L.R. *The Works of Pindar* (with English commentary). 3 vols. London, 1930–32.

Gow, A. S. F. *Theocritus* (with English commentary). 2 vols. Cambridge, England, 1952.

Jebb, R. C. *Bacchylides: The Poems and Fragments* (with English commentary). Cambridge, England, 1905.

Mackail, J. W. *Select Epigrams from the Greek Anthology.* 3d ed. London, 1911.

Nisetich, Frank J. *Pindar's Victory Odes.* Baltimore, 1980.

Page, Denys. *Sappho and Alcaeus* (with English commentary). Oxford, 1955.

Bibliography

————.*Select Papyri: Vol. 3, Literary Papyri: Poetry*. Rev. ed. London and Cambridge, Mass., 1942.

Paton, W. R. *The Greek Anthology*. 5 vols. London and New York, 1916–18

Translations without Greek Text

Barnard, Mary. *Sappho*. Berkeley and Los Angeles, 1958.

Davenport, G. *Carmina Archilochi*. Berkeley, 1964.

————.*Sappho: Poems and Fragments*. Ann Arbor, Mich., 1965.

Fagles, Robert. *Bacchylides: Complete Poems*. Intro. and notes by A. M. Parry. New Haven, 1961.

Fitts, Dudley. *Poems from the Greek Anthology*. New York, 1938.

Groden, S. Q. *The Poems of Sappho*. Indianapolis, 1966.

Higham, T. F., and C. M. Bowra. *The Oxford Book of Greek Verse in Translation*. Oxford, 1938.

Lattimore, Richmond. *Greek Lyrics*. 2d ed. Chicago, 1960.

————.*The Odes of Pindar*. Chicago, 1947.

Mills, Barriss. *The Idylls of Theokritos*. West Lafayette, Ind., 1963.

Studies in English

Bowra, C. M. *Early Greek Elegists*. Cambridge, Mass., 1938.

————.*Greek Lyric Poetry*. 2d ed. Oxford, 1961.

————.*Pindar*. Oxford, 1964.

Burn, Andrew R. *The Lyric Age of Greece*. London, 1960.

Burnett, Anne Pippin. *Three Archaic Poets: Archilochus, Alcaeus, Sappho*. Cambridge, Mass., 1983.

Burton, R. W. B. *Pindar's Pythian Odes*. Oxford, 1962.

Bury, J. B. *The Nemean Odes of Pindar*. London, 1890; rep. 1965.

————.*The Isthmian Odes of Pindar*. London, 1890; rep. 1965.

Campbell, D. A. *Greek Lyric Poetry*. London, 1967; rep. 1976.

_____.*The Golden Lyre: The Themes of the Greek Lyric Poets.* London, 1983.

Farnell, L. R. *Critical Commentary to the Works of Pindar.* London, 1932; rep. 1961.

Fränkel, H. *Early Greek Poetry and Philosophy*, trans. Hadas and Willis. Oxford, 1975.

Gerber, D. E. *Euterpe.* Amsterdam, 1970.

Gildersteve, B. L. *Pindar: The Olympian and Pythian Odes.* New York, 1890; rep. 1970.

Kirkwood, G. M. *Early Greek Monody.* Ithaca, N.Y., 1974.

Körte, Alfred. *Hellenistic Poetry*, trans. Hammer and Hadas. New York, 1929.

Lefkowitz, M. R. *The Victory Ode.* Park Ridge, N. J., 1977.

Lloyd-Jones, H. *Females of the Species: Semonides on Women.* London, 1975.

Mackail, J. W. *Lectures on Greek Poetry.* London and New York, 1926.

Martin, Hubert. *Alcaeus.* New York, 1972.

Norwood, Gilbert. *Pindar.* Berkeley and Los Angeles, 1945.

Page, Denys. *Alcman: The Partheneion.* Oxford, 1951.

_____.*Corinna.* London, 1953.

Rankin, H. D. *Archilochus of Paros.* Park Ridge, N.J., 1977.

Snell, B. *The Discovery of the Mind*, trans. T. G. Rosenmeyer. Cambridge, Mass., 1953.

Webster, T. B. L. *Greek Art and Literature, 700–530 B.C.* New York, 1960.

West, Martin L. *Studies in Greek Elegy and Iambus.* Berlin, 1974.

Concordance

◇◇

Barnstone Archilochos	Edmonds	Diehl	West
1	21, 21A	18	21-2
2	52	54	102
3	97A	79	HI 115-16
4	51	53	116
5	53	55	105-6
6	54	56	91(214-15)
7	4	5a	4, 46
8	23	21	213
9	43	43	212
10	11	12	8
11	9, 13	7	13
12	12	10	9(10-11)
13	74	74	122(1-9)
14	160		
15	29	25	30-31
16	17	15	331
17	72	72	119
18	47	34	252
19	97	102	43
20	184	1 (adespota)	
21	142		
22	56	58	130
23	61	63	107
24	118	103	201
25	1		
26	2		
27	3		
28	103	112	191
29	6	6	5
30	58	60	114
31	25	22	19
32	14	13	15
33	19	17	325
34	71	71	118
35	84, 85	104, 118	193, 196
36	68	69	125
37	35	37	45
38	114	51, 117	93-98; 192
39	48A	50	330
40	78	78	124
41	8	9	14
42	65	66	126

[335]

Concordance

Barnstone	Edmonds	Diehl	West
43	97B	80	Hi 117
44	22, 13	20, 10	215, 9(10-11), 11
45	66	67a	128-29
46	18	16	325
47	33	32	297
48	31	27	205
49	88	94	177, 180
50	27	30	26 (3-5)
51	30	26	48(5-6)
52	94, 143	88	172, 223
53	10	11	12
54	63	64	133

Kallinos

55	1	1	1
56	2	2	2

Tyrtaios

57	10	6, 7	10(1-14), 10(15-32)
58	14	11	14

Semonides

59	1	1	1
60	3	3	3
61	2	2	2
62	6	6	6
63	*Sim.* 97	29	*Sim. eleg.* 8(85)

Terpandros

			Page
64	1	1	698
65	3	*Carm. Pop.* 49	941
66	6		

Alkman

67	70, 25	93, 92	40, 39
68	36	58	89
69	47	37	56
70	56	54	93
71	49		
72	1	1	1
73	28	15	82
74	64	59	90
75	2B	2	2
76	16	24	60
77	2A	13	16
78	130	101, 102	59
79	46	49	17
80	138	55	19

Concordance

BARNSTONE	EDMONDS	DIEHL	PAGE	
81	137	56	20	
82	139	53	92	
83	61	105	91	
84	142	110	102	
85	89	72	79	
86	24	35	55	
87	131	36	58	
88	39, 17, 19, 20	64, 65, 62, 19	54, 170, 53, 35	
89	26	94	26	
90	67	109	125	
91	50	40	28	
92	164		176	
93	13	7	14c	

			LOBEL AND PAGE	
Alkaios				
94	166	98	Z44	
95	14	78	B2	
96	157, 158	90, 91	Z14, 11	
97	161	94	Z23	
98	163	96	Z22	
99	156	70	C1	
100	159	92	Z39	
101	133	50	Z27	
102	85	103	Z36	
103	141	135	Z21	
104	81, 92, 175	101.	Z37	
105	17	77	B13	
106	120	74	B10	
107	1	1	Z1	
108	18	142	Z41	
109	86, 92, 175	67, 123, 139	A10B	
110	19	54	Z34	
111	28, 29			
112	69	42	D11	
113	77A	117	F5	
114	160	87	Z24	
115	37, 38	30, 118, 119, 120	Z2, A6	
116	76	27	D16	
117	50	31	H2	
118	70	43	D12	
119	122	73	B6	

				CAMPBELL
Sappho				
120	80	103	118	118
121	1a			
122		Suppl. pp. 39, 70	98a	98a
123	74	108	120	120
124	38	27a	16	16

Concordance

Barnstone	Edmonds	Diehl	Lobel and Page	Campbell
125	111	94		168B
126	27	19	38	38
127	54	50	47	47
128	2	2	(Page II)	31
129	53	47	52	52
130	139	118	143	143
131	78	113	145	145
132	12	11	160	160
133	3	4	34	34
134	19	15	123	123
135	94	Alc. 94	Alc. 347b	Alc. 347b
136	16	13	42	42
137	138	121	136	136
138	32	133	104b	104b
139	133	156		168C
140	69	56	54	54
141	86	98	96	96
142	82	95	92	92
143	83	96	94	94
144	81	137	131	131
145	48	40, 41	49	49
146	43	34a	24a	24a
147	1	1	(Page I)	1
148	(Bowra, p. 196)	5, 6	2	2
149	40	28	(Page VI)	17
150	135	114	102	102
151	134	156		
152	75	110	159	159
153	31		198	198
154	103	107	140	140
155	87	99	101	101
156	123	87	134	134
157	7, 8	8	40	40
158	9	9	33	33
159	24	145	i.a. 23	i.a. 23
160	33		200	200
161	68	57	53	53
162	101	90	128	128
163	129	154	127	127
164	10	10	32	32
165	128	134	126	126
166	126	144b	133 (16A)	133b
167	55	143	144	144
168	150, 151	116, 117	105 a, c	105a, c
169	30		125	125
171	161	127	115	115
172	(Bowra, p. 221)	39	30	30
173	65	54	43	43
174	147			

Concordance

BARNSTONE	EDMONDS	DIEHL	LOBEL AND PAGE	CAMPBELL
175	163	130	113	113
176	155, 156, 158	128	112, 116	112, 116
177	148 (11. 2-7)	123	111	111
178	146	135, 136	141	141
179	160, 16a	129, 128	117, 112, 116	117, 112, 116
180	154	124	110	110
181	52	46	51	51
182	84a		197	197
183	112, 114	88, 93	154, i.a. 16	154
184	157			
185	164	131	114	114
186	159	53	107	104
187	66	55 a, b	44	44
188	(Lobel, p. 80)	98	96	96
189	89	48	48	48
190	121	150	155	155
191	125	144a	133 (16)	133a
192	98	61	57	57
193	51	45	i.a. 5	i.a. 5
194	73	62	i.a. 11	i.a. 11
195	70	Alc. 9a	Alc. 349b	Alc. 349b
196	140	119	142	142
197	122	86	135	135
198	100	92	148	148
199	71	58	55	55
200	120	151	138	138
201	Alc. 124, Sa. 119	Alc. 63, Sa. 149	Alc. 384, Sa. 137	137
202	58	49	50	50
203	45	36	22, 9-19	22, 9-19
204	23	20	36	36
205	41	31	20	20
206	72	60	56	56
207	110		204	204
208	20	17	39	39
209	105	85	100	100
210	21	142	152	152
211	56, 57	42	46	46
212	61, 60, 59, 62	138, 139	156, 167	156, 167
213	148 (11. 9-11)	115	106	106
214	117	80	81b	81b
215	115	63	82a	8
216	93	141	i.a. (1. 2)	i.a.
217	137	126	158	158
218	50A (App.)	156B	139	139
219	(Robinson, 122)		196	196
220	142	51	i.a. 25	i.a. 2
221	22	18	129 (1. 2)	129a
222	29	147	163	163
223	18	14	37	37

Concordance

BARNSTONE	EDMONDS	DIEHL	LOBEL AND PAGE	CAMPBELL
224	107	111	122	122
225	96	140	i.a. 5 (1. 3)	i.a.5c
226	13	37	26 (11. 2-4)	26, 2-4
227	106	52	146	14B
228	141, 141A	125, 106	149, 151	149, 151
229	46	38	27	27
230	44	35	23	23
231	130	152	132	132
232		Suppl. pp. 39, 70	98b	98b
233		70	71	71
234	36	25	(Page V)	5
235	37	26	15	15
236	118	65a	58	58
237	118B (App.)	67	63	63
238	118A (App.)	66	62	62
239	145	159		
240	116	64	91	91
241	113A, B		201 i.a. 18	i.a. 18
242	91	(Bergk)	131	
243	144	158		i.a. 27
244	(i.a.)			44A
246	97	105	166	166
247	99	100	121	121
248	28		172, 188	172, 188
249	124	146	129 (1. 1)	129a, b
250	14	12	41	41
251	149	120	104a	104a
252	85	97	95	95
253	42	32	21	21
254	108	109	150	150
255	11		193	193
256	76, 77	59	147	147
257	Lyra Graeca III, p. 438	Fr. Mel. Mon. Adesp. 18		
258	34	24	4	4
259	om.	68	65	65
260	177	16	157	157

Solon

BARNSTONE	EDMONDS	DIEHL		
261	36	24		
262	28a	4		
263	9	10		
264	32	23		
265	24	14		
266	15	4		
267	1	2		
268	21	22		

Concordance

BARNSTONE	EDMONDS	DIEHL	WEST
269	41	27	30
270	25	12	25
271	17	17	17
272	14	15	14
273	27	19	27

Mimnermos

274	1	1	1
275	3	3	3
276	(Greek Anthology IX 50)		
277	6	8	8
278	7	11	11-112
279	12	7	7
280	14	13	14
281	8	10	12
282	2	2	2
283	10	12	9

Phokylides

284	9	11	
285	3	2	

Asios

286	1	1	

Stesichoros

287	87		256
288	18	11	192
289	43	15	219
290	15	10	187
291	2	2	179a
292	5	4	184
293	8	6	185
294	12	17	223
295	52, 53, 54	22, 23, 24	232, 244, 245
296	36, 37, 38	12, 13, 14	210, 212, 211

Ibykos

297	1	6	286
298	9	11	303b
299	2	7	287
300	4, 5	9, 10	317
301	7	13	315
302	6	8	288
303	65		339
304	3	12	314
305	34	2	285
306	28	23	313
307	23	21	321

Concordance

Barnstone	Knox	Diehl	West
Hipponax			
308	78	70	120-21
309	54	3	42
310	1	12	19
311	68	45	28
312	57, 59, 60	24a, b, 25	32, 34
313	61	20	15
314	89	77	128-29
315	67	42	39, 49
316		(Andrados 92)	30
317	69	67	

	Edmonds	Diehl	Lobel and Page
Anakreon			
318	1	1	348
319	47	34	398
320	25	52, 53	378, 379
321	15	5	358
322	84	88	417
323	75	27	396
324	48, 49	45, 46	413, 414
325	21	17	376
326	104	79	428
327	122		446
328	138		439
329	97	54	388
330	4	4	360
331	116		
332	9	11	363
333	36	20	377
334	101	87	424
335	6	6	362
336	150		
337	158		
338	89	92	443
339	149		
340	162		
341	29	60	437
342	68	65	416
343	69	44	395
344	56	37	410

			West
Xenophanes			
345	1	1	1
346	3	3	3
347	23	19	
348	34	30	
349	6a	6	7-7a
350	18	16	
351	14, 15, 16	12, 13, 14	14 (Diehl 14)

Concordance

BARNSTONE	EDMONDS	DIEHL	LOBEL AND PAGE
352	30	26	
353	32	28	
354	27	23	
355	29	25	
356	11	10	
357	28	24	

Simonides

BARNSTONE	EDMONDS	DIEHL	LOBEL AND PAGE
358	129	122	
359	126	121	
360	133	116	
361	21	5	531
362	116	87	
363	65	37	579
364	124	95	
365	119	92	
366	117	88	
367	122	120	
368	120	83	
369	141	84	
370	136	97	
371	128	119	
372	95	53	
373	142	80	
374	27	13	543
375	159	142	
376	37	20	508
377	181	148	
378	39	23	509
379	152	140	
380	144	129	
381	60	28	571
382	156	138	
383	70	56	604
384	22	6	521
385	73	45	586
386	26	7	523
387	139	85	
388	98		648
389	32, 33	10, 11	526, 527

Lasos

BARNSTONE	EDMONDS	DIEHL	LOBEL AND PAGE
390	1	1	702

Line numbers standard in all editions

Theognis

391	1069-1070
392	183-192
393	181-182
394	173-178

Concordance

Concordance

Barnstone	Edmonds		
Bakchylides			
427	7		
428	75		
429	11		
430	15		
431	12		

Barnstone	Edmonds	Diehl	Page
Praxilla			
432	1	2	747
433	5	3	754
434	2	1	748
435	4		750
Parrhasios			
436	2	2	
437	3	3	
Hippon			
438	1	1	
Melanippides			
439	1	1	757
Timotheos			
440	15	11	800
Platon (Plato)			
441	2	5	
442	1	4	
443	8	3	
444	7	2	
445	6	1	
446	11	15	
447	4	7	
448	5	8	
449	17	24	
450	(Greek Anthology IX 51)	30	
451	14	28	
452	12	17	
453	16	16	
454	(Greek Anthology XVI 13)	27	
455	(Greek Anthology IX 823)	26	
456	18	14	
457	13	10	
458	9	9	

Concordance

BARNSTONE	EDMONDS	DIEHL
459	(Greek Anthology VII 268)	29
460	14	28
461	3	6

GREEK ANTHOLOGY

Diphilos
462	XI 439

Anyte
463	IX 313
464	VII 538
465	IX 314

Kallimachos
466	VII 453
467	VII 517
468	VII 80
469	VII 318
470	VII 277

Theokritos
471	IX 437
472	IX 338
473	VI 177
474	VI 336
475	(Idyll 7, 11, 135-146)

Leonidas of Tarentum
476	X 1
477	XVI 230

Asklepiades
478	V 169
479	V 85
480	V 210
481	V 162
482	V 64

Mnasalkas
483	IX 333

Theodoridas
484	VII 282

Poem numbers standard

Moschos
485	IV

Concordance

Concordance

Concordance

Concordance

Concordance

BARNSTONE	EDMONDS	DIEHL	LOBEL AND PAGE	CAMPBELL
615			99b	99b
616	(Treu, pp. 161-64	102	Alc. 304	44A
617		78	73a	73a
618		65	68a	68a
619		Rhein. Mus. 1944	86	86
620		76	70	70
621		56	60	60
622			i.a. 103b	(i.a.)
623		69	67a	67a
624			99a	99a